PARENTS, TEACHERS, AND CHILDREN:
Prospects for Choice
in American Education

PARENTS, TEACHERS, AND CHILDREN: Prospects for Choice in American Education

James S. Coleman
John E. Coons
William H. Cornog
Denis P. Doyle
E. Babette Edwards
Nathan Glazer
Andrew M. Greeley
R. Kent Greenawalt
Marvin Lazerson
William C. McCready
Michael Novak
John P. O'Dwyer
Robert Singleton
Thomas Sowell
Stephen D. Sugarman
Richard E. Wagner

Institute for Contemporary Studies
San Francisco, California

The Institute wishes to thank the following copyright holders for the privilege of quoting from their works:

Atheneum Publishers, New York—for the passages from John Higham, "Ethnic Pluralism in Modern American Thought," in chapter 10 of *Send These to Me: Jews and Other Immigrants in Urban American* (1975).

The Institute on Pluralism and Group Identity of the American Jewish Committee, New York—for the passage from the *The Schools and Group Identity: Education for a New Pluralism,* ed. Judith Herman (1974).

The New York University History of Education Society, New York—for the passage from Ronald K. Goodenow, "The Progressive Educator, Race and Ethnicity in the Depression Years: An Overview," *History of Education Quarterly* 15 (1975).

Copies of this book may be purchased from the Institute for $5.95 plus 75¢ postage and handling charges and sales tax where applicable. All inquiries, book orders, and catalog requests should be addressed to the Institute for Contemporary Studies, Suite 811, 260 California Street, San Francisco, California 94111——(415)-398-3010.

Library of Congress Catalog Number: 77-79164
ISBN 0-917616-18-9

TABLE OF CONTENTS

ERRATA

Page 271, line 34: *For* of cosmopolitan *read* of cosmopolitanism and pluralism. The liberal mind always aspired to, and felt most at home in, a cosmopolitan

CONTRIBUTORS

James S. Coleman
Professor of Sociology, University of Chicago

John E. Coons
Professor of Law, University of California, Berkeley

William H. Cornog
*Superintendent Emeritus, New Trier Township High School
Winnetka, Illinois*

Denis P. Doyle
Chief, School Finance Division, National Institute of Education

E. Babette Edwards
Administrator, Harlem Parents Union

Nathan Glazer
Professor of Education and Sociology, Harvard University

Andrew M. Greeley
*Director, Center for the Study of American Pluralism, National
Opinion Research Center, University of Chicago*

R. Kent Greenawalt
Professor of Law, Columbia University

Marvin Lazerson
Associate Professor of Education, University of British Columbia

William C. McCready
Associate Program Director, Center for the Study of American Pluralism, National Opinion Research Center, University of Chicago

Michael Novak
Watson-Ledden Distinguished Professor of Religious Studies, Syracuse University

John P. O'Dwyer
M.A., Teacher in Elementary Education/Reading

Robert Singleton
Director, Education Finance Reform Project, Los Angeles

Thomas Sowell
Fellow, Center for Advanced Study in the Behavioral Sciences, Stanford University; Professor of Economics, University of California, Los Angeles

Stephen D. Sugarman
Professor of Law, University of California, Berkeley

Richard E. Wagner
Professor of Economics, Virginia Polytechnic Institute and State University

PREFACE

Toward the end of the 1960s increasing general concern about American public education moved the federal government to become formally involved in experiments for increasing educational choice. Unfortunately, the open discussions that accompanied the experiments were cast in the adversary tensions of the period; serious consideration of educational choice was therefore aborted.

Despite disappointments in the early "voucher experiments," educational choice has maintained an intense following among a surprisingly diverse group of educators, academics, and community leaders; that following has been encouraged by a more general interest in social tolerance and cultural pluralism in American society as a whole, an interest which has arisen in an attempt to repair the social trust which was damaged so badly toward the end of the 1960s and at Watergate.

This book takes the narrow subject of educational choice into the broader reaches of cultural pluralism and social trust. The sixteen authors come from broadly diverse backgrounds; from different perspectives they offer some profound observations about American education and about American society in general. In exploring themes such as the role of the family and the interdependence of unity and diversity, they touch issues of critical importance as America moves into her third century.

Perhaps most important, the authors have tried to remove the discussion of educational choice from the adversary mode so characteristic of public discussions on social policy, and have tried to approach their subject in a positive and constructive manner. In this regard, we are particularly pleased to include in the book two special appendices—the first a model statute drafted by Berkeley law professors Stephen Sugarman and John Coons, and the second an *amicus* brief filed in the school desegregation case of *Crawford v. Los Angeles Unified School District*—setting forth practical, affirmative proposals on how choice and voluntarism may be used to encourage social policies to which society is committed, without resorting to compulsion. We are glad to include them, since they reflect a general understanding that the solution of most, if not all, social problems ultimately depends on consent and cannot be imposed.

The Institute trusts that this book will be valuable to those concerned about American education, as well as to those concerned about the general health of American society.

H. Monroe Browne

President,
Institute for Contemporary Studies

San Francisco, California
June 1977

JAMES S. COLEMAN

INTRODUCTION:

CHOICE IN
AMERICAN EDUCATION

European duality and the U. S. common school. Economic and technological changes. The end of the common school. Suburban and central-city schools. Residential and racial constraints on educational choice. Government-imposed desegregation. Expanding educational choice. The remaining issues.

Public education in America has a history unlike that of any country in Europe. From the outset, European education was two-tiered: one set of schools for the elite, another for the masses. This dual school system took different forms in England, France, Germany, and elsewhere. But everywhere, whether in the *lycée,* the *Gymnasium,* the Grammar School, or another form, it was marked by richer, more academic, and more intensive curricula for children of the elite, and by a longer period of schooling.

1

American public education was, from its beginning, a single system, founded on the ideology of a single "common school" to which children of all economic levels and all groups would be sent. Only in the South was there a parallel to the dual school systems of Europe, and that duality required a racial distinction for its sustenance. Everywhere else there was a single system, with only minor aberrations. For example, the East coast, mimicking Europe and always less egalitarian than the rest of the country, maintained and still maintains a number of private schools for the elite; the same is true in parts of California. Throughout other parts of the country private secondary academies were numerous seventy-five years ago, but vanished when public secondary schools came into being. Another aberration has been the religious schools, primarily Catholic. But because Catholics have seldom been an economic elite in American communities, Catholic schools have not constituted a way of separating the elite from the masses. And finally, the ideal of the common school was always better realized in towns, small cities, and rural areas than in large cities.

The general idea of the common school did not mean, of course, that schools were fully egalitarian. Within the school, children from lower socioeconomic groups were likely to fare less well; the general social structure of the community impressed itself on the functioning of the school. Nevertheless, the difference between these schools and the class-stratified schools of Europe was marked, just as the general assumption of equal opportunity in America was markedly different from the European assumption that every man had his station.

The idea of the common school in America was an important part of the ideology underlying American development. It was part of the ideology which finds expression in the steadfast declaration by many Americans that there are no social classes here, the ideology which gave birth to Horatio Alger, the ideology which insists that each American should have an opportunity equal to that of all others, the ideology which in the *Brown* decision of 1954 led the Supreme Court to outlaw dual school systems for blacks and whites.

However, there have been changes, economic and technological, which undermine the idea of the common school and the
idea of equal opportunity through education which underlies it.
The technological changes have been in transportation, principally the automobile. The existence of the automobile has
meant that, economic questions aside, the place of work and the
place of residence are no longer tied together. Automobiles have
made possible the physical separation of work and residence by
rather long distances. The economic changes have been a
general increase in affluence, which allows families (given that
the car frees them from living near work) to choose where they
will live, and to repeat that choice several times during their existence as their economic conditions change.

The end result has come to be communities far more economically homogeneous than before World War II; suburbs which
differ sharply in economic level from one another as well as
from the central city. Racial segregation by residence has also
become far more possible than in the past, and maintains itself
despite sharp reductions in racial prejudice and discrimination
in nearly all walks of life.

The effects of this residential fractionation along economic
and racial lines makes itself felt in the schools. While residence
and workplace are no longer tied together for the adult members
of the family, residence and schooling are tied together for the
family's children. This is in part due to the naturally smaller
radius of movement that young children have—making the
"neighborhood school" a likely institution, while the "neighborhood office" or the "neighborhood factory" is not— but it is in
part due to school policies. These policies characteristically limit
the child to attendance at a particular school, the one into which
he is zoned by his residence. This is often the closest school (his
"neighborhood school"), and otherwise one of the closest.

With families sorting themselves out residentially along economic and racial lines, and with schools tied to residence, the
end result is the demise of the common school attended by
children from all economic levels. In its place is the elite suburban school, in effect a homogeneous private school supported

by public funds, the middle-income suburban school, the low-income suburban school, and central-city schools of several types—low-income white schools, middle-income white schools, and low or middle-income black schools.

Perhaps this makes no difference: perhaps the economic or racial or educational or cultural level of the children with whom a child attends school is unimportant for the education he gets. But this seems unlikely. Even if children don't learn from one another and through competing with one another (which is unlikely), the teacher must teach to the level of the class, making a child's learning dependent on others in his class. Parents, children, and school staff recognize this: a school is regarded as a "good school" or "bad school" more on the basis of its student body than anything else.

If parents, children, and teachers are right and a "good school" is largely made a good school by its student body, then the residential patterns I have just described destroy the traditional idea of equal opportunity through education. The existence of choice about where one will live, conditioned by economic or racial constraints which make the range of choice of some greater than that of others, coupled with the absence of choice of school, limits a child's opportunity by the economic level or the race of his parents. Indeed, the only children whose choice of school is not constrained by the residence of their families are those whose families have enough money to pay for private school tuition. Only they have the choice which allows their educational opportunity to be unconstrained. They are limited neither by economic constraints nor by residence.

In recent years there have been various attempts to overcome the inequalities of educational opportunity. Ordinarily these have been in the name of racial equality, and most often they have been imposed by the courts as implementation of school desegregation policies. The simplest and most straightforward of these have been the removal of artificial constraints against attending a nearby school, constraints that had been imposed on account of race. Beyond such policies, however, the actions have taken the form of imposing additional constraints; that is, assignment to schools at some distance from the child's residence in order to bring about racial balance.

Such policies, although currently used to reduce racial segregation in the schools, are a prototype for general policies to bring about a return to the common school attended by all social levels. As affluence and mobility become even greater than at present, and as American families become even more able to separate themselves residentially by economic strata, the reaction to this separation and stratification grows. It may take the form of reactions against inequalities in school financing, as in the *Serrano* case in California or the *Rodriguez* case in Texas. And it may take the form of reaction against schools made homogeneous by residence, as in a Duluth, Minnesota, plan to bring about socioeconomic—not racial—integration. Public opposition aborted this plan before it was implemented. But whatever form it takes, it constitutes an egalitarian reaction against the process which allows those with economic resources increasingly to separate their children from others, either by separating themselves residentially or by using their additional wealth to remove their children from the public schools altogether.

The egalitarian reactions I have described above all seek to reimpose, by governmental action, those constraints which in a different technological era made possible a common school attended by all. By introducing these governmental constraints (whether through busing or through gerrymandering school attendance zones), the policies sharpen the disparity between an increasing residential mobility and freedom and a decreasing freedom and choice in the public schools. It is not surprising, then, that these policies, when used to implement racial integration of the schools, have brought about both residential flight from the affected districts and flight from the public schools to private schools.

There is another egalitarian response to this process of self-segregation through economic resources, and it is this response which constitutes the focus of this book. The response lies not in reducing the scope of choice in education, but expanding it;

not in imposing additional constraints upon public school attendance, but in removing current constraints which act differen-
tially upon families with money and those without. The logic
behind this response is straightforward: the combination of
geographic constraints on school attendance together with
differential economic resources have allowed those with money
to escape the common school and increase the stratification
among schools. Increasing the constraints on school attendance,
as recent policies have done, only increases the power of this
combination to create a stratified school system. (This is evident
in the aftereffects of court orders to bring about busing in central
cities: it is the affluent whites who leave the city's public schools
for the suburbs or private schools, leaving the poor whites and
the poor blacks to experience the constraints imposed by the
busing orders.) Removing those constraints, by giving every
child the possibility of attending any school regardless of his
family's economic level, reduces the power of economic
resources to make a stratified school system.

This would probably not have been true in the past, when residence was constrained to be far more physically proximate to
work. In pre-automobile times, residential areas were more economically heterogeneous, and it is very possible that separating
school from residence (as is true, for example, in England)
would have made for a more economically stratified school
system, rather than one less stratified. But conditions have
changed, and with them the effects of government policy.

The matter today is very straightforward. The greater the constraints imposed on school attendance—short of dictating place
of residence and prohibiting attendance at private school—the
greater the educational opportunity gap between those who have
money to escape the constraints and those who do not. Thus as
with many governmental policies, those policies which attempt
to fix rigid attendance patterns by race or residence have a perverse effect. The perverse effect only intensifies the efforts of
policymakers to impose broader constraints, and the result is a
vicious circle, all the while increasing the gap in educational opportunity between those with money and those without.

Once it is recognized that educational opportunity is increased by expanding the educational choices of all to approximate those of the economically affluent, then the general policy approach is clear. It consists of providing families and their children with entitlements, rather than services. They are then free to choose which services they will use. This is the policy employed in some other areas of governmental activity, though not all. It is the policy used in Medicare (in which the individual is free to choose his doctor and hospital) and in food stamps (where the recipient is free to spend his stamps at any grocery), but not in publicly supported housing (where the recipient is provided with governmentally supplied "public housing").* It is not wholly clear why one pattern develops in one area and another pattern in a different area. For example, in lieu of food stamps, food for the poor could first be purchased from producers by the government and then distributed from government warehouses. Or housing for the poor could be provided through housing allowances usable for rent, like food stamps are for food.

Having the general idea of entitlements or vouchers in education does not, unfortunately, solve all the problems. There are several issues of importance that must be successfully resolved. Some of these will be discussed briefly here; they are covered in more detail in the ensuing chapters.

FULL VOUCHERS VS. PUBLIC-SECTOR VOUCHERS

First there is the question of how broadly the entitlement or voucher may be used. Inherent in the concept is the idea that private schools as well as public schools are eligible to participate in a voucher system; but some of the effects of a voucher may be realized by choice within the public system itself. If the

---

*It is interesting to note, however, that there are currently in progress two social experiments to test the feasibility of housing allowances or entitlements as an alternative to public housing developments. The concept is like that for entitlements in education: the recipient may use the entitlement in partial payment of rent or mortgage for the apartment or house he chooses. It differs, however, in that its availability is restricted to low-income families.

competition among the schools within a system is appropriately structured (with principals and teachers rewarded for success in attracting children), then the resulting market system would have some similarity to that of a full voucher. Indeed, the educational experiment at Alum Rock School District in San Jose which is known as a "voucher experiment" includes only public schools, though the initial design included private schools. Perhaps the greatest danger to the idea of a voucher or entitlement that may arise by restricting it to public schools is the likelihood of collusion among schools under the same superintendent to reduce their own uncertainty at the expense of the options available to children (e.g., by restricting transfers).

RACIAL INSTABILITY WITHIN SCHOOLS

A most important question for any system that leaves choice of school in the hands of parent and child is that of racial instability. Will whites or blacks who live in the attendance zone of an integrated school use the free choice to escape integration? The question is especially relevant for those districts which have gerrymandered attendance zones to increase racial balance, so that many children live closer to a school other than the one they attend.

The answer is that probably under some circumstances they would use the choice in this way. This does not mean, of course, that there would be less integration with a voucher scheme than at present. There could very well be more, due to the choices of those living in racially homogeneous attendance zones.

It is important to note that even if such a segregating tendency were virulent among parents and children, this does not mean that a voucher system need lead to segregation. A simple provision in the voucher program could insure that the schools would be at least as integrated as before. The provision would read that no child could choose to attend a school with a higher proportion of his own race than the attendance area of the public school he would have otherwise attended.

Some voucher purists would object to such a constraint, and I do not advocate it here. I merely introduce it to show that most of the freedom introduced by the voucher or entitlement can remain even when constraints are imposed to prevent segregation.

IDEOLOGICAL EXTREMISM
AND RELIGIOUS INSULARITY

This possibility of racial homogeneity in schools with free choice is only a special case of a more general issue. Especially when private schools are eligible to receive vouchers, schools may spring up which inculcate values seen to be "dangerous," and attract a radical left or radical right clientele. Even the participation of religious schools in a voucher system would raise for some the spectre of schools (voluntarily) segregated by religion.

This concern with ideological extremism or religious segregation derives directly from the conception of public schools as an instrument of national cohesion, akin to the idea of the school as the melting pot of America. This is indeed a matter which for some is decisive against entitlements or vouchers. And it is clearly a matter which should be given the greatest discussion, since the schools are an increasingly important instrument in the socialization of the next generation. It is not, however, certain what would happen if a voucher system were in operation; for one thing, there would probably be greater consistency between parental ideology or world view and that of the school, as is suggested by the comparison at present between private and public schools.

Yet the discussion of this issue should be placed in the broader context of a discourse concerning the limits of diversity in a free society. Where should those limits lie? At present, there are curious anomalies between the wide range of literature and film on the one hand and the narrow range of schools on the other.

ACCREDITATION AND BLURRING THE
DISTINCTION BETWEEN PUBLIC AND PRIVATE

When private schools begin to receive public funds, they come more closely under public scrutiny and find themselves subject to greater government regulation than before. Private colleges and universities have learned this in recent years.

The particular form that such government oversight or regulation takes may be inappropriate, but the principle could hardly be otherwise. The public has a legitimate interest in the functioning of organizations supported by taxes. This is above and beyond the interest they have in what happens to the next generation, an interest which leads to the current accreditation procedures for private schools.

The new additional interest under a voucher or entitlement system would and should lead to greater regulation. The question is, how much greater? And how is the regulation to be exercised? These are not simple questions, and it might be that the appropriate answers would evolve out of the trial and error of common practice. On the other hand, government regulation once in place is difficult to remove even when it is self-defeating. Thus attention should be addressed to the kind of accreditation procedures that would insure the independence of the non-public schools. Some lessons might be learned from the experience of the British with the direct grant schools.

AUTHORITY OVER ADMISSIONS

The question of who should have authority over admissions when a child applies to a school is another difficult issue. In the "private sector" that authority currently rests with the school's administrative staff, while in the "public sector" neither school nor student may choose.

Obviously the two would move closer together under a voucher system: public schools would have greater freedom to expel a child, just as the child would have greater freedom to leave a school. And obviously, there would be some constraints on the private school's admissions policy. But what kind?

The answer to this question depends in part on resolution of issues discussed earlier, such as the racial instability issue.

Again, I will not attempt to resolve the issue, but only to point it out.

SUPPLEMENTATION BY PARENTS AND COMPENSATORY PAYMENTS BY GOVERNMENT

Two issues which are closely allied are these: (a) should parents be allowed to supplement the government-provided voucher payment if they want to attend a school more expensive than the voucher allowance? and (b) should the government be allowed to supplement the voucher allowance for "disadvantaged children"? These questions are similar, though they occur at opposite ends of the income ladder. Some advocates of voucher systems believe that both should be permitted, some believe that one should be, and some believe that neither should be allowed.

At the extreme, if both were allowed, one could visualize that for the upper-middle classes most of their education would come from family supplementation, while most of the education for the lower classes would arise from compensatory governmental supplements. But there are devices which would inhibit both of these extremes. I will not go into them here, but only indicate that it appears most reasonable that either *both* supplementations be allowed or that *neither* government nor family supplements be allowed. In the latter case, it could be particularly difficult to prevent private supplementation.

INFORMATION AND ACCOUNTABILITY

One of the clear virtues of any system where the child and family have a free choice of school is the fact that accountability is intrinsic. A child can leave a school if he or his parents no longer like it. But this choice, in order to be effective in improving the performance of schools and increasing the benefits to their clients, must be informed. A voucher or entitlement system without adequate information about school performance is an invitation to inequality, since some parents are well equipped to inform themselves and make good choices, while others are not.

Information about school performance where children are assigned to particular schools is interesting to parents, but not of much value, since there is little they can do short of moving. But it is crucial where children and families have choice, just as product information is critical to any consumer choice. The schools now obtain detailed information on the children's performance; it would perhaps not be inappropriate for the children and their families to have parallel information on the school's performance.

CONCLUSION

In this chapter I have attempted to indicate some of the reasons that make free choice among schools—whether by voucher, entitlement, or some other means—a viable pattern for education and the future. Some would say it is the *only* viable pattern. The chapters that follow will examine the arguments for expanding choice in education and will consider the issues that must be resolved in introducing a choice system in education at any level—local, state, or federal.

AMERICAN EDUCATION: PAST AND PRESENT

I

MARVIN LAZERSON

CONSENSUS AND CONFLICT IN AMERICAN EDUCATION: HISTORICAL PERSPECTIVES*

Educational development before and after the American Revolution. Classification of citizenship and the drive toward homogeneity. Nineteenth century: religious discrimination and economic progress; social control and labor management; family responsibilities and the immigrant urban poor. Schooling and the work ethic. Industrial demands vs. ethnicity. The economic benefits of education. Multicultural influence on the schools—a losing battle. Conflict and compromise between parochial and public schools. Ethnicity and education: Slovaks and Italians; exclusion and persistence of Native Americans and blacks. The educational bureaucracy vs. ethnic pluralism.

*The author wishes to thank the Immigration History Research Center, University of Minnesota, and the University of British Columbia Graduate Research Committee for their support.

15

It would be hard to distinguish America's beliefs about its schools from the nation's beliefs about itself. The ideology of schooling has paralleled the more general ideology of American life; assumptions about equality of opportunity, success, the nature of group relations, among others have marked political and economic debates as well as educational discussions. As in American life more generally, social changes and alternative expectations have also produced tensions and contradictions in the ideology and practices of schooling, whether in the form of residential segregation that limits the possibility of truly common schools or in the impact of economic status, race, and sex on what is taught and learned within schools. Much of this becames clear when we review the commonalities and diversities of American education over the last two hundred years.

CULTURAL HOMOGENEITY AND THE WORK ETHIC

During the nineteenth century, Americans altered their beliefs about the role of schooling. While schools had gradually assumed greater importance during the previous century, in 1800 most schooling arrangements still remained ad hoc and unsystematized, and of limited importance in the lives of most youth. Traditional expectations were strong that the most important learning took place within families, at work, and in religious institutions. Schools were places where basic literacy was extended, familial and communal moral codes reinforced, and where youth and young adults might enhance their job prospects through the learning of specific skills. But their position was clearly secondary to the apprenticeships, household labor, familial, and religious environments that dominated the household and rural economies of colonial America (Kaestle 1974; Axtell 1974; Demos 1970).

In the half century after the Revolution these informal learning arrangements came under attack, the outcome a newly enhanced importance for schools as the major formal agency in the transmission of cultural values to the young. On one level, this transformation was related to the ideology of republican citizenship that emerged with the Revolution. Concern for the uniqueness and tenuousness of the American experiment, fear of Old World corruption, and the desire to establish a unified nation and a national character fostered numerous proposals for institutions to assure the creation of patriotic citizens. The need, to quote Benjamin Rush, a signer of the Declaration of Independence, was to "effect a revolution in principles, opinions, and manners," to "adapt our modes of teaching to the peculiar form of our government" (Tyack 1967; Rudolph 1965). This concern was neither unique to America nor limited to schooling. The nation states of Europe manifested similar concerns, and calls for a uniquely American literature, art, and architecture were common. But increasingly the school became a focus of American identity, not as an agent of the national state—the Revolution after all was fought against excessive state authority and Americans were too committed to decentralized institutions and voluntarism to support a national system of schools—but as an expression of patriotic citizenship, as the place where the young learned how to be Americans.

The meaning of citizenship, however, was complicated. Tensions and conflict over definitions and applications were the substance of nineteenth century politics and social reform movements. Accommodations had to be made to regional and local variations, to ethnic and religious differences. Citizenship for whites obviously differed from its application to blacks and Native Americans. Women were not so much citizens as the mothers of future citizens. Preparing the young for republican citizenship thus meant that public school systems had to provide both a common set of definitions and a means of acknowledging the diversity of American life.

To a great extent the schools did this by denying the diversity. Despite moments of dissent, even a Civil War, the United States, students were told, had achieved a consensus on all moral, political, and economic issues. The diverse peoples populating America had to overcome their distinctive characteristics and inherent inferiorities. One means was to identify as Protestants. Although denominational competition had undermined attempts to create an established church even before the

Revolution, Americans nonetheless expected their society to be religious, and they assumed it would be Protestant. The absence of an established church, however, raised serious problems about how to inculcate religious values. In terms of schooling, the question was simply put: how could religious education be made secure when the state was committed to nonsectarianism? The answer led Americans to distinguish between denominational affiliation and general moral values applicable to society as a whole. This distinction allowed for the adoption of a common denominator, Protestantism, that stood above doctrinal conflicts. In the process, public education became America's established church. One did not have to be Protestant to be American—although it helped—but one did have to pay psychological deference to Protestantism. Under these conditions, the possibilities of a culturally plural society were severely circumscribed (Smith 1967; Tyack 1966).

Nineteenth century schoolchildren thus learned that Catholicism was a false religion, fostering tyranny, superstition, and greed. The projected image of Jews changed during the nineteenth century from a distinctly religious to a racial group, their quest for material goods portrayed in sinister terms and identified with urban vices. Religion was often subordinated to racial and national characteristics. Blacks were at best happy children, thoughtless, subject to violent passions, and lacking those qualities necessary for full citizenship. Native Americans were also inferior to whites; they were either "noble savages" or, if they resisted the march of progress westward, simply savages. In either case, their extinction was inevitable. The Irish were impulsive, violent, fond of drink, and impoverished. The French were frivolous and Catholic, although they had produced Lafayette and Napoleon. Worst of the white immigrants were the Southern Europeans: racially homogeneous, indolent, and Catholic. While other groups, especially the English and Germans, received more generous treatment, nineteenth century schoolbooks taught American children harsh stereotypes about racial and ethnic minorities. The lesson was clear: while individuals could become Americans by identifying with white,

Anglo-Saxon, Protestant values, they could only approximate true Americanness. A hierarchy of Americanism had been created (Elson 1964; Carlson 1975).

The best Americans were not simply those who equated Protestant values with patriotism and rejected distinctive nationality and ethnic traits. They were also economically successful. To assure economic success, the school was to integrate Protestant morality with secular advancement. Even more it had to establish success as a peculiarly individual accomplishment, attached neither to one's family or communal group. The task was not easy, for it involved reassessing the meaning of the family and traditional modes of work behavior.

Colonial Americans had endeavored to limit the disruptive effects of a transient, unattached work force and of technological growth on their communities. The breakup during the eighteenth and early nineteenth centuries of apprenticeships, the release of large numbers of the poor from communities, the growth of a floating wage labor force, and the abandonment of mercantilist state economic regulations, however, had disrupted traditional mechanisms for providing labor and for restraining disorderly and deviant behavior. The resulting stresses led to a search for new institutions of social control and labor management. In the South this took its most pronounced form in an intensified commitment to a precapitalist work structure—the plantation system and slavery. Outside the South the search for new institutional controls was manifest in the establishment of professional police and fire forces, reformatories for delinquents, prisons, workhouses, and mental asylums, and in the founding of common school systems (Genovese 1969; Rothman 1971; Jones 1975).

The institutional transformation of mid-nineteenth century American society was largely justified on two interrelated grounds: the failings of the family and the need to impose new patterns of work behavior. Although the former had been a complaint since the early colonial period, its nineteenth century manifestation rested on the disappearance of the household economy. As the basic unit of production, the household once linked the economic structure, communal institutions, and family members into a complex web of interrelationships. The separation of work and home, however, sharpened the boundaries between family and community, intensifying the family's role in the socialization of its children. Whereas large numbers of children had once left their families to enter other families in a state of quasi-independence as apprentices and domestic servants, during the nineteenth century they began to stay home for longer periods, lengthening the state of childhood. One consequence of this was to emphasize the responsiblity of the nuclear family for the socialization of its young. Parents, especially mothers, now stood with the awesome burden of assuring their children's success or took responsibility for their failures (Katz 1976; Dawley 1976).

The intensified responsibilities of nineteenth century child rearing was of especial concern to observers of the urban poor. As the Secretary of the New York Association for Improving the Condition of the Poor wrote in 1851:

> So sadly has the character of the poor deteriorated of late years in this city from the immense influx of foreigners.... immigrants have the same right to come here as had the first colonists; but they have no right to burden us with pauperism, nor to deteriorate our morals, or to endanger our institutions.

The worst of the imigrants' sins was their failure to raise their children adequately. Adult depravity made immigrant families "nurseries of indolence, debauchery, and intemperance," prevented adequate role models from developing, denied children schooling, and, most of all, inculcated values hostile to the work ethic. In part, the critics of immigrant life were right. Poverty made it difficult to engage in respectable working and middle class behavior. Able to earn only limited wages, subjected to a fluctuating labor market, and without a public welfare system, the unskilled and semiskilled were often thrown back on the very limited availability of philanthropic charity or their own group or kin for their survival. But the conflict was more complex than the critics suggested, for at issue was a deep tension between the demands of industrial capitalism and the values of an essentially rural, preindustrial population (Schlossman 1974).

Preindustrial work patterns were casual—in agriculture, dependent upon the seasons and land; among artisans, upon independent control over hours and products. Household and group cohesion dominated expectations. These shaped the rhythm of labor. Intense involvement followed by idleness, a host of rituals and festivals, interrupted work schedules. These were the patterns that native rural migrants, European immigrants, black slaves, and Native Americans carried with them. Industrial capitalism, however, demanded a new morality, one that depended upon consistency and regularity and an individualist ethic of self-control, self-discipline, and self-improvement. Many of the phrases that described this morality were not new; their meanings were. Once industry simply referred to hard work. By the mid-nineteenth century it meant "devotion to a methodical work routine" dictated by the clock and the sale of wage labor as a commodity (Dawley and Faler 1976; Gutman 1973).

The implications of these developments for schooling were momentous. In order to smooth the transition between family and the new economic order, schools had to adopt bureaucratic and factory-like procedures. Differing cultural values and familial behavior patterns made ethnic groups and families the enemy. The most effective public schooling was that which separated children of the poor from their families. And the responsibility schools were accorded for the resolution of social and moral problems opened public education to a host of ameliorative cure-alls that bore little relationship to the substantive social problems of American society (Tyack 1974; Katz 1971; Lazerson 1971).

EDUCATION AND SOCIAL CONFLICT

Anyone who views the tensions and conflicts that have marked American education quickly recognizes that while the schools have been dominated by a broad consensus on the issues of cultural homogeneity and the work ethic of industrial capitalism, that consensus neither triumphed immediately nor without conflict. Alternatives were always posed, the consensus itself was often inconsistent and ambiguous, and modifications occurred. Around such issues as work, biculturalism and bilingualism, Catholic parochial schools, the education of Americans of color, and school achievement, groups have conflicted with the dominant ethic—occasionally winning, sometimes revising parts of the ethic, but often conforming or losing. What remains striking, however, is that America's diversity suggested other ways to run the schools, alternative assumptions under which the educational system might function.

Work Values and Schooling

The implementation of technological and capitalist social relations of production varied over time and from place to place. Traditional work patterns continued in certain regions, among some groups, and within occupations. In particular, while ethnic and familial ties were often the conduit through which individuals found work, they were also the basis for resistance to the dominance of the individualist work ethic. The ethic itself was modified by the strength of nonindustrialized, often premodern, families and cultures, what Herbert Gutman has called the "tough familial and kin ties [that] made possible the transmission and adoption of European working-class cultural patterns and beliefs to industrializing America." This was especially apparent at the turn of this century when the new dominance of the factory required a dramatic resocialization of the work force (Gutman 1973, p. 563).[1]

When critics thus pointed to the disorganization of working class and immigrant life and to the "culture of poverty" that surrounded it they were only partially accurate. The street gangs, youth neither at work nor in school, and industrial protest were more than assorted acts of criminality and alienation, more than simply the moral failings of the poor. Rather they often revealed the tensions between strong cultural traditions, the necessities of survival amidst urban poverty, and the functioning of the economic system. They were part of a process that included benevolent societies, ethnic churches and political organizations, working class saloons, and communal festivals as cushions against the demands of the industrial workplace.

Cultural conflicts over the nature of work dramatically affected the expansion of schooling in the nineteenth and twentieth centuries. They underlay reformer demands that schools act as moral stewards, that education overcome the baneful effects of family life, and that schooling become the mechanism to create a sober and deferential workforce. They fueled the periodic outbursts of Americanization, as well as the movements to centralize, bureaucratize, and professionalize school systems. And they shaped the pressure to take the schools "out of politics," thereby withdrawing educational decision-making from local communities and urban wards (Tyack 1974; Bowles and Gintis 1976).

For those who went to school and aspired to being successful, adopting more acceptable codes of conduct was imperative. By the early twentieth century, schools provided a means to that end. Lessons learned could be translated into economic reward. With limited amounts of schooling, young women could enter the new women's white-collar and middle-class occupations of teaching, office work, and nursing. In an uncertain and fluid economy, secondary schools became places where middle class adolescents could have the security of living at home while gaining the education necessary to retain or advance beyond their parental status. By the 1920s, programs to tie schools to the occupational structure proliferated. For many, such vocational courses distinguished those with middle class aspirations from the working class; for others, they represented a way of learning job skills. But however one viewed courses preparing youth for work, it was becoming clear that staying in school itself was the wisest career decision (Katz 1976; Lazerson and Grubb 1974).

Biculturalism and Bilingualism

Most immigrants to America wanted to become Americans. But
it is also clear that many wanted some continuity between their
ethnic cultures and the dominant culture of their new environment. They did not wish to see their children's American
citizenship gained at the expense of deep and open hostility
toward the culture and language of their former homeland. For
much of the nineteenth century, the structure of American
education allowed immigrant groups to retain some balance and
to incorporate linguistic and cultural traditions into the schools.
In urban as well as rural areas, schools were decentralized and
locally controlled, often blending public and private supports.
Because of this, schools tended to be highly responsive to ethnic
and political pressures, and immigrant groups could successfully
assert that the preservation of their cultural identity was a legitimate responsibility of public education (Tyack 1974, pp. 13-27).

Usually this preservation took the form of instruction in a
language other than or in addition to English. Wherever immigrant groups possessed sufficient political power—be they
Italian, Polish, Czech, French, German—foreign languages were
introduced into elementary and secondary schools either as separate studies or as languages of instruction. The most successful
group in this regard were the Germans. In cities where they constituted a significant political force, German became a regular
part of the school curriculum. In Cincinnati, children in the first
four grades wishing to do so (about 14,000 in 1899) could split
their school week between an English teacher and the German
teacher. During the mid-1870s St. Louis's Superintendent of
Schools William T. Harris, soon to become U.S. Commissioner
of Education, defended his city's bilingual program by claiming
that "national memories and aspirations, family traditions,
customs, and habits, moral and religious observances—cannot
be suddenly removed or changed without disastrously weakening the personality" (Tyack 1974, pp. 104-9; Troen 1975).

Yet despite these successes in ethnic pluralism, pressure to
convert to a culturally homogeneous system proved too great.

Assimilation and identification with America intensified latent and sometimes overt conflict between earlier immigrants like the Irish and Germans and the more newly arrived Southern and Eastern Europeans. Americanization programs, especially around World War I, combined with the bureaucratization of school systems to make it politically more difficult to force adaptation to subgroup requests. By the first decades of the twentieth century, bilingualism and biculturalism in the public schools were rapidly disappearing. Groups like the Poles, Croatians, and others who identified their language with their national identity were forced outside the public system to preserve either. The symbolic battle between one standard of belief and pluralistic forms of education was being resolved, and pluralism was in full retreat (Higham 1958).

The Catholic Alternatives

From the mid-nineteenth century, Catholics sought to control their children's education, defending themselves against anti-Catholicism and seeking public funds for their schools. Church councils called for schools to provide Catholic children with a Catholic education. European religious orders reinforced the immigrant's traditional values, and provided the labor to run the schools at subsistence wages. The process of founding parochial schools, however, varied from community to community. In Marquette, Michigan, Catholics established schools as a logical extension of church and family education, and not in protest against the public school's Protestantism or agnosticism. In New York City during the 1850s, Bishop John Hughes inveighed against the "Socialism, Red Republicanism, Universalism, Deism, Atheism [and] Pantheism" of the public schools, and moved to establish separate parochial schools in the wake of Catholic/Protestant and native/foreign-born conflicts (Ravitch 1974, ch. 1-7; Graham 1975, pp. 74, 86-90).

Important as these mid-nineteenth century developments were in laying the foundation for future growth, they were not part of a consolidated drive toward parochial schooling. A

variety of strategies for integrating secular and religious values
were available, while the decentralized structure of education
and the blurred distinctions between public and private allowed
for informal options to meet group needs. In the four decades
after 1870 that situation dramatically altered. As informal decentralized schools changed to centralized bureaucratic systems,
the influence of local interest groups waned. Simultaneously,
schooling itself took on new importance; high rates of voluntary
attendance were reinforced by the passage of compulsory attendance legislation. By the 1890s three out of five parishes had established parochial schools as alternatives to the public system,
many of the schools maintained only with great economic
difficulty. And increasing numbers of Catholics had concluded
that support for the local parochial school was an excellent,
perhaps the best, way of expressing their religious convictions
(Cross 1965).

Two aspects of the origins and subsequent development of
parochial schooling are particularly relevant here. First, the
system was born of conflicts between Catholics and Protestants
and between groups within the church. Second, once the commitment to an alternative system was made, certainly by 1920,
Catholics tended to minimize differences between parochial and
public schooling; the former appeared more and more like the
latter.

During the nineteenth century, anti-Catholicism was frequently tied to anti-foreignism and, as we have seen, school people often assumed that one could not simultaneously be a good
American and a good Catholic. Of special importance at the end
of the century was the collapse of a number of attempted de-
tentes between Catholic authorities and public school officials:
plans to allow nuns and priests to teach in public schools,
transfers of property that would give public school authorities
use of the parochial school buildings in return for a continued
Catholic atmosphere, and released time experiments. These
compromises were invariably undermined by Catholics dis-
trustful of public institutions and opposed to "Americanizers"
like Archbishop John Ireland and by non-Catholics and public

school educators unwilling to accommodate to minority group sentiments (Morrissey 1975).

Differences within the church among nationality groups were also of major importance in the proliferation of parochial schools. The church had typically been organized into territorial parishes with all Catholics who lived within a given geographic area members of that parish. After 1870, however, the arrival of large numbers of Polish, Southern Slav, and Italian Catholics, when added to the nationalist-oriented German Catholics, forced the largely Irish hierarchy into a de facto acceptance of parishes along national and language lines. In Chicago, where the phenomenon was striking, the number of foreign-language parishes grew from 9 of 25 parishes (36 percent) in 1869 to 38 of 80 (47.5 percent) in 1889 to 62 of 117 (53.9 percent) a decade later. By 1902, 55 percent of the city's Catholic parochial children were in ethnically designated schools. While the situation varied by city and nationality group, those organized in nationality parishes were often unwilling to send their children to the public schools or to the parochial school of another nationality, where they were often unwanted anyway. Italians resisted Irish schools. Poles distrusted Irish and Germans. Lithuanians complained of having their children taught by "Polish Sisters." These groups, except for the Italians, proceeded to set up their own school alternatives. (Sanders 1976, pp. 32-61; Shanabruck 1975).

Conflict was not the only basis upon which parochial schools were established. Many Catholics arrived in America with the belief that education should be an extension of family life, and they supported the idea that the school should be under church auspices. But in historical retrospect, conflict—between Catholics and Protestants and among nationalities within Catholicism—appears as the crucial determinent in the origins of the parochial school system in America.

While the parochial system originated as a religious and ethnic alternative to public education, equally striking has been the pressure on that system to conform as closely as possible to the public schools. From World War I on, Catholic educators have emphasized the "American-ness" of their parochial schools, and that the values taught there are those held in common by most Americans, save for distinctions of religious preference. Moreover, as the class composition of the American Catholic community changed, parochial schools ceased to be primarily for lower and working class children and, since World War II at least, have tended to enroll the newly emerging suburban middle classes. This is not to suggest that parochial schools and public schools became exactly the same. But while there were differences, parochial and public schools in the same localities came to share striking resemblances. In cities like Chicago and New York high proportions of public school teachers and administrators were from Catholic families and parochial schools. What began as an explicitly different system has wound up considerably less different than Catholics and non-Catholics believed likely seventy-five years ago (Sanders 1976, pp. 108-213; Greeley and Rossi 1966; Greeley et al., 1976).

Ethnic Culture and School Achievement

The cultural values of American ethnic groups and the demands of school achievement have frequently been in conflict. While there are many reasons for differential school achievement among groups—economic status, previous cultural background, the availability of rewards through schooling, levels of discrimination, and the attitudes and climates of individual schools and teachers—at least some of the differences can be attributed to the discrepancies between what was expected and rewarded by ethnic and family cultures, and what was demanded by school authorities. Jews, Scandinavians, and Rumanians showed strong commitments to public education, cultural values congruent with public school expectations, and high school achievement levels. Other groups manifested different patterns. An examination of two of these, Slavic and Southern Italian immigrants, suggests much about the conflicts and limits of public education in America (Olneck and Lazerson 1974; Cohen 1970; Barton 1975).

To many Slavic immigrants, education's responsibility was to strengthen family and ethnic ties, especially those of language, religion, and shared work income. Only through strong and unified families and cultural groups could future security be assured. For many, language and religion were inseparable; their retention had been essential to protect the Poles, Croats, Slovaks, and other minorities of the Austro-Hungarian Empire from assimilation and deracination. Schools could play an important role in this process. They could be places, as one Slovak writer put it, where children learn "to think in Slovak, and know the culture of their nation and love for their people" (Bodnar 1976; Stolarik 1974, esp. pp. 149-83).

The tension between immigrant parents and public school officials over cultural values quickly led to the proliferation of private nationality group and parochial schools. But even more striking, and more important in terms of school achievement, were the poverty and the assumptions about schooling and work that Slavic parents carried with them. For many, education was not designed to enhance economic mobility; that was what work was for. To get ahead—indeed, simply to survive—one did not stay in school; instead one entered the labor force, and, as much as possible, one's wages became part of the family budget. Children were thus members of a collective necessary for family survival—a value reinforced by the reality of low incomes and the unskilled, largely industrial jobs with very limited opportunities for occupational mobility their parents held. Slavic children were pressed out of school and into work as quickly as possible. Only where schooling amounted to learning an immediately useful skill or trade could extended attendance be justified (Scott and Tilly 1975).

The necessities of economic survival, the importance of national language and religion, and cultural values that gave priority to family unity and family needs, placed Slavic children among the lowest public school achievers. Many dropped out before the sixth grade; very few stayed to high school. In Chicago in 1910, while 5 percent of all black children and 6 percent of all Polish Jewish children were in high school, only 1 percent of the Poles and Slovaks were enrolled, and the proportions were worse in Cleveland. As late as 1950 in Pennsylvania, the state with the largest influx of Slavs, median years of schooling for Slavs was the lowest among the state's ethnic groups. Even when parochial school statistics are included, the data in city after city show only limited improvements in school attendance and achievement for Slovak children.

Southern Italians also showed low rates of school achievement. School authorities complained that Italian children were unruly and truant, dropout levels were high, and there seemed to be little enthusiasm among Southern Italian parents for advancing their children's academic careers. There were undoubtedly many reasons for this, ranging from hostility to Southern Italians by school people to the economic pressures that required early school leaving. But it is also clear that Southern Italian cultural values conflicted with the demands of formal schooling in America, and in that conflict the Italian child either had to change or was dropped by the wayside.

Italians of the *contadino* or the peasant class of southern Italy arrived in America with cultural patterns conditioned by chronic poverty, by a rigid social structure, and by exploitation of frequently absent landlords. In a world heavily stacked against them, the *contadini* found in their families the sole refuge within which trust and loyalty could be cultivated. The world was "us," the family versus "them"—the official institutions, the state, the outsiders. To survive required complete loyalty to "us" with as little contact as possible with "them" (Vecolli 1964; Banfield 1958).

Schools, in this context, were alien institutions maintained by the upper classes at the *contadini's* expense. Few peasant children went beyond the third grade, and they received little incentive from their teachers to achieve further. Nor was formal education supported by the church. Catholicism in Southern Italy was marked by mysticism, the supernatural, and emotional identification with the patron saints. Rarely was the Italian peasant expected to be able to read the prayer book. Knowledge—religious and secular—was based on community folklore not written texts, to be learned not debated or analyzed (Vecolli 1969).

This background ill-disposed Southern Italian immigrants to respond favorably to American schools. Schooling was seen as a direct challenge to family values and parental control. The dominant concern of many Southern Italian parents seems to have been that the school would indoctrinate their children with ideas antagonistic to the traditional codes of family life. Reporting on the dilemma of being Italian in New York's public schools, a sociologist wrote that "it is in the school that the one institution which is an integral part of his nature and devotion—his home—is constantly subjected to objections." In addition, schooling, especially for adolescents, conflicted with the economic needs and expectations of Southern Italian families. Once old enough to contribute, Italian youth were expected to work (Covello 1967; Bromsen 1935).

Southern Italians and Slavs did change in America as they grasped the opportunities to become middle class. But for at least a generation, their strong familial cultures combined with economic poverty to accerbate conflict with public schooling, their needs often met by disinterest or hostility on the part of American educators. The conflict was not unique to these groups; but Southern Italians and Slavs clearly suffered from American education's inability to respond sensitively to familial and communal values or to provide secure learning environments for children caught in the conflict of cultures.

Americans of Color and the Melting Pot

In the conflict between white and nonwhite Americans over socialization and educational achievement, one finds the supreme irony. The ideology of public schooling required that as many as possible be brought into the public schools as the only sure way to achieve a common socialization process. But from the beginning nonwhite Americans were excluded. Race was the line that could not be crossed in the melting pot of the common school.

By the mid-nineteenth century white policy toward Native Americans consisted of two phases: expulsion from tribal lands and genocide against those who resisted. The assumption was that education to the white man's ways would slow the pace of westward expansion and was unlikely to be effective anyway. After the Civil War the economic costs of Indian wars and some public outcry led to a policy of land allotments to individual Indians, in direct violation of tribal communal landholdings, and to the establishment of federal boarding schools for native youth. The schools were explicitly designed to break traditional tribal and group identities. As the founder of the Hampton Institute, Samuel Chapman Armstrong put it upon admitting Native Americans to his school, "in missionary operations the world over, the boarding school is used as affording the best leverage on the races. The savage or semi-savage needs a training that covers the twenty four hours of the day." Because it was assumed that Native Americans were averse to work, they were given heavy doses of manual labor, at Hampton even more than required of black students. Coeducation was encouraged, an attempt to foster marriage across tribal lines to create families distinct from tribes. Native dress was replaced by Western clothing, and Indian students were urged to shun Indian ways and to "walk the white man's road." The view was nicely summarized by the U.S. Commissioner of Indian Affairs in 1902, when he wrote that Indian dances and feasts were "subterfuges to cover degrading acts and to disguise immoral purposes" (Kerber 1975: Hendric 1976).

To anyone who looked the educational provisions were a travesty. Corporal punishment was rampant; kidnapping and other coercive measures to require attendance were common, made more likely by having boarding school budgets dependent upon enrollment. Salaries for teachers at Native American schools were substantially lower than those of public school teachers, while poor living conditions and geographic isolation compounded difficulties of recruitment. After 1885, centralized operational procedures were developed for boarding and day schools—uniform curriculum, uniform examination and grading, uniform rates of financing. Enrollments and attendance were low; frequently native children were caught between totally inadequate reservation and boarding schools and seeking access to district public schools where they were usually unwanted. By the time a "new deal" for Indians was proclaimed during the 1930s, Native Americans had become the outcasts of American society (Hendrick 1976; DeLoria 1970).

For black Americans the processes of exclusion and participation were more complicated. Whereas Indians wished to be left alone, blacks sought participation. In the antebellum South, a tightening web of controls intensified restrictions upon learning in the slave quarters; masters were forbidden to allow slaves to learn to read and write. For slaves, the transmission of knowledge depended upon the strength of communal and family ties, religion, an oral tradition, the skills learned on the job, and through the selective imitation of white ways. Although neither enslaved nor forbidden to learn, blacks in the pre-Civil War North were either excluded from common schools or forced into underfinanced segregated schools, often no more than basements in church buildings. In New York City, the proportion of black to white students in the public schools was 1 to 40; the proportion of expenditures from the school fund was 1 to 1,600. In Boston, a coalition of blacks and white abolitionists attacked that city's policy of segregating the races in the late 1840s. In the Roberts Case that set the precedent for Jim Crow, the Massachusetts court declared that separate but equal facilities were acceptable, a decision only overturned by the state legislature in 1855. In most major cities, however, integration did not proceed that far. At best, blacks could expect minor improvements in their schools, largely designed to undercut pressures from black parents for access to white schools (Genovese 1974; Schultz 1973; Litwack 1961).

Yet commitment to schooling among blacks was high. Black voluntary groups provided places for the young and adults to become literate; literary societies, manual training groups, and other self-help agencies organized programs whereby northern blacks could receive an education. After the Civil War that commitment became even more apparent when emancipated slaves flocked to schools to gain some learning. Using available funds from Reconstruction governments, setting up their own schools, attending the Freedmen's Bureau schools or those of white missionary societies, it seemed as Booker T. Washington put it, that a "whole race [was] trying to go to school." The expectation that schooling would translate into economic opportunity and lay the basis for equality of treatment, however, soon proved mistaken. With the end of Reconstruction in the 1870s and the growing movement among whites to erode what limited political and economic gains blacks had made, the expansion of educational opportunity was severely limited (Washington 1963; Bond 1969; Harlan 1969).

The combination of black faith in education, white resistance, and the limited returns blacks received from schooling could be seen in the city of St. Louis. With the white community intensely hostile to them and with little economic or political power, blacks were kept outside the common school systems before the Civil War. Not until 1865 were they legally entitled to public funds, and then their schools were segregated and poorly financed. But with little white support, the black community built its own facilities, successfully used a boycott to gain black teachers for their schools, and unsuccessfully asked that black public schools be designated by the names of great black figures. And they attended school in striking numbers; black enrollment exceeded or equalled that of white working class students. Their commitment, however, was not translated into opportunities for social mobility. The overwhelming number of blacks (97 percent in 1891) held unskilled or semiskilled jobs. For blacks, going to school was neither cultivated nor rewarded by the white community (Troen 1975).

By the first decades of this century, blatant exclusion of blacks from educational institutions had been replaced by more subtle measures. The growth of large urban ghettoes effectively segregated black children from the rest of the city. The rhetoric of special programs and educational conditions for blacks centered less upon distinctions of race than upon the need for schools to be realistic and relevant, to concentrate upon fitting the student to the realities of the economic and social marketplace and to the realities of scientific measures of intelligence. This took a variety of forms.

> Educational tests showed that Black children had low mental levels and therefore they were unfit for rigorous academic learning.
>
> Since discrimination in the economy was such that Blacks could not get good jobs, schools should therefore train Black children for the jobs they could get: girls would receive training for domestic service; boys for unskilled menial labor.
>
> Blacks, it was argued, grew up in immoral atmospheres. The schooling of Black children, therefore, should emphasize basic moral values absent from their home life and neighborhoods. (Anderson 1973; Tyack 1974, pp. 109-25, 217-29)

The black response to the processes of exclusion varied. Some, like Booker T. Washington, publicly acknowledged the legitimacy of education for second-class citizenship, even as he worked more privately for progress in civil rights. Washington's most outspoken critic, W.E.B. DuBois, agitated for an explicitly egalitarian education for blacks and whites. At local levels, conflict over education often revolved around the issue of integrated versus segregated schools. Sometimes black communities worked for entry into white schools, the participation of their children on an equal basis with whites. In some cases, the demand was for separate but equal schools, places where black children could be taught by blacks and where they would be free from the hostility and prejudices of white children and white teachers. Whatever the politics of any particular situation, however, blacks showed a willingness to use a multiplicity of techniques to win their case: court action against school boards, public pleas and lobbying, school boycotts, all attempts to force the white power structure to respond (Harlan 1972; Meier and Rudwick 1967a, 1967b).

Exclusion and education for second-class citizenship touched all native and immigrant peoples of color. While similar expectations affected other ethnic groups and the poor generally, for nonwhites exclusion from the melting pot was more total, more systematic, and more discriminatory. If the goal of American public education was to adjust the individual to the realities of society, it was America's people of color for whom the realities were most oppressive.

CONCLUSION

Since the mid-nineteenth century America has sought political unity by an ideological commitment to cultural homogeneity. The trauma of a Civil War, the disorganizing effects of industrial capitalism and large-scale immigration, and the tensions of racism made Americans unwilling to acknowledge a citizenship that stressed diversity. But political unity based on cultural homogeneity has occurred only by discriminating against some, segregating others, and denying the possibilities of alternative ways of life.

Partially out of the commitment to homogeneity, public education was reshaped at the end of the nineteenth century into a bureaucratic administrative structure that made the schools highly resistant to ethnic pluralism. The two processes—bureaucratic structures and the denial of pluralism—were thus closely intertwined historically. American schooling before the mid-nineteenth century was eclectic, ah hoc, consumer oriented. That tradition has been all but lost. To reassert it would require explicit commitments to multiculturalism as essential to American life *and* a bureaucratic reorganization allowing for considerably more decentralized decision making. Without these it is unlikely that varied cultural values and styles will be acceptable in public education.

II

JOHN P. O'DWYER

CLASSROOM COLLAGE: ONE PERSPECTIVE

Introduction. The kids: class size; diversity in the classroom. The conditions: classroom, supplies, and materials; support services. The content: the problem with public standards; time constraints. Teacher as diagnostician: the problems; individual differences. Deficiencies in administrative control. Lack of teacher incentives and parent expectations.

INTRODUCTION

I suppose I have to be considered part of the new blood in public education, one of those who received his teacher training during the late 1960s and early 1970s. I've been teaching since 1967 when my graduate student stipend depended on my conducting three discussion sections a week in Western Civilization. Deciding, however, that my fascination with history would not feed

37

my family, I transferred my knowledge to the high school domain and student-taught in an upper-middle class high school
while looking for a real job.

Finally, during the last week of August 1969, I was hired by a
suburban Sacramento junior high school; the administrator and
I mutually agreed that we were, at best, each other's second
choice. After two years of teaching 7th grade social studies and
math and 8th grade science, I quit—strategically retreating to
college where I obtained an M.A. in Reading.

While a student, I also taught nursery school; but again, $3,300
is a belt-tightening wage. So I relocated in the San Francisco Bay
Area where I had grown up and, after a one-year search, signed a
contract with a suburban East Bay school district.

In three years I have had three assignments: Reading
Resource Specialist, 3rd Grade Teacher, and Kindergarten
Teacher. None of these assignments has been in a "bad"
school—inner city, predominately minority, or low socioeconomic status—the kind where armed guards are required in
high school halls. None has been exclusively with remedial,
behavior problem, or special education children. My classroom
assignments have been average for districts where achievement
was slightly below average.

In this chapter I have drawn upon this experience to present
one teacher's perspective on the obstacles to teaching effectively
in the public education system. To some extent, these obstacles
result from the failure of the system to adjust to a clientele
which is often more mobile, more diverse, and better educated
than the neighborhood-centered populations of the 1950s. More
important is its failure to define responsibility for the education
of the child. Issues concerning expectations, standards, accountability, and control go unresolved as the respective roles of
parents, teachers, and government remain confused.

To give shape to my role as a teacher, I have focused on the
August *angst* familiar to many teachers, the questions which
must be answered to prepare for the school year. Assuming your
assignment is known (no certainty, since transfers and the creation of multigrade classes are still possible to accommodate

sudden vacancies or shifts in student population), you begin to sort the pieces: Whom do you have and how many? Which room are you assigned to? What supplies, texts, specialists, etc., are available? The answers are important, since they shape your existence for the next ten months.

THE KIDS

Class Size

When my assignment is finally unveiled, usually in late July, I make haste to obtain an up-to-date class list. Then I count. This is not ignorant superstition. I am aware of the controversy and literature on class size; it has been discussed for centuries, even receiving mention by Herodotus. The bulk of the evidence would seem to indicate that, as an isolated variable, class size cannot be the villain held accountable for low achievement scores (Klitgaard and Hall 1973; NEA 1968; Shapson 1972; Coleman 1966).

Public education is a human process in which class size is an inextricable part of the dynamic. Controlling factors, such as threat of expulsion or parent support, cannot be guaranteed. Perhaps this is why the subject continues to rank as a critical concern on teacher polls. It is why I worry about "how many." Bluntly put, how would you like to have 38 thirteen-year-olds assigned to your home—attendance: compulsory?

Obviously, a classroom is more flexible than a home; but more bodies still mean increased competition for space. In my junior high classroom where 38 students were assigned, there were only 34 student desks. The overflow used my desk or stood. Fortunately, truancy was high and attendance low, so this situation seldom occurred.

Last year, though, "who got it first" was a major issue, the disputes often ending with Lenny and Sondra each holding half of the gameboard or Bob stealing the assignment sheet so he alone could use it. Ever try getting 32 eight-year-olds to share eleven lockers crammed into just sixteen feet of wall space? "That's my hook!" "He pushed me!" "Somebody stole my hot dog money!" Crowding commonly creates conflict (Shapiro 1975, pp. 437-41).[1]

To reduce conflicts successfully, and certainly to *teach* anything, students and teacher must reach some agreement—at a minimum, a respect for the rules; more hopefully, genuine rapport. Remember, school is compulsory. In my 3rd grade class at least one-quarter of the kids would have preferred not attending; three were practiced truants. By the 7th grade, when cars and sex are beckoning, how many children are really interested in the difference between a democracy and a republic?

Remember the Get-the-Substitute game? You switch seats and answer to the wrong name. You swap answers and copy homework openly. You whisper loudly. Large classes can be almost as unproductive, unless there is respect and rapport. Yet consider my junior high school position: I saw 228 students a day, 38 in each forty-five minute instructional period. That gave me a bit more than a minute per student each day, multiplied by two hundred instructional days—a total of slightly more than three hours per student per year in which to establish any sort of human contact, much less respect or rapport. It took me almost three months just to learn their names.

Each student represents a time cost—preparation, correction, testing, makeup. Even if you have enough space and materials, even if you have good rapport, there's no shortcut to responsibly eliminate the work an additional student represents. Simply, if you have 30 students instead of 20, you have 50 percent more paper to shuffle. You compromise by preparing less specifically, correcting less often, ignoring makeup. It is a direct relationship: more kids mean quantitatively more work for the teacher and qualitatively less individual attention, academically and behaviorally, for the students.

Diversity in the Classroom

All students, however, are not created equal. Some demand more—more discipline, more instruction, more attention of all kinds. I should have discerned this when a probation officer brought Eric to class on the first day of my junior high school assignment. By midday, though, when Richard declared, "I ain't picking up no paper for no ---- honky teacher!" I'd an inkling that these were not the polite and respectful students I had anticipated. Now, after counting heads, I always check to see *which* students have been assigned to me (Ohlson 1977).[2]

Not that I have any control over these assignments. In my school, as in many, someone in the administration (the school secretary, if no one else is around) handles student placement. The intent is to balance teacher load, ensuring that no teacher has significantly more students or an excess of known "problem" children. Creating an ethnic or sexual balance is given passing consideration, but factors like SES (socioeconomic status) or learning modes/teaching styles are given none.

The result is a heterogeneous group of children who present disparate profiles of background, expectation, attitude, and ability. Some degree of diversity, of course, is helpful, enriching the classroom experience with unique student perspective and experience. But how do you please both the Steinmuns, advocates of a nutrition-oriented snack program, and the Browns, who described class nonparticipation in Hot Dog Day as "heartbreaking"? How can Herman be expected to join in classroom clean-up when at home such tasks are derided as "woman's work"? If such petty problems consume teacher time and energy, consider the impact of such disparity on important instructional concerns.

Forty percent of my students come from a low-income (not welfare) housing project; yet these students account for 73 percent of the absences. How do you teach, or even plan for, Michael who has missed thirty-three of the first sixty-six days this year—and has come tardy fifteen of the times he attended? Last year Donald held the record with fifty-one absences for the year, more than one per week.

The test scores present a similar picture: children from the project score 15-20 points less than children from other parts of the community of standardized tests in reading, math, and language. In theory, a range of abilities and achievement levels is helpful for providing cross-fertilization of ideas. In practice, you must be equally prepared to teach Danny, who has his own library card, and Tina, who doesn't know what a library is.[3]

Behaviorally, the differences may be amusing, irritating, and sometimes sad. First recess last year I dismissed the class and 3rd grade Joseph jumped out through the window. Later gaffes included his bringing a knife to school and throwing a chair during a fight. His method of initiating "play" was punching. He wasn't a malicious boy; he just didn't know any other way. Similarly, Mr. Bradley, father of a kindergarten boy who had been beaten up on the way home from school, asked me in all seriousness if it would be appropriate for Tod to bring a club to school to protect himself. I'm trying to teach the child to raise his hand; at home he's learning how to handle a club!

While project children present a particular set of problems, other parts of the community are not trouble-free. On the edge of town is a new, fairly expensive ($45,000+) development. The families moving in are upwardly mobile, and frequently both parents work. School is dismissed at 2:45, however, leaving many children unsupervised until 6:00. Older children often are left in charge of younger ones; in my 3rd grade class, four children (eight- and nine-year-olds) were the older ones.

The results are both behavioral and academic: bright, exposed Kevin—who had the latest in TV-advertised toys, who took tap lessons, who went skiing—was finally referred to Guidance after he lowered his pants on the playground. This was the finale of a three-month long escalation of attention-getting behaviors. Five times he had evaded discipline for various infractions, and always his parents had protected him by insisting an "apology" would suffice. Meanwhile, they paid even less attention to Kevin's skills which, after an unsupervised summer, had slipped a full grade level.

Sondra's case is also telling: although she had entered kindergarten on the 98th percentile, she was retained at the end of 3rd grade because her skills had dropped to the 35th percentile. Sondra still sucked her thumb, wet her pants, and threw temper tantrums in class; but after school she went home to take care of 1st grade Greg until her parents returned.

The community where I work is a predominantly white (77 percent), middle income (1975 median: $10,267) area. The majority of project dwellers are not welfare recipients; there are few of the familiar problems—racial tensions, severe unemployment, non-English speaking or single parent families (83 percent of the school's children come from two-parent families; only one child does not speak English).[4] Looks good on paper, but the statistics belie the differences in the children. Which ones will know what a puzzle is for? How many will be able to understand simple verbal directions? Which parents are likely to support your discipline policies or help out in class? How each child will settle into the classroom situation, the amount and kinds of attention he will demand, are related to his environment. Albeit neither unerring nor a determiner, the address is still one predictor of the child.

THE CONDITIONS

Classroom, Supplies, and Materials

Assignment confirmed, class list reviewed, I try to get a firm commitment on a room—"Are you putting me in Mrs. Bregan's room for sure?" Seems trivial, except that last year I was moved from Room 10 to Room 2 to Room 8 in a span of ten days—books, boxes, treasured objects, and all.

After finally settling in Room 8, I spent a week (my own time) collecting the proper furniture and materials to equip a kindergarten room. Like many others, our school is participating in a state program which stresses small group instruction, i.e., the teacher and several students working together around a table. Most of the school's equipment, however, is still desks. Naturally, we teachers compete for the choice items. Anything not clearly labeled with another teacher's name is *mine*. Once those items are claimed, we just shove the desks together into small instructional clumps.

After pilfering enough to piece together a classroom and supplementing the school's furniture with my own soft touches such as rugs and pillows, I usually spend another week (my own time) going through supply catalogues and filling out requisitions. Then, order pad in hand, I go in to lobby the principal for his signature.

It is important to present these requisitions as soon as possible, preferably by late June. Hopefully, at this time, competition from the other teachers for available funds will be low. Hopefully, too, the funds will not yet be spent by the administrator himself (last year our principal spent $3,000 to equip a new kindergarten; the tables and chairs he selected were too large for many of my 3rd graders). Finally, early action is necessary to ensure that your order will arrive before Thanksgiving.

In late August, following a brief respite, preparations are completed by a raid on the stockroom. Again, early action is advisable, since by Christmas shortages are likely and by Easter crucial items, like pencils and glue, may be unobtainable. Last year we were told in November that the supply budget for the year had already been spent.

These shortages, such as running out of pencils, can be a big thing. Normally, the teacher is to issue each child one pencil a month. Please be aware that the eraser may only last the first hour and that no eraser ever makes it twenty class days. By day ten, a pencil *with* eraser is highly valued and a major source of social conflict. In my junior high class, during the last two weeks of each month I would go around to each child who had neglected to bring a pencil and trade one I had purchased for an article of his clothing, usually a shoe. I'd pile all this stuff on my desk and exchange it after the work period. Yes, it did happen once that a student lost one of my pencils. I made him hobble out to his locker, sans shoe, to get another pencil to exchange for his shoe.

The same year the school ran out of toilet paper in mid-May. The administration asked the children to bring it from home, which they did—rolls and rolls of it. Since the roll tissue did not fit the school's sheet dispensers, however, the kids were soon enjoying glorious throwing matches which left the school festooned with toilet paper and the bathrooms still bare.

Many of these problems could be resolved by granting each teacher his own supply budget, a lump sum to be spent as needed on instructional supplies; a few schools already do this. In mine, though, it is the school secretary who orders everything from toilet paper to ruled news. Perhaps that is why we started this year with a three-year supply of index cards and a three-month supply of red paint.

Support Services

The school secretary is part of an amorphous collective known as "support services." She doesn't type for me; she doesn't file or maintain records for me. What she does do, fairly frequently, is interrupt me via the school's PA system. Just as the lion is about to eat the Christian in the read-aloud story, the speaker at the front of the room will blare: "Remind Franklin that he has a dental appointment." The announcement that "Mary's lunch is in the office" may disrupt the work of an entire class. One directive caught the class several minutes into a recess period. Rain was pouring torrentially outside when the message came: "Do not send the children outside for recess."

The remainder of the support team is made up of specialists assigned to serve as resources in areas such as reading or music. A good specialist can help the teacher build an effective program—providing appropriate materials with instructions on how to use them, sometimes working with children who need special assistance. The Math Specialist at my school, for instance, has spent one hour a day for a month in my class helping me to implement a new program. Too often, though, the specialist's effectiveness is thwarted by an overload of paper work, meetings, and duties, coupled with inexperience. Ten specialists have worked at my school over a three-year period; only half had previous experience as specialists. Perhaps to compensate, they give inservices.

An inservice sounds like an efficient way to disseminate information: a presentation of materials, methods, and theories to the teachers en masse. In reality, it is usually a mandatory, two-hour lecture at the end of the day, when specialists or guest speakers discourse in educational abstractions, e.g., "The Possible Difficulties in Remediating Impairment of the Visual Modality." This to teachers fresh from a barrage of double negatives and garbled locutions ("Me go home now?"), who still have to correct, lesson plan, and prepare materials for the next instructional day. One specialist was elated when three (out of twenty) teachers actually used materials provided at an inservice. If my response rate was only 15 percent, I'd seriously reexamine my presentations.

Specialists, secretaries, supplies, teaching materials, freshly painted classrooms—it all sounds like so much. Yet in September it may seem so inadequate. Services may be misapplied or impractical. Supplies may not stretch quite far enough. All I can count on, aside from a shipment of grade-level texts, is a sufficiency of chairs and desks and a sickly-green square of a classroom.

THE CONTENT

The Problem with Public Standards

What shall I teach? Certainly there is no lack of advice on this subject. State and local guides recommend a variety of subjects for inclusion in the elementary curriculum—typically, reading, mathematics, language arts, social science, science, art, music, and physical education. These subjects can each be divided into several topics, each by itself suitable for extensive study. The Language Arts, for example, include speaking, listening, handwriting, spelling, grammar, and composition. Likewise, the Social Sciences may include history, political science, anthropology, economics, philosophy, etc. Indeed, curriculum guides often provide charts showing how themes within a subject are to be introduced, developed, and interrelated throughout the grades. Fortunately, the legislators stop short of mandating that teachers actually use these guides.

My county guide recommends that I teach reading, math, language, science, social studies, and PE on a daily basis. To this, add or subtract several quirks of community. In my present position, this means that holiday observances are transformed into extravaganzas. The Halloween party is no mere candy fest just before dismissal. Instead, it is a two-hour party with games, refreshments, and costumes, followed by a parade through town. At Thanksgiving there is a kindergarten parade and feast; Easter has egg-rolling and kite-flying contests.

The locale of my previous position, where 42 percent of the students bore Spanish surnames, dictated obviously different concerns. Ethnic studies—like unionism, pollution, even nutrition—can become the subject of controversy. (I have been labeled a "health food freak" because I believe PTA cupcake/hot dog sales undermine the school's efforts at nutrition education.) The only trouble I encountered, however, arose when I tried to follow a state-approved text which included the topic of evolution. About 10 percent of the community were members of the Jehovah's Witnesses, and students would bring tracts to class in angry rebuttal of the text. Finally, when one disapproving parent began dropping in to listen, I took to taping my lectures as a precautionary measure.

After considering community curriculum demands, the teaching requirements that come with state and federal projects are factored in. My school receives Title I Compensatory Education funds; in exchange, I am supposed to provide more instruction to identified students, those who test below the 50th percentile. In addition, I am to provide an individualized, "diagnostic/prescriptive" learning environment, since my school receives state Early Childhood Education funds. ECE also adds affective and multicultural education to the curriculum list.

Time Constraints

Now that it's clear what should be taught, let's see how it fits

into the school day. Assume that the child attends school from
8:30 to 2:30; that looks like a six-hour day. Deducting for the obvious breaks—a one-hour lunch, three ten-minute recesses, a
ten-minute snack period, and two ten-minute cleanup periods—
still leaves a four-hour day. When you subtract the start-up costs
for each activity (get a pencil, get a book, sit down, find your
place)—multiplied by the inefficient pace of children—and
throw in additional lost minutes for the time spent refereeing or
paper-shuffling, the day diminishes to a fraction of what is indicated by the published school schedule. You'll be close if you
count on three hours—maybe as much as two hundred
minutes—of actual instructional time. And that's ignoring holi-
days, assemblies, library visits, health screening, and other
special events.

These time constraints make some pruning of the curriculum
unavoidable. Naturally, basics receive prime consideration.
Since reading (and probably math and language as well) requires
at *least* three instructional groupings to accommodate different
achievement levels, most of the morning is absorbed by these
subjects. Other subjects are squeezed into the remaining afternoon time, when the kids are restless, inattentive, or just plain
tired.

Teacher as a Diagnostician: The Problem of Materials

The precise content of the program is a compromise between
the time, the children, and the available materials. As a junior
high school instructor, I was supposed to be teaching about the
nations and capital cities of Europe; yet fully one-quarter of my
students could not identify Sacramento as the capital of California, though it was less than ten miles away. Should I really teach
comparative communities in the four climate zones, as indicated
in the 3rd grade social studies guide, when 68 percent of the
children have never been more than fifty miles from home?

I see myself, in part, as a diagnostician: through testing and
observation discovering what the children already know and
where they are weak. I stumbled onto this approach when

assigned to teach 7th grade mathematics. The text began with a review of fractions and decimals, but only three of my students had really mastered multiplication and division. Four students were still weak on the addition and subtraction combinations below ten. So late one Friday afternoon I had a janitor admit me to the textbook warehouse and salvaged from boxes marked "India" sufficient elementary texts to suit the different levels of achievement among my students.

Most commercially available programs present similar suitability problems. Ideally, topics should be presented several times in a variety of ways. Students should see about, talk about, read about, and write about the subject as part of the learning process. But when texts and activities rely on grade-level reading or writing skills, the material may be inappropriate for whole group use.

The science program for an 8th grade course I taught is a good example. The text was a professor's dream of what every child should know about his planet, complete with beautiful illustrations and charts, definitions and questions, suggested activities and projects. On the first page the earth was described as an "oblate spheroid," a description which was 100 percent successful in baffling both the children and their teacher. The text was soon relegated to the picture-book/reference category and received little use throughout the year.

Many recent materials, especially in reading, have been redesigned to stress specific skill instruction and, hence, provide greater flexibility. The instructional pattern is to pretest, teach, and retest. Thus, it is hoped, the materials will be suitable for all the children in the class.

Sounds good, but where do I start? The district-adopted reading program has forty-four skills for the kindergarten level. Combine this with the ECE project reading continuum, which has sixteen kindergarten skills (not all duplicates). Following the pattern of pretest-teach-retest, then, these four- to six-year-olds are expected to *master* more than one new skill a week in reading alone.

At this pace, it is no surprise that much may be covered with

little being learned. Materials frequently offer inadeqate practice for skill mastery. The teaching guide to the 3rd grade reader
used last year, for instance, called for me to teach antonyms; but
the accompanying workbook furnished only one page on the
subject. Correspondingly, the math workbook used in the 2nd
grade spent only four pages introducing "carrying." Additional
practice was spread sparsely over the last third of the book. In
September only 2 out of 32 children entering my class remembered how to "carry."

Teacher as Improviser

Science, health, social studies, and spelling are still commonly
taught in whole group fashion using district-adopted commercial programs. Where materials are too unsuitable, however, the
teacher may be left to invent a program from what he can
scrounge and what he can make. Last year's health book, which
was too hard for many of the children, was replaced by a series
of films, prints, projects, and books on nutrition, disease preven-
tion, and safety.

The problems of this eclectic approach are both administrative and substantive. Since my junior high school had only four
projectors serving twenty teachers, I volunteered for the position of "audiovisual coordinator" to ensure that I would have a
working projector when needed. What do you do, though, when
you are supposed to teach a unit on Ancient Greece and the
county film library has nothing listed under Plato, Socrates, or
Aristotle? (You have the students give "TV" presentations
using boxes and pictures cut from old copies of *Life* and *National Geographic*.)

This "cut and paste" approach is also time-consuming and
frustrating. Sometimes topics must be dropped for lack of
materials; my district, for example, has few environmental
education films suitable for kindergarten. But the alternative,
whole group and textbooks, is equally grim. When the task is inappropriate (too hard or too easy) the children don't attend:
they doze; they dream; they disrupt. Learning is halted when

the teacher must attend to distraction and discipline rather than to instruction.

Special Problems: Individual Differences

For children with special problems, whole group instruction may be counterproductive: if a child has a speech or hearing problem and is taught to read by a phonics method, if he has a vision problem and is pushed to memorize sight words, the instructional response may be aversion. Perhaps these considerations appear extreme, since they would seem to refer to only a small percentage of the student population. Hardly, as detailed in Table 1.[5] The totals reflect the number of *different* children in my classes over the last two years who have had normal physical difficulties requiring some accommodation in instructional technique. Only two of these children were identified as "educationally handicapped," and all received the bulk of their instruction in a normal classroom situation. And these were just the children who had physical problems.

What should I do with Robert, who is seeing a psychiatrist at age five after setting fire to his house three times? What about nine-year-old Denise, whose psychiatrist gave up, saying "I can do no more until the family life changes"? Isolated examples? Not especially so. Third grade Jerry missed a year of school after being kidnapped by his father; six-year-old Tim was molested on his way home from school. Each of my classes has included two to four kids like these, and my teaching assignments have been in areas that are close to average; my kindergarten children scored only two points below average on a standardized readiness test.

More common are the children whose parents are too busy, too demanding, too combative, or too drunk. These children are distracted from the curricula by basic necessity—hunger, fatigue, insecurity, fear. Occasionally school becomes a haven. Karen, for instance, is responsible for her own breakfast, clothing, and transportation to school. She attends regularly but is frequently tardy. I no longer report her, however; after all,

Table 1

Students with Special Problems

Specific Problem	1975-1976 (average=27)	1976-1977 (average=23)
Hearing loss	2	2
Visual impairment	2	4
Speech	1	2
Hyperactivity	2	1
Other (severe allergies, dominance)	3	2
Total	10	11

Karen is only five. Other children are less enchanted; school for them is another routine of childhood.

Recipe for a normal class: start with approximately 27 children. Sprinkle liberally with physical problems. Add a handful of "home-related factors" and a dash of emotional disturbance. Fold in a range of abilities and achievements. Mix well. In the final analysis, it is the children who qualify the classroom experience. Curriculum guides, parent demands, text suggestions, carefully prepared lesson plans—all must suffer the little children.

THE PLURALISTIC CLASSROOM

The Role of Parents

On 8 September my musings are replaced by bodies, bulletins, records and forms, yelling, coughing, milk tickets, and yard duty. The first month is placement time for the children; they undergo a battery of standardized and school-developed tests. It is catch-up time for me; I add seats, adjust chairs, meet with parents, consult files, and perform other minor tasks necessary to adjust theory to practice.

Almost inadvertently an operational program creeps into existence. By mid-November I surface to the reality of parent conferences: I have twenty-three sets of parents to please, as well as the principal, the project director, the Governing Board, and the State ECE Monitor and Review Team. Parent reactions are mixed. Stacy's mom thinks I work the kids too hard; Peter's parents want to see more papers coming home. The Allens want more music and craft. The Steinmuns want more nutrition education. Missy's mom is so glad that I'm a *man* teacher; Tina's wants to know *what happened* to Miss Hoover.

My role during these conferences is almost political. I try to inform and encourage the parents about their children, while mollifying their concerns about the program. Usually the conferences result in little change; a tally of comments from twenty-three different families rarely provides sufficient basis for program revision.

Then, too, parent comments are not necessarily reliable indicators of what the parent wants. The American Dream in education is, of course, that all children will score *above* the national average, particularly in reading. Parents in our district share in this dream and express disapproval if the children don't come home with bundles of phonics worksheets.

But at home the kids don't read. Only six of the children in my kindergarten class have ever been to the local library. Why should they? Their parents would rather watch television. In two years, only two parents have borrowed material from the classroom Parent's Education shelf, which includes craft, cooking, and some general interest reading, as well as educational books. The children model what they see; they watch television (one parent did ask, though, whether six hours a day was too much television).

The gap between comments and commitment is obvious in

other areas. In conferences last year, many parents praised my concern with student work habits. Yet only half the parents saw to it that their child completed his weekly spelling homework, even after notes went home explaining the homework program and soliciting parent assistance. Parents complain to the school when their children are involved in fights on the playground or are beaten up on the way home; but according to a 1975 survey, 68 percent of the parents encourage their children to fight as the first recourse if threatened. "What would your parents tell you to do if someone hit you?" I asked some brawling 3rd graders, trying to lend greater authority to my position. "Hit 'em back harder" was their response.

The Administration

If some parents are guilty of failing to reconcile individual with institutional values, the policymakers are equally culpable in their failure to provide any consistent implementation of intent. The Governing Board of my district, for instance, has involved the teachers in the state's Early Childhood Education program. Nevertheless, the business manager for the district refuses funds for a variety of items either implied by the project's goals or explicitly identified in its needs assessment. Thus, although 75 percent of the parents indicated that TV is the only cultural medium available to their children, each teacher is allotted only 1.5 field trips for the entire year. Similarly, while parent involvement is a major component of ECE, parent-teacher communication is not encouraged. Last year, since over half of my students' parents worked during school hours, I would contact them from my home to discuss pressing academic or disciplinary matters. Vouchers for phone reimbursement were returned, though, with a note attached suggesting I mail home letters instead.

Board support for a policy—at least in its applied, classroom form—seems to stop whenever a parent protests. Present board members are advocates of the Back-to-Basics movement and have initiated research into establishing a fundamental school. When a parent complained of my policy of keeping children after school until they had completed two-thirds of their daily assignment, however, I was told to change my policy.

Kevin was transferred after thirteen phone calls and two parent meetings concerning his behavior. In each conversation, the parents would assure me of support; but in Kevin's own words, "They didn't do nothing." Office referrals similarly achieved nothing. When, as a last resort, I suspended Kevin for the day the administration balked. Both parents worked; suspension would inconvenience them. So Kevin played in the school library all day and was transferred to another class the next day, without consultation. One hour after the transfer his new teacher referred him to the office for correction.

The principal defended Kevin's transfer as a consumer choice. Some transfers, it is true, are consumer choices: many parents support parochial education on this basis. But what about Scott's "social" promotions? His parents refused retention after kindergarten, 1st, and 2nd grades. Now in 3rd grade, Scott's skills are at least two years retarded.

Parent rights are popular with our administration. The attendant responsibilities, however, are not. A child may be driving *me*—and the rest of the class—crazy; yet the office may not even phone his parents if I refer him. "How do you feel about being in trouble?" I asked one 3rd grader. He shrugged. "They just put the pink slip in my folder with the others. So what?" The parents' responsibilities seem to end with enrollment. Once enrolled, the kids can (and some do) cheat, steal, lie, cut class, and ignore work—and the school will still serve them.

CONCLUSION: TEACHER INCENTIVES FOR IMPROVEMENT

The only coherent interpretation of educational policy I can derive from my personal experience is: avoid controversy. The administration seems satisfied as long as you manage your class efficiently—turn in your register on time, maintain student files, attend meetings, keep the children quiet and the annoyed parents appeased. Indeed, most parents are content with the appearance of education, regular progress through workbooks and texts. Some seem to equate school attendance with school achievement (one set of parents was genuinely shocked last year to learn that their 3rd grade daughter had 1st grade math skills).

Improvement in education is possible, but why bother? Last year I averaged a sixty-three-hour workweek. I spent an *un*reimbursed $350 on furniture, teaching materials, supplies, and phone bills. As a result, the children gained an average of fourteen months on standardized achievement tests. I was elated. But I received no bonus; class conditions did not improve. I received no commendations nor any other form of recognition—aside from confrontations with six different parents (three involving the administration) over academic and disciplinary policies.

Incentives for improvement simply do not exist. Teachers' pay scales are based on a formula which considers longevity of service and additional education rather than performance. Award or honorarium programs commonly are limited to PTA-sponsored retirement or "Teacher of the Year" luncheons.

Discussions of professionalism are, in the main, rhetorical. The teacher is blatantly a district employee. For instance, I'd estimate that almost $45,000 is spent for my class, but I have discretionary use of none.[6] It is the teacher who has the most intimate knowledge of a child's educational needs, yet he typically will have no control and little influence over grade level assignment, room assignment, student placement, class size, scheduling, standardized testing, transfers, promotions, retentions, or budget allocations (including equipment, supplies, and the use of support services).[7]

Program development usually proceeds from the dictates of classroom survival, with a measure of personal drive and satisfaction. The pleasant image of parent and teacher earnestly working together under the smiling glance of the passing principal is myth. Few parents pursue such a relationship (about one to three a year in my experience). Most are uncomfortable, slightly defensive, and inarticulate concerning their educational goals for their child. They expect education to be a modified version of their own schooling. Only a handful request a specific teacher for their child; even fewer select a specific school. Parents mainly seem to relate to education with resignation: school just happens to kids.

The administration does little to promote a more active parent role: the system tends towards inertia. No viable mechanism exists to help or encourage parents to articulate educational goals for their child.[8] The schools themselves frequently lack any distinctly defined educational philosophy (indeed, programs are often adopted district-wide), leaving parents without alternatives. Standards for admission and promotion are usually nonexistent; but then neither are standards of health, attendance, or discipline widely enforced. If schools expect little of parents beyond taxes and enrollment, neither do they promise much beyond the availability of classrooms, books, and teachers.

For the individual teacher to promise more is, at best, quixotic. As parent conferences should suggest, teachers presently lack the control, the time, and the resources to respond adequately to the diversity of parent expectation. The families I serve represent a spectrum of attitude, expectation, and approach to education, but the political mechanism seems incapable of translating their needs into an integrated, effective policy. I entered education believing I'd be a professional in charge of young children's education; ten years later I feel a little naive about my high aspirations and a little betrayed about my minimum expectations. I feel that I've described a building which has stood for a hundred years and become a bit shaky, a classroom which desperately needs earthquake-proofing.

I have a fantasy of the teacher as a private practitioner teaching students whose parents basically agree on an approach to education. Standards (admissions, promotions, discipline) would be contractually stipulated; administrative services would be contracted for as a member of a collective. While in execution this fantasy might prove inadequate, faltering over large capital outlay expenses or state mandates, at least it considers the problems of defined responsibilities and a diverse clientele. It is indeed illusory for the present system to continue to pursue its goal of mass education without recognizing or resolving these problems.

IIIA

E. BABETTE EDWARDS

WHY A HARLEM PARENTS UNION?

Equalizing pressures exerted by organized professional educators. Community educational services vs. a centralized educational bureaucracy. Parent-student concern for quality. Lack of school cooperation with parents. Problems of communication in a poverty-level community of ethnic minorities. Control of educational financing as a means of improving educational quality.

The primary goal of the Harlem Parents Union has been to help parents help their children to get the best education possible. The philosophy behind the founding of the organization was that parents and children are an unprotected group of consumers who must depend on a highly organized, self-regulating, heavily funded, and authoritarian school system to provide public education. Since all paid workers in the school system, from principals to janitors, are aggressively represented by organizations devoted to their own interests, it seems natural that parents and students should also be represented.

I have always believed that parents are consumers with a vital interest in their children's academic achievement and must exert a controlling presence in the public school system. I submit that the record of the public school system in teaching black children is nothing short of disgraceful, and that the schools make every effort—both obvious and subtle—to discredit significant parent participation. I also believe that only an informed parent body can demand and make the basic changes necessary to achieve excellence in education.

The purposes of the Harlem Parents Union are several: to challenge the widespread notion that home conditions are responsible for poor academic achievement in isolated minority communities; to fill the information vacuum for parents in one such community, District No. 5 in the Central Harlem area of New York City; to provide intensive education to parent groups about the public school system and how to cope with it; to act as a central core for encouraging effective parent involvement in the schools; to provide a vital educational consumer advocacy center for parents and parents associations for schools in the district; to disseminate information about consumer interests in the community to the outside media; to monitor the academic progress of children, the quality of education in the individual schools, and in the district as a whole; and to challenge the basic negative pedagogical attitudes expressed in the professional educational community.

We are aware that many call the problems before us insuperable. We ourselves have experienced the formidable opposition that "mere parents" face when attempting to equalize the power disparity and to increase parent participation in the schools. For we represent parents who have no vested interest in the school system other than the children they love.

As an organization, we feel we are uniquely qualified to carry out our program. We have long experience as an indigenous parent and student advocacy group, with deep roots in the community and its concerns; and also with a practical and theoretical knowledge of the educational system. We feel that we shall succeed because of our humane, committed, and flexible approach to community educational problems.

As parents, the organization perceives the need for drastic educational change in a community in which, according to the School Ranks Report, New York City Board of Education, 87 percent of its children are below grade level in basic skills in addition to having other educational problems. But as parents we move with caution and deliberation. Decisions are made on the basis of what is, what should be, what can be—without recourse either to "movement" rhetoric or to the pseudoscientific rhetoric emanating from majority-sponsored studies.

We speak from twelve years of work in the Central Harlem community—work which is truly of, by, and for the parents and children of this community. On the overtly political level, Harlem Parents have struggled for integrated education through regular channels, and when those were closed, through peaceful demonstrations, school boycotts, etc. In despair at continuing de facto segregation and substandard schools, we initiated the concept of community control which the Board of Education later translated into decentralization. Decentralization left contract negotiations, finances, and other major decisions in the hands of the central authority and was a grave disappointment to advocates of community control.

Through all the political struggles and failures, Harlem Parents worked with parents and children on an individual level, providing referral and advocacy services, study groups and workshops advising people of their educational rights and teaching them how to cope with the school bureaucracy, and most recently, after-school tutoring. Over the years, Harlem Parents has worked with thousands of people on all kinds of problems relating directly and indirectly to the education of minority children. In addition, we are recognized by educators and sociologists throughout the country as a leading indigenous authority on minority public education.

The observations presented herein are as those of a community general practitioner who knows the complaints and histories of all his patients firsthand, and from experience has become a reliable diagnostician. He can truly be said to be the leading authority on the health of his community, and while he keeps up (as this organization does) on the literature produced by the profession outside the community, he tests all of it against Mr. Jones's gallbladder. If some of our experiences and conclusions seem to be undocumented in a formal sense, they are, nevertheless, based on intensive communication with thousands of community people.

THE PROBLEM

According to information published by the Board of Education of the City of New York, 87 percent of the elementary and junior high school students in Community School District No. 5 have scored considerably below grade on standardized reading and mathematics examinations.

In their efforts to explain away what must otherwise be seen as their own professional failure, teachers, principals, and other officials working in the city's public school system claim that the majority of black and Puerto Rican children are "unteachable" because of inadequacies in their homes. They cite poverty, "broken" families, and indifference and ignorance on the part of parents as factors impeding student motivation and academic progress.

Poverty is, indeed, debilitating to parents and children alike, but historically poor people have been successfully educated in America's public schools. Many teachers now working in the school system came, themselves, from poor families. As for the breakdown of family life, this phenomenon is endemic throughout the society, cutting across all social and economic lines, and there is no clear evidence that children of single parents fare worse academically than those of nuclear families.

So we are left with accusations of neglect and ignorance. The history of the movement for integrated education, for community control of schools, etc., should leave no doubt as to black parents' concern about the education of their children. In our long experience of working with parents in Central Harlem, we have observed an avid, and often tragic, concern among them with respect to their children's academic progress. Our after-school tutoring center attracted more than twice the students we were able to handle, and all of them were brought to the center by their parents. Very little publicity was given to the existence of this program in District No. 5, because as soon as the first mention of it went out we were flooded with applications. In a school district serving approximately 18,000 children, we would estimate that at least one-half the parent population would apply for extra educational services for their children if such were available. We are often swamped by requests from parents to help them negotiate for their children with school authorities. But it is true that there is a lack of *official* parent involvement in the schools, e.g., in parent associations.

From time to time, principals, teachers, and their unions decry this lack of involvement, but we have found these complaints to be merely lip service. Any sustained involvement by enlightened parents is viewed as a threat by school officials, and such parents are labeled "trouble-makers," "militants," etc. It soon becomes apparent to parents that the kind of "involvement" considered desirable by economic interest groups (i.e. principals, the United Federation of Teachers, etc.) takes the form of participating in cake sales and other kinds of busywork designed to give parents the illusion of participation. But when parents show a *real* interest in what goes on in the schools— when they question the competence of teachers, the validity of teaching methods, the curricula—their "public servants" make every effort to discourage them from further activity. One of the disadvantages of poverty is that it imposes an economy on people's time, and parents in Central Harlem have little time for illusions. They quickly smell out phoniness.

While complaining that parents are ignorant, either the schools make little or no effort to alleviate the situation, or they make a deliberate effort to keep parents in the dark. Communications are generally confined to "open school days," notes to parents about students' "disciplinary" infringements, and report cards. Parents are often given unwarranted reassurance about their children's achievements during the school year, only to be informed at the end of the year that they'll be left back due to failure. Reading and other textbooks, when they are issued to children at all in District No. 5, are kept in the classroom, effectively preventing parents from assisting children in these areas of study.

Recently it was necessary to enact laws to permit parents access to their children's school records and to insure the confidentiality of these records. The very need for such a law is an indication of the strenuous effort made by school officials to keep parents at a distance.

Parents are made to feel unwelcome in the schools except at official functions, and their attempts to obtain necessary information about their children's rights and progress usually meet with indifference if not outright hostility. Too many questions can and do result in subtle and not-so-subtle reprisals against their children. Guidance counselors, frequently poorly trained, approach verbal and nonverbal criticism of teachers by children as evidence of emotional disturbance, seldom looking into the possibility that the criticism might be just; the counselors are equally defensive about parental criticism. Black and Puerto Rican parents, already oppressed into a sense of inferiority by the attitude of the society as a whole, are particularly sensitive to aloofness in professionals and easily discouraged by it. Their classic response is to retreat into acceptance of authority, no matter how it offends their common sense, and to despair about their own abilities to guide their children's futures.

The above is a sketch of some of the mechanics of deliberately inculcated ignorance. Hoping to help their children somehow to function within a system of seemingly mindless authority where "behavior" is rated—and often *graded*—above achievement, they tend to imitate the authoritarian mode in their own homes, teaching their children to obey without question, and reinforcing the antithesis of democratic education. Children, finding a total lack of support for their intuitions, either fall into a dull, apathetic conformity or rebel against all rules imposed on them, sensible and otherwise. Aggravating this situation is the fact that among the information withheld from parents in this community is a knowledge of psychological theory formulated and developed during the past century. The books on this subject, read as a matter of course by middle-class parents, are inaccessible to the majority of black and Puerto Rican parents because of their own reading deficiencies resulting from a backward educational system. Guidance counselors, instead of acquainting them with some of the ideas which have created a virtual revolution in middle-class child rearing, condescend to what they interpret as "black culture" and/or reinforce the general defensiveness of a bureaucratic school system which regards all challenge as a threat.

The Harlem Parents Union was established to address these real areas of parental "ignorance" and the resulting lack of involvement by parents in the schools. Meeting the educational and advocacy needs of so many people (short of an act of Congress) is extremely difficult. But we do reach out into the community as a whole, with information, and keep the individualized effort within the bounds of reasonable expectation.

It is our hope that through our leadership training workshops, parent-student advocacy referral programs, and effective information dissemination, we will produce a core of parents so well informed and so self-confident that they will provide a formidable presence in school collective bargaining. To a limited extent we have achieved an effective presence, but a *formidable* presence is still a goal for the future.

One way in which parents, particularly poor parents, can establish a formidable presence is to assume control of the financial levers. Education vouchers are one such mechanism. Introducing an element of competition for the education dollar would give parents the power to act as change agents to improve the quality of educational services.

IIIB

WILLIAM C. McCREADY

PAROCHIAL SCHOOLS: THE "FREE CHOICE" ALTERNATIVE

Early Protestant-Catholic conflicts. Ethnic influences and parochial schools. The role of the parish in the Catholic community. The neighborhood and pluralism. Parish schools and community needs. An alternative to public education. Community subsidies. The Chancery Church and the Parish Church: diversity of views. Free choice and sectarian schools. The implications for social trust.

INTRODUCTION: WHY DID THEY GET STARTED?

Many American Catholics have traditionally been wary of the public or common school. Such suspicions were probably encouraged by the early historical fusion of the Protestant Church with the public school during the intensely nativistic period of the 1830s. If Catholic children could be prevented from attending parochial school, so the conventional wisdom held, then there was a chance they might grow up with the ability to think for themselves instead of acceding to papal whims. In *A Plea for the West,* Lyman Beecher of Lane Theological stated the argument in unequivocal language: "It is equally clear that the conflict which is to decide the destiny of the west will be a conflict of institutions for the education of her sons, for purposes of superstition or evangelical light, of despotism or liberty" (Beecher 1835, p. 12). In the face of such virulent nativism Catholic parents were highly motivated to create their own school system as an alternative to that system which utterly failed to show any respect or appreciation for either their religious or cultural heritage.

Although nativism was one force which promoted the growth of the alternative parochial school system, another came from the diversity of the Catholic immigrants themselves. Many of the larger cities had "national" parishes as well as those founded by the diocese. These "national" parishes were designed by religious orders to serve the needs of the Poles, Italians, Germans, and others, and were totally independent of the diocesan structure. The merging of these parishes, and the destruction of some of them, is a part of the history of American Catholicism that need not concern us here save to remind us that the strain between pluralistic and monistic definitions of culture were at work both in the church and in the larger society. The people who comprised parishes, both national and diocesan, have always defended themselves against those who would collapse or merge them together, and this attitude has been most intense with regard to the parish schools. In order to understand why people resist having their school closed or their parish merged, we need to examine the role of the parish in their lives, and the role of the school in the parish.

The waves of immigrants that came to this country from the mid-1800s relied on needed institutions which mediated between them and the larger host society. For Catholic immigrants the church frequently played that role. Our forebears had needs which shaped the structure of local parishes. The parish became a power center and a refuge and provided a point of stability and familiarity in a strange and alien culture. Frequently the parish and the political precinct went hand in hand to make jobs available to immigrants who would have gone unemployed because of nativist bigotry. Parish houses became "welfare agencies" when the government would not contribute to the well being of "those kinds of people," and they became settlement centers, counseling resources, family service agencies, and, rather quickly, centers of education all rolled into one.

Parochial education was both a conservative and progressive force at one and the same time. Its simultaneous goals were to prevent the faith of the immigrants from being unduly influenced by American Protestantism and to assist the immigrants and their children in moving out of the slums and tenements and into the more "respectable" social strata. As measured by both of these standards, it was an unqualified success. The parish school has been at the core of the parish structure in this country, and in many ways has represented the social bond of the parishioners more completely than the parish church itself. The school is likely to create more loyalty to the parish than vice versa, and that is the major reason for the continued support of the schools in the face of rising costs and the indifference of the "official" church.

CONTINUED SUPPORT: WHAT KEEPS THEM GOING

In the 1974 study by the National Opinion Research Center (NORC) concerning American Catholics and their attitudes toward parochial education, 90 percent of the Catholic responded that they were in favor of continuing the parochial school system and that it was doing a good job (Greeley, McCready, McCourt 1976, p. 239). In the same study 80 percent of the respondents said that they would be willing to give more money to keep their parish school open if they had to. These "intentional contributions" totaled $1.8 billion available for the support of local parish schools (Greeley et al. 1976, p. 258). Why do these schools engender such support and loyalty from the people who use them?

I would identify three elements which contribute to the support of parochial schools and which may be identified in other
unique settings as well. First, people have a sense that the
schools belong to them; Catholics can truly speak of them as
being "our schools." For many people, their parish school is the
lynchpin of their sense of belonging to a neighborhood or community. Urban life has been and continues to be beset by strains
toward dehumanization caused by the necessity of having large
bureaucratic institutions in order to handle the sheer volume of
administrative decisions which must be made almost daily. The
best way of counteracting this dehumanization so far devised by
man has been the urban neighborhood. Neighborhoods, for
Catholics, have been a combination of parish and precinct
which provided places of both religious and political belonging.
(Religious belonging is sometimes called faith, and political
belonging is sometimes called clout.) The neighborhood also
served as a training ground for the means to make one's way in
society. Jobs were frequently attained by making a "connection," that is by being referred through a system of informal
relationships between people who trusted each other. There
were faults in neighborhoods, and there are certainly failings in
our contemporary neighborhoods; but the real question is what
the alternative may be. There may be better ways to humanize
urban life than building strong neighborhoods, but as of now we
do not seem to know what they are.

The neighborhood is where "our kind of people" live. This
does not have to mean socially homogeneous people, people of
the same ethnic, racial, or religious group. In fact the phrase
"our kind of people" is more and more coming to mean people
who appreciate diversity in their social environment. In many
contemporary urban neighborhoods, people who do not want
the sameness of the suburbs consider themselves to have a common bond and therefore have developed a pluralistic conception
of "our kind of people." The underlying principle which holds
the loyalty of the neighbors is their general agreement that the
piece of real estate which they call their neighborhood is something that is extremely important and that is inhabited by the

best people in the world. The sense that this terribly important place is "ours" is closely identified with the sense that the parochial school is also "ours." Loyalty to the neighborhood and to the school are closely linked to each other, and each reinforces the other.

Second, people have continued to support parochial education because the schools are much more responsive to local control than are most public schools. In Chicago, for example, there are about 500,000 children in public schools and about 250,000 in parochial schools. Yet the public school administration consists of more than 3,000 full-time professionals while the archdiocesan school board employs only 35 or so. This means that if you have a complaint or an innovative idea for the public schools, it may take months before it is brought to the attention of someone with the authority to act on the matter. On the other hand, if some action needs to be taken in the parochial school it is generally the principal, pastor, or the local parish school board who need to be mobilized; and they are right there in the neighborhood.

Local control is closely related to the previously discussed sense of the schools being "ours" because, on a continuum from no-trust to a great-deal-of-trust, people are likely to be more trustful of educational administrations comprised of neighbors than of those comprised of strangers. And if people trust their educators they are more likely to be involved in the activity of education and more likely to have positive feelings about the schools long after their own children have left them. This reservoir of goodwill toward the parochial schools has yet to be tapped fully by the church, but the NORC study demonstrated that it was there nonetheless.

Third, Catholics, and increasingly others—particularly inner-city minority families—continue to support parochial schools because they work. Just how they work is defined differently by different groups of people, and many Catholics would be hard pressed to detail in what way the schools are successful, but they are correct in thinking that their schools work very well. One of the surprising findings of the NORC study was that the parochial schools were even more important for the church and the society in 1974 than they were in 1963, when the first part of the study had been done.

Parochial education did not reverse the trend of lower levels of attendance at mass or the popular opposition to the official church position on birth control, but it did have other major influences. Those with more Catholic school exposure remained closer to the church during the tumultuous decade, and this was especially true for young men. And since it is likely that these men as they enter fatherhood will be important influences on the religious socialization of their children, this effect of parochial education must be considered vital for the future of the church (McCready and McCready 1973, pp. 58-68). A more immediate benefit stems from the fact that those who attended parochial schools are more likely to give money to the church in a time when sources of revenue are drying up. Finally, the society as a whole benefited from parochial education since graduates are more likely to be racially tolerant than the average, and they also are more likely to face tragic circumstances with hope rather than with cynicism or easy superficialities (Greeley et al. 1976, Table 6.18, p. 193).

These findings are not known by most of the Catholics in the country, but then they probably didn't need a sociological study to tell them that their schools had done a good job and were worth keeping; they already know this in a very gut sense, and that is one reason they resist the notion that the time is past for the parochial school. These data merely support their sense that the schools, like their neighborhoods, are valuable and worth keeping. However, given the ambiguities within the church and the complexities of the external social situation, the future of parochial education is in doubt. Support for the system needs to find additional justification in order to reinforce the traditional motives we have just discussed.

FREE CHOICE IN A PLURALISTIC SOCIETY: WHAT WILL KEEP IT GOING?

Increasingly Catholics are exposed to the idea that they have something very special to offer American society, and that it comes in two attractive packages. Several authors in this volume address themselves to the fact that parochial schools offer a choice to public education, and that "choice" is a good thing to have, given our constitutional concern for liberty. Second, Catholics are being told that their tradition of subsidiarity is currently in favor as a defense against creeping bureaucracy. These two democratic principles, freedom of choice and subsidiarity, strengthen the contemporary foundation for parochial education, providing the Catholic Church acknowledges their existence. That, as the Englishman said, is the rub.

Outside observers of the Catholic Church in America are seriously mistaken when they assume that there is a unified church. There are actually at least two churches within the general category. The first might be called the "Chancery Church," since most of its members work there and those who don't would like to. The second could be called the "Parish Church," since that is where its members live. The Chancery Church is a monistic structure with one eye placed firmly on Rome. The Parish Church is very pluralistic and diverse, usually cares little for the concerns of Rome, and expresses the twin principles of freedom of choice and subsidiarity much better than the Chancery Church.

The two churches receive very differently the news that the parochial schools have worked and that they continue to be supported by Catholics around the country. The Chancery Church generally criticizes the messengers bringing the news, and reacts defensively whenever the topic of popular support for liberalizing the official position on birth control comes up. The Parish Church, on the other hand, reacts by wondering why the Chancery Church does not support its belief that parochial schools are valuable. The Chancery Church listens to the discussion which says that the parochial school tradition has something of value to offer our society and wonders what Rome thinks; the Parish Church listens to the same discussion and wonders why the first isn't really paying attention.

CONCLUSION

The long Catholic tradition of support for a separate school system is particularly important at a time of growing general interest in expanding freedom of educational choice. The Catholic experience has important consequences for non-Catholics in at least two ways. First, parochial schools are increasingly offering educational alternatives to the public school systems for blacks and Hispanics in the inner cities of our major metropolitan centers. The public systems are being drowned in their own bureaucratic structures, and political infighting occupies more and more of the school year. The role of Catholic schools as "new minority academies" needs to explored and evaluated, but the possibilities for the future are exciting.

Second, parochial schools are the only alternatives to public education which encourage diversity and pluralism in our society, and are available in significant quantities. Catholic schools are not only diverse from public schools, but often from each other—a circumstance made possible by the fact that many parish schools are under the local control of an elected parish school board and are not subordinate to a central diocesan authority. If pluralism and free choice are to become realities in American education, the parochial school model will play an important part in the movement toward reform.

Rising costs and hesitant leadership have placed severe financial constraints on the parochial system at the present time; but the willingness of Catholics to support the parish school is as strong as ever, and ways will be found to activate that support. The schools were built by people who had far fewer resources than most contemporary Catholics, and the schools will be maintained despite current obstacles. If the Chancery Church should totally withdraw support and begin to close schools and to refuse to build new ones, the Parish Church can be counted on to continue supporting the school system which has served it so well (Greeley el al. 1976, p. 239).

Finally, it will be instructive to watch the fledgling movement for choice in education—and for public finance mechanisms that encourage choice—in dealing with parents who wish to have their children in sectarian schools. The issue will pivot on judgments about the relationship of diversity to the common good, a relationship which provides the "hidden agenda" for most free-choice debates in our society. The problem of social trust looks in two directions: if society trusts people to make their own choices, they may feel greater trust toward society and toward others within it. On the other hand, if society strictly limits their choices, the implications for trust in the larger society and in its institutions may be severe.

Having stated our commitment to choice and pluralism, the issue becomes what kinds of choices and pluralism we are willing to permit. In conditions of expanding choice—genuinely free choice—it would be interesting to see how current public, private, and parochial schools evolve, and what new educational alternatives develop.

IIIC

ROBERT SINGLETON

CALIFORNIA: THE SELF-DETERMINATION IN EDUCATION ACT, 1968

Low income and minority parent support for expanded choice in education. State government investigation of disparities in educational opportunity. Community participation in advisory board. Responses to Watts survey. The importance of choice and competition for equal opportunity in education.

Public discussions of choice in education are often haunted by the suspicion that poor and minority parents may be less rational than their rich and middle income Anglo counterparts in choices about schooling for their children. This view is understandable, since it tends to come from people who occupy the high and upper-middle income classes themselves.

In 1968, the California legislature created a rare opportunity to observe and study the attitudes of low income and minority groups toward education, especially their ideas about how public education might be improved and be made more responsive to their needs.

The results of the experience revealed that lower income and minority parents have aspirations for their children's educations that are very similar to the aspirations of higher income groups—and that the choices they tend to make are also remarkably similar. The results indicated overwhelming support by low income and minority group parents for expanded choice in education, as well as increased competition with the existing public education delivery system in the ghettoes and poor areas of the cities.

BACKGROUND AND INTRODUCTION

After the assassination of Martin Luther King in April 1968, the California Legislature State Assembly, by Concurrent Resolution, created a special Subcommittee on Urban Problems of the Assembly Ways and Means Committee to commemorate the ideals of the slain leader by employing the state's resources to address the same problems to the fullest extent consistent with legal and constitutional constraints.

At its initial meeting the subcommittee selected equality of educational opportunity as its most urgent and appropriate first thrust. To develop a meaningful legislative proposal, Subcommittee Chairman Leon Ralph announced that interim hearings would be held in several high impact communities of the state.[1] At the same time he requested the Assembly Office of Research to undertake a preliminary study of the problem in large ghettos of the state, and to assist in forming an advisory board made up of activist poor and minority parents and reformers in education.

I was asked by the chairman to help organize the advisory board, to research disparities in educational opportunity between the ghettos and the privileged areas of the larger cities of

California, and to participate in planned committee hearings on the question of equality of educational opportunity in the poor and privileged areas of Californian cities. I later got help from the UCLA Survey Research Center[2] to survey the attitudes of community residents who would be affected by the advisory board legislative proposal. The latter task was in order to validate the advisory board's representativeness against expected criticisms of its makeup.

To identify the most qualified people for the advisory board, a "telescoping panel" was established in which five likely candidates in each city were asked to name five more, who were in turn asked to name five more. Resumes on the five people most frequently named in any community were submitted for final selection by the subcommittee. The resulting advisory board was a collection of minority and poor persons who had credibility at both the grass roots and establishment levels.

DELIBERATIONS OF THE ADVISORY BOARD

An important part of the advisory board's investigations included special seminars which preceded each business meeting, and which considered both the present educational system and proposed alternatives to it.

Seminar leaders ranged over a wide array of topics from the state of education technology and the Coleman Report findings to decentralization and community control. A subject of intense interest was the Ocean Hill-Brownsville crisis in New York, which was raging at the time. The subcommittee chairman promised to invite Rhody McCoy and others of his calibre to the hearings which would follow the advisory board deliberations. From the deliberations, a preliminary plan would be presented to the subcommittee for investigation by hearings.[3]

After the seminars, the board met at least as many times again to discuss alternative delivery systems for education with proponents of competing systems, many of which had been encouraged by the recent passage of legislation waiving the entire California State Education Code for innovative programs in education.[4]

Proponents presented a wide array of possible alternatives, most with a persuasive model for innovative change. Some argued for secession from existing local boards of education and the formation of miniboards composed of clusters of high schools and their feeder schools that were falling below a reasonable standard; some argued that the miniboard was doomed to copy the mistakes of the full board, and proposed the takeover be followed by a turnover of the schools to a learning corporation (of the kind which abounded prior to the Rand Corporation review) (Hall 1972). Still other presenters argued in favor of legislation which would make available the equivalent of the cost of a child's education in the form of a voucher, to be redeemed at a school of the household's choice.

ADVISORY BOARD RECOMMENDATIONS TO THE SUBCOMMITTEE

All presentations and proposals that the board found most impressive had one element in common: that the sorry state of education in ghetto schools probably results from the monopolistic hold that the public schools have on poor and minority children. Children of the well-to-do have two forms of mobility which are closed to the poor and which serve to keep some semblance of competition alive in privileged neighborhoods: rich and middle class households can either move across district boundaries or send their children to private schools. Race and poverty effectively close both options to the poor and minority pupils.

In its debriefing meetings with the subcommittee just prior to drafting the model legislation, the advisory board indicated that it could see no reason to eliminate any of the alternative models. Indeed, they concluded that the spirit of competition with the existing system could be extended to competition among the alternative competing systems as well. Accordingly, it was recommended that the model legislation be drafted to include all four options. Communities with failing schools could then adopt the option most applicable to its circumstance.

The advisory board proposed that the legislation be named "The Parental Choice in Education Act of 1968."[5]

THE MODEL LEGISLATION

The subcommittee members were visibly impressed that the parents and low income community activists on the advisory board could recommend so sophisticated a program of innovation in education. It was a result they had not anticipated. The subcommittee sent its final legislation to the Legislative Counsel for drafting and to the Legislative Analyst for its fiscal digest in practically the same form as developed by the advisory board.[6]

The board proposed that an arbitrary standard of achievement be set by the State Office of Compensatory Education.[7] Parents with children in urban high schools and feeder schools which fall below that standard would be eligible for the choices made available by the legislation. The director of the office would be responsible for notifying the parents, and he would also be responsible for calculating the affected portion of the district's budget, which the County Superintendent would then impound until the choice process was completed.[8]

The choices would be as follows:

1. Parents could choose to apply to the County Superintendent directly for a voucher equivalent to the district current cost of education. This voucher could then be used in private or public schools of the family's choice.

2. Parents could choose to form their own school district. In this case, the County Superintendent would appoint a temporary "elections board" which would oversee the elections and then dissolve itself.

3. Parents could choose to pool their vouchers and hire an education corporation approved by the state.

4. Parents could choose to pool their vouchers and themselves become an education corporation to compete with both public and private schools with their own (approved) education programs.

THE ATTITUDINAL SURVEY

Anticipating inevitable attacks on the representativeness of
both the advisory board and its recommendations, a survey was
designed and implemented in the Watts area of Los Angeles
with the assistance and close supervision of the UCLA Survey
Research Center.[9] By the time the survey was planned, the legislative proposal had become a bill, AB 2118 (Ralph 1968), and its
name was changed to the "Self-Determination in Education
Act."

The survey population was a systematic probability sample of
450 occupied household units drawn from the ten census tracts
which encompass the Watts area. A total of 236 interviews were
completed, for a return rate of 52 percent. The face-to-face, in-
house interviews were conducted by twenty black UCLA students who had been specially trained for the purpose. The
modal interview time was twenty minutes.[10]

The questions in the survey instrument, in brief, asked
whether the respondent (1) had heard of the bill; (2) favored the
concept; (3) favored a change in governance; (4) favored a
locally elected school board; (5) thought the present board was
doing a good or poor job; and (6) ranked the schools in Watts
above or below average.

While the vast majority were unfamiliar with the bill (70.9
percent), after a brief explanation of its provisions 79.3 percent
responded in favor. A simplified chi-square test established the
independence of their responses to the first two questions,
which dealt with the bill and its content; thus it mattered not
whether people had heard of AB 2118 or not.

When queried regarding the group which does the best job in
running the schools, the present school board received only 12.9
percent approval from the respondents. A potential self-determination school board received 30.6 percent.[11]

Those who thought the self-determination school board
would make a difference numbered 73.8 percent, and 66.0 percent thought things would change for the better if AB 2118 were
to pass. Moreover, 49.9 percent responded that the schools were

below average, while only 6.4 percent felt that the schools were above average in Watts.

The survey established beyond a doubt that the community was overwhelmingly in favor of increased choice in education, of competition with the status quo in education, and of a chance to make their schools more responsive to local needs.

CONCLUSIONS

The assumptions widely held by middle and upper income groups that the poor and minority communities will make perverse choices regarding education for their children are greatly exaggerated. As Coons and Sugarman note later in this book, any reforms expanding choice in education could provide safeguards in individual cases. But the experience of the 1968 Advisory Board suggests that such individual safeguards would be needed far less often than one might think. The important point is that an advisory board to a legislative subcommittee deliberately comprised of poor and minority group activists in education proved itself capable of comprehending the merits of complicated choices. After long deliberation, they preferred choices which would increase the degree of competition in the education systems offered to their children.

Not only was the advisory board rational and consistent in its support of increased competition and choice in education, but a survey of residents in one of the affected communities revealed substantial agreement with the advisory board recommendations.[12]

There is no reason to believe that the results would be different today. The need for expanding choice and competition remains as strong now as it was then. Choice is the critical element in parent participation; without choice, low income and minority groups will continue to feel equal opportunity in education is an unredeemed promise.

IV

NATHAN GLAZER

PUBLIC EDUCATION AND AMERICAN PLURALISM

Ethnic and racial diversity in the two World Wars. Intercultural education. Recent demands for greater recognition of ethnic identities in education. Tolerances vs. recognition and respect. The achievement issue. State power of funding and legislation. Bilingualism and changes in textbook content. Complexities of application and the role of choice.

It is no simple task to outline the degree to which intercultural or multicultural or multiethnic (or, also relevant to our inquiry, bilingualism) perspectives have taken hold in American elementary and secondary education. That they have taken hold, in law and practice, cannot be denied. But it is difficult to say how far the practice extends, with what degree of sophistication and commitment, short of elaborate investigation which unfortunately cannot be undertaken here. Later on there will be some statistics—how many programs, how much money, by what levels of government.

Before that the stage must be set, and that is best done by contrasting the attitude to American ethnic and racial diversity prevalent in the two World Wars. For even by the later 1940s it is clear that a substantial change had come over American education's view of how it should respond to cultural diversity. This is true however backward that period may appear from the perspective of the heightened rhetoric, demands, and expectations of the later 1960s and the more sober commitments of the later 1970s.

WORLD WAR I

In the first World War the United States went through a period of hysterical affirmation of Americanism and oneness. The teaching of German was briefly driven out of the schools, the use of German words or terms was banned, any form of dual loyalty which threatened a total commitment to the United States and its allies was viewed with fierce suspicion, the foreign language press was closely monitored for disloyalty. After the war the great suspicion continued, now directed against Bolshevism rather than Germanism. Immigrants from Eastern Europe who showed any attachment to socialism, anarchism, and communism came under severe attack; many were deported; socialists elected to office were denied their seats.

This is an old story, often told. In this environment, to take account of the cultural differences of school children—which would mean for the public schools to acknowledge the distinctive background of Germans, Hungarians, Jews, Czechs, Russians, and the like—seemed simply out of the question. It is true that the major founding statements of cultural pluralism—by Horace Kallen and, of lesser significance but great interest, Randolph Bourne—came out of the dispute over hyphenated Americanism during the war. These statements, in their hope for an America that was an orchestra of many nations and cultures, were before their time (Kallen 1924; Bourne 1956; Higham 1975).[1]

Ethnic loyalty was considered a drawback to a full national effort to fight World War I, for our enemies were Germany and multiethnic Austria-Hungary; and, soon after our entry, multiethnic Russia exited from the war under Bolshevik rule to become what seemed like an ally of our enemies. (The ethnic loyalties of the English-origin Americans did not seem to be ethnic, but simply American.) Even in World War I there were, of course, ethnic loyalties that could have been drawn upon to assist the allied cause in America—Czechs had no attachment to the Austro-Hungarian Empire, Italians were on the allied side, and so on. It was ideology as well as practical considerations that led to the criticism of "hyphenated Americanism" and dual loyalties. The war had come in the full flood of immigration, and the problem of forging common loyalties, a common American nation, was inevitably seen as a severe one. No political leader was inclined to encourage ethnic loyalties during World War I.

After the war, a public commitment to ethnic pluralism seemed an equally vain hope. This was the age of the Red Scare and the Ku Klux Klan. Nor did matters improve with the sudden collapse of the Klan and the apparent weakening of anti-foreign prejudices as a major force in American politics with the onset of the great depression, when other issues seized public attention and when the working man and the middle classes were concerned with more important things than the maintenance of cultural and linguistic heritages.

WORLD WAR II AND "INTERCULTURAL EDUCATION"

The rise of Hitler and the coming of the second World War again made the relationship of the various foreign stocks paramount to American life and national interests. But this time ethnic loyalties seemed for the most part something that could support our allies and our own national interests, rather than something to be viewed with suspicion. Americans of German, Italian, and Japanese origin could again be seen as potential enemies. But Germans had been chastened by the experience of

World War I; the Italians were not seen as very political; Japanese were circumspect—though that did not save them from forced relocation. Almost every other ethnic strand seemed to have good reasons for opposing Hitler and Nazism. The voluminous writings of the Yugoslav immigrant, Louis Adamic, best symbolize the coinciding in the second World War of a reawakening of pride and commitment to ethnic heritage with the great national effort of the war (Adamic 1938, 1940, 1941, 1942, 1945; Christian 1971).[2]

Nazism and World War II gave rise to curricular innovation in what was then called "intercultural education." There were two themes in intercultural education: the first was that one should not be ashamed of one's heritage; the second and more important one was that all should be tolerant of racial, religious, and cultural differences. In effect, intercultural education was America's answer to Hitler's preaching of group hatred. The second theme, that of tolerance, outweighed the first, that of the celebration of heritage and diversity.

Whereas the first founding statements of cultural pluralism of World War I had no impact on the schools, the second wave of interest created organizations, publications, new curricula, and extensive discussion. There existed during this period a Center for Intergroup Education in Cooperating Schools of the American Council on Education, a Service Bureau of Intercultural Education, a Common Council for American Unity, a newsletter, *Intercultural Education News,* edited by William Heard Kilpatrick, and other journals presenting material on intercultural education (Goodenow 1975; Vickery and Cole 1943; Taba and Van Til 1945; IECS 1949, 1951, 1952; AASA 1947; NEA 1942).[3]

The content of intercultural education was rather thin. It should be seen as a response to the frightfully dangerous upsurge of racism that the rapid explosion of Nazi power stimulated all over the world—and in the United States, too, though our own domestic roots of racism were strong enough. One of the chief keynotes of intercultural education was tolerance, enlisted in the fight against prejudice. Intercultural education concentrated on the processes that might counter current intolerance of other peoples and cultures; what end it envisaged for a diverse America was less clear. One suspects that to advocates of intercultural education the picture of a decent America consisted of one in which Americans of whatever origin were really very much alike, and were not discriminated against for their origins, religion, or vestigial cultural differences. Certainly there was no notion that it was the task of the public schools to present or preserve a full-bodied version of ethnic cultures. It was enough to teach tolerance of whatever existed.

Thus, the intercultural education version of cultural pluralism would seem very weak to us today. Indeed, the notion of cultural pluralism itself was rejected in one influential formulation of intercultural education as, on the other extreme, was assimilation. The new middle path was labeled "cultural democracy." Vickery and Cole (1943, pp. 34-35), whose presentation of intercultural education we are following, present three fundamental propositions to define their approach:

1. That there are certain essential democratic loyalties and beliefs, as well as practices which have been established for the general welfare, which all Americans should have in common....

2. That the dominant majority group can rightly require individuals and minorities neither to isolate themselves from the community and nation as a whole, nor to cling to ways of living which are incongruent with democratic practice.

The majority, however, is called upon to be careful in distinguishing between undemocratic beliefs and practices and

those which are only different. . . . The latter the majority is required to honor, though not necessarily to adopt. Nor can the majority justly make conformity to the dominant culture pattern or membership in the dominant race a requirement for full and equal participation. . . .

3. That individuals . . . should be free to practice and perpetuate such of their group's traditional values, folkways and customs as

do not conflict with essential democratic principles; or to repudi-
ate their ancestral ways of living and thus to lose themselves in
the population as a whole.

Goodenow (1975, pp. 375-76) gives a somewhat similar
evaluation of the intercultural education movement:

> In part, however, intercultural programs suffered from the
> progressive spirit of the times. Their endeavors were only partly
> successful because they were highly committed to an ideology of
> national unity, democracy, and tolerance that would resist
> authoritarianism at home and abroad and defend America's na-
> tional interests. Attacking anti-Semitism and other forms of in-
> tolerance the interculturalists focused upon international and
> cross-cultural aspects of racism and noted the "commonness" of
> all men to the point where they blurred the differences between
> ethnic groups. Drawing on anthropological and biological
> research they often failed to consider the structural and institu-
> tional nature of racism in the United States. Indeed, by placing
> considerable stress upon the past cultural contributions of
> ethnics and others to American life, pluralism was portrayed as
> a static phenomenon. Virtually no attempt was made to suggest
> that these groups could themselves shape the nature of Ameri-
> can society.

His article is particularly valuable for describing the attitudes of
the intercultural education movement towards the problems of
blacks, and their reaction to intercultural education. Blacks had
been ignored in earlier writings on cultural pluralism: these
came out of the experiences of European immigrants, and particularly Jews. John Higham (1975, p. 208) writes of Horace
Kallen:

> He liked to describe the American ensemble as an orchestra; but
> there was a fatal elision when he wrote that America could
> become "an orchestration of mankind" by perfecting "the
> cooperative harmonies of European civilization." Nothing in
> Kallen's writings gave away the magnitude of that elision. In the
> fullest statement of his argument there was only a single,
> obscure footnote on the point. "I do not discuss the influence of
> the negro," Kallen confessed in fine print. "This is at once too
> considerable and too recondite in its processes for casual men-
> tion. It requires separate analysis." The pluralist thesis from the
> outset was encapsulated in white ethnocentrism.

There was considerably more interest in non-European racial minority groups among the intercultural educators. But a good part of even this interest was stimulated by a European event, the rise of Nazi racism, which evoked a defense of racial equality and tolerance in the United States.

National loyalty comes first; there is no great virtue to sticking to group customs and practices, even though they should be tolerated. Clearly, a good deal was going to change in the next upsurge of commitment to ethnic heritage in the later 1960s.

CULTURAL PLURALISM SINCE THE 1960S

In this stage, the one we are living through, there is little talk of striking a middle path between "assimilation" and "cultural pluralism." Cultural pluralism itself is the correct path, and presumably if one wants to protect one's reputation for moderation, one must create another extreme pole which one can reject, one we could label "separatism." It is interesting to contrast the Cole-Vickery principles we have just quoted with a document of the 1970s, a statement by the American Association of Colleges of Teacher Education. We should note first that the term "intercultural education," with its variant of "intergroup education," is now a thing of the past. The issue is no longer to teach tolerance for other groups (though that is not totally ignored); the new term is multicultural or bicultural education. Consider now the language of the early 1970s (Herman 1974, p. 27):[4]

> Multicultural education rejects the view that schools should seek to melt away cultural differences or the view that schools should merely tolerate cultural pluralism. . . . Cultural pluralism is a concept that aims toward a heightened sense of being and a wholeness of the entire society based on the unique strengths of each of its parts. . . . Schools and colleges must assure that their total educational process and educational content reflect a commitment to cultural pluralism.

Consider also another authoritative statement on multiethnic education, "Curriculum Guidelines for Multiethnic Education," of the National Council for Social Studies (1976). The four major principles upon which this statement is based are :

1. Ethnic diversity should be recognized and respected at individual, group, and societal levels.

2. Ethnic diversity provides a basis for societal cohesiveness and survival.

3. Equality of opportunity should be afforded to members of all ethnic groups.

4. Ethnic identification should be optional for individuals.

Four major differences should be noted in contrasting the new multiethnic education with the intercultural education of thirty years ago.

First, the new development has emerged directly out of the demands of minority groups for recognition. There was the explosive impact of the "black power" slogan and all it carried in its train—the demands of Mexican Americans and Puerto Ricans, of Asian Americans, of American Indians, and then the "new pluralism" of the white ethnic groups with their demands for equal time and equal recognition. In contrast, there was little in the way of demands by racial and ethnic groups themselves in the inspiration for intercultural education. Or, if any one group was involved, it was the Jewish group, frightened at the rise of anti-Semitism. Undoubtedly Negroes were worse off than Jews, but they did not face in the 1940s and 1950s any marked increase of antiblack prejudice and discrimination. Jewish defense agencies played a substantial role in launching and supporting intercultural education. And in sponsoring major research on anti-Semitism, on ethnocentrism generally, and on authoritarian and prejudiced attitudes, they provided much of the intellectual base and many of the concepts that were behind intercultural education. But we should not exaggerate the Jewish role: academic anthropologists and social psychologists were perhaps rather more important in providing this intellectual and conceptual base.

The point to be noted is that the intercultural education movement of the 1940s was in large measure something devised by elites—academic scholars, liberal church organizations, intergroup relations organizations—for a mass that they believed was imminently available for prejudiced and antidemocratic social movements. The movement of the later 1960s and early 1970s, on the other hand, grew directly from the demands of group leaders—leaders of black and other minority groups. The academic and religious leaders and intergroup relations agencies were dragged into the train of these new demands, and they themselves did not initiate the movement for multicultural education.

A second major difference, and the major reason for the new multiethnic education, is the poor achievement in education of certain groups, a record which is then used to deny entitlement to further education, jobs, promotions, and, in short, a better life. This issue played no role in either the cultural pluralism proposed by Kallen (Kallen was also a Jew and a Zionist, and poor educational achievement is clearly not a Jewish problem), nor did it play any role in intercultural education: in this movement there was no suggestion that what was being proposed would generally improve attitudes toward the education of minority groups and their educational achievement.

A third major difference: the issue of tolerance as such has almost disappeared. Attitudes and prejudice are no longer the center of attention: one now demands "recognition" and "respect," which are somewhat different from mere tolerance. A number of new elements have supplanted tolerance as central foci in multicultural education. First, there is an emphasis on individual and group wholeness, health, identity; a "heightened sense of being," "respect," "cohesiveness and survival." Ethnic identity, the ethnic group, is good: it should not be merely tolerated. Second, there is an emphasis on an expanded equality of opportunity—which in the present moment is translated to mean an equality of achievement, of result, of entitlement, and an intolerance of substantial difference in the credits derived from education and used as the basis for higher occupation, income, and prestige. This is an inevitable corollary from the second point of difference: that multicultural education derives from a concern with the educational deficiency of minority groups.

And finally the fourth major difference: the state is now actively involved in the new multicultural education. It pays for much of it, requires a good deal of it, and surrounds it with state regulation and enforcement. This is a new twist indeed.

ROLE OF THE STATE

The cultural pluralists of World War I wanted little enough from the state: they wanted it to stop imposing forceful assimilation. The intercultural educators of the 1940s wanted a bit more: it was the responsibility of the state to assist in education for tolerance of other groups; after all, intolerance was one of the chief weapons of the enemy, and weakened the common war effort. The new multicultural education emerges at a time when the state role generally is far more extensive and has assumed much greater power than in the past. The minority groups that began the demand for an education to support cultural difference were, to begin with, poor and without an organization that would permit them to launch extensive programs of after-school and weekend education, as had some other groups. The state in any case engrossed far more resources in the later 1960s than it had in the 1940s or the 1920s, and it was generally expected that if there was something good to be done, one should get the state to do it.

The role of voluntary groups, it would appear, had shrunk to the function of putting pressure on the state so that it provided the money. But of course if the state provides money something new enters the situation: the state, disposing of state power, must carefully define what it is that it is supporting, what it expects from it, who is eligible for it, and who is required to do it. This is not to say that the state cannot do what voluntary private

organizations can do. It can support research, curricular innovation, experiment. But there is a quid pro quo for state support.
And this must inevitably shape the concrete reality of
multiethnic education today.

To sum up, the multiethnic education of the later 1960s and
1970s is based on a heightened self-consciousness and militancy
of ethnic groups; it is strongly motivated by a sense of failure to
achieve in the educational system; it emphasizes the value of
group identity for mental health, group cohesion, and individual
achievement; and it demands and receives state support for
multiethnic education, both by means of legislation and administrative rulings that require local school systems to do something, and by means of budgetary support provided from state
and federal sources for the purpose.

And because the state is now deeply involved, what we have
today is not simply another phase in a series of explosions of interest in relating to ethnic heritage or maintaining it: once
government enters, as it has today, it is clear we have a tendency
in education that is firmly fixed. Government does not easily
withdraw from a field once it has entered upon it. In the past,
cultural pluralism and intercultural education was the concern
of groups of intellectuals, of leaders of voluntary organizations,
of organized elements within ethnic groups. Programs had to be
developed and advocated without government assistance.
Voluntary budgets have to be raised anew each year. But government budgets, once established, possess a dynamic of their own.
In the past, when individuals and group leaders lost interest in
ethnic education, then activity generally declined: there was no
one to keep up the pressure. Once a program is incorporated in
legislation and budgets, however, one can expect the program to
keep going even if the number and intensity of lobbying activity
for it declines: there are now, after all, paid agents of government who have developed an interest in the program and are
there to see that it does not die.

PHASES OF MULTIETHNIC EDUCATION

Multiethnic education is, of course, no fixed matter; in the nature of the case it could not be. We have already moved through a number of phases in the years since the black power and black pride explosion once again placed ethnic concerns on the educational agenda. We have seen a number of excesses and false turnings. One wonders, for example, whether there are many courses in Swahili still being given; this was advocated on the assumption that it was an equivalent of the advocacy of the teaching of Italian and of Hebrew by Italian and Jewish groups in New York State, but there is, as a matter of fact, no single African language that can play the role Italian did for Italians, Hebrew for Jews. Since the history of these past ten hectic years has to be reconstructed from raw materials, one can give no clear description of the phases through which the multiethnic education movement has gone, but a few overlapping phases can be discerned.

The first phase, beginning in the early 1960s, emphasized advocacy of group pride by the minority groups that most strongly felt their oppression. In this phase, the only minority groups that counted were blacks, Mexican Americans and Puerto Ricans, and Asian Americans. In this phase, America was scourged for its racism; self-deprecation and self-hatred were in the air, for it was the period of the Vietnam war and the black urban riots. In the second phase, it was argued that learning about America's iniquitous treatment of minority groups was something that everyone needed, majority groups as well as minority groups. History books were criticized, and new texts were created. English curricula were overhauled, and works of minority authors describing minority experience were added to the required readings. In the third phase, the issue of language was raised, particularly for the Spanish-speaking students; a bilingual education act was passed as early as 1968, strengthened in 1974. In the fourth phase, white ethnic groups also entered the scene; they, too, wanted their ethnic experience to be noted. Just as the bilingual thrust was marked by federal legislation, so too was the white ethnic thrust: an Ethnic Heritage Studies Program was first proposed in 1970, passed in 1972, funded in 1973, and implemented in 1974.

We have thus moved from minority studies for the most oppressed; to minority studies, integrated into the curriculum, for
all; to bilingual studies; to ethnic studies for all. What has
emerged sharply is a national commitment to facilitating the
maintenance of the ethnic heritage and, rather more significantly, a commitment that *requires* that school authorities take
into account ethnic and linguistic difference in education. It may
seem too strong to assert that we have moved from *facilitating*
to *requiring,* but if we look at the history of bilingual education
requirements, I believe we will see that this is not an inaccurate
characterization of what has happened.

EXPANDING GOVERNMENT REQUIREMENTS

The story, like much in the strange history of policy affecting
racial and ethnic groups in the United States in the last decade,
begins with the Civil Rights Act of 1964, Title VI: "No person in
the United States shall, on grounds of race, color, or national
origin, be excluded from participation in, be denied the benefits
of, or be subjected to discrimination under any program or activity receiving Federal financial assistance." The next year the
Elementary and Secondary Education Act of 1965 gave teeth to
this general prohibition of discrimination by providing for the
first time substantial federal financial aid to school districts.
Next, concern over the poor education of Spanish-speaking
minority groups led to the passage of the Bilingual Education
Act in 1968, offering funds for new educational approaches to
meet the need of children of limited English-speaking ability;
these funds were to be used in school systems with high concentrations of children from low-income families. The sums involved were not large: $118 million were spent between 1969
and 1973.

While bilingual education thus developed as an effort to improve the education of children of foreign-language background,
simultaneously new requirements were imposed on school districts on the basis of the Civil Rights Act of 1964. In May 1970
we had an "interpretative memorandum" from the Director for

Civil Rights of the Department of Health, Education, and Welfare (HEW). He referred to "compliance reviews" undertaken to enforce the ban on discrimination in Title VI of the Civil Rights Act of 1964; and these have revealed, in school districts with large Spanish-surnamed populations, "a number of practices which have the effect of denying equality of educational opportunity to Spanish-surnamed pupils. Similar practices which have the effect of discrimination on the ground of national origin exist in other locations with respect to disadvantaged pupils from other national origin-minority groups, for example, Chinese and Portuguese." The HEW office described its major areas of concern. The first was that "where inability to speak and understand the English language excludes national origin-minority group children from effective participation in the educational program . . . the district must take affirmative steps to rectify the language deficiency in order to open the instructional program to these students." School districts must not assign these students "to classes for the mentally retarded on the basis of criteria which essentially measure or evaluate English language skills." They must not deny them access to college preparatory classes for the same reason. Grouping or tracking to deal with language problems should not become permanent tracks. School districts are responsible for proper notification of parents, a notification which may have to be provided in languages other than English.

In the *Lau* case (1974), the Supreme Court entered the fray as to what was required. Presumably no more than the above: where a student could not get advantage from an English-language program because he only understood Chinese, some "appropriate relief" should be furnished. The HEW Office of Civil Rights (OCR), having seen its earlier, moderate statement as to what was required quoted approvingly by the Supreme Court, proceeded further:

> In order to facilitate efforts by both State Education Agencies and this Office to secure voluntary compliance with current Title VI requirements [after *Lau*], this Office designated a Task

> Force to develop an outline of those educational approaches which would constitute appropriate "affirmative steps" to be taken by a non-complying school district "to open its instructional program" to students foreclosed currently from effective participation therein.

The outline was attached: and we see a further expansion of what the law requires. Culture now enters the scene. A school district, having determined which language or languages students speak and how well, must then determine the students' educational needs,

> and then prescribe an education program utilizing the most effective teaching style to satisfy diagnosed educational needs. The determination of which teaching style(s) are to be used will be based on the cognitive and affective domains and should include an assessment of the responsiveness of students to different types of cognitive learning styles and incentive motivational styles—e.g., competitive v. cooperative learning patterns. The diagnostic measures must include diagnoses of problems related to areas or subjects required of other students in the school program *and* [sic] prescriptive measures must serve to bring the linguistically/culturally different student(s) to the educational performance level that is expected by the Local Education Agency (LEA) and State of nonminority students.

The issue is no longer merely one of language use; we now have a problem of differential responsiveness by students of different cultures to various teaching styles. Schools should be responsive to cultural as well as language facility differences among students. Simply bringing the student up to adequate facility in English has become only one of a number of possible approaches a school district may implement. In addition to "transitional bilingual education," it may undertake a "Bilingual/Bicultural Program" or a "Multilingual/Multicultural Program." While it is not mandated, one acceptable affirmative response to the presence of students of different language backgrounds is education in the language "and culture" of the individual student. "The end product is a student who can function, totally, in both languages and cultures."

In 1974, finally, the Bilingual Education Act of that year,

> recognizing (1) that there are large numbers of children of
> limited English-speaking ability; (2) that many such children
> have a cultural heritage which differs from that of English-
> speaking; (3) that a primary means by which a child learns is
> through the use of such child's language and cultural heritage,

and so on, declared it to be the policy of the United States "to encourage the establishment and operation, where appropriate, of
educational programs using bilingual educational practices and
techniques" (CLE 1975, pp. 222-40).[5]

And so Congress itself in 1974 capped a movement that began
with its own Civil Rights Act ten years earlier, and which
seemed then to be directed only against discrimination in
federal programs. This became defined (or redefined, since no
one in 1964, one may assume, realized that nondiscrimination
meant educational programs adapted to the presumed cultural
differences of students in this multicultural nation) as
taking into account cultural as well as language differences by
both the Office of Civil Rights and the courts.

What we see in these documents which establish the law is a
pulling and hauling between a number of different concepts of
bilingual and bicultural education. One concept, which begins to
emerge in the OCR document of 1970, is that education should
be appropriate to a student's needs; if a student cannot speak
English, some adaptation must be made so that the student gets
something from the educational process. Here we see bilingualism as a means to an effective education. We see the same
reasoning in the Supreme Court's *Lau* decision. But by 1974 and
1975 a second concept has entered the scene. Language inability
is a rather clear notion. Now we deal with "culture" as a barrier
to educational achievement, and educational programs must not
only be in language that can reach the child but in a cultural
mode that can reach the child.

A third concept sees bilingual and bicultural education as no
longer simply a means to a common educational achievement;
there is at least the implication that educational programs

should maintain distinctive cultures, along with their distinctive languages. The Ethnic Heritage Studies Program Act of 1972 proposes a mild version of this in its Section 901, Title IX (Herman 1974, p. 77):

> In recognition of the heterogeneous composition of the nation and of the fact that in a multiethnic society a greater understanding of the contributions of one's own heritage and those of one's fellow citizens can contribute to a more harmonious, patriotic, and committed populace, and in recognition of the principle that all persons in the educational institutions of the Nation should have an opportunity to learn about the differing and unique contributions to the national heritage made by each ethnic group, it is the purpose of this title to provide assistance designed to afford to students opportunities to learn about the nature of their own cultural heritage, and to study the contributions of the cultural heritages of the other ethnic groups of the Nation.

No one in this version is *required* to study his or her ethnic heritage; no school system is *required* to provide it. It is only assisted insofar as it wishes to do so, within the limits of the small sums that have been made available for this program.

But a fourth concept does carry with it some element of compulsion: this is the concept of bilingual/bicultural education as something which it is the *right* of students to get, and the obligation of school systems to provide—rights and obligations deriving not from legislation dealing with bilingualism and ethnic heritage, but from interpretations of what nondiscrimination requires under the Civil Rights Act of 1964. It is only in the multicultural education that derives from authority under this act that we can see compulsion employed. It should be made clear that the compulsion is imposed on states and school systems, not on individual students. These must be counted and their language facility tested to see if a program adapted to their language capacities and cultural mode of learning should be developed; once a minimal figure of students who may need bilingual/bicultural education is reached and a program is triggered, a school system *must* provide a program; there is no requirement that a student *may* be compelled to enroll in it. (And yet, why does one count the students?)

GROWING BODY OF STATE LAW

In describing the course of federal legislation dealing with multicultural education, it should be made clear that we have been dealing with only one body of law and regulation. There are fifty states, and parallel changes in law have occured there. Many of these require some kind of education to take account of cultural heritage. The strongest laws are those which mandate some kind of multicultural education. According to Judith Herman (1974, pp. 58-60):

> Those states where legislation mandates the teaching of ethnic material vary in their inclusiveness. New Jersey requires that Black history be a part of the two-year American history curriculum; Illinois, on the other hand, says that" . . . the teaching of history shall include a study of the role and contribution of American Negroes and other ethnic groups including but not restricted to Polish, Lithuanian, German, Hungarian, Irish, Bohemian, Russian, Albanian, Italian, Czechoslovakian, French, Scots, etc."
>
> This Illinois law was passed in 1967 but almost no action was taken until 1972, when the State Superintendent of Public Instruction, Michael Bakalis, established the Office of Ethnic Studies . . . .
>
> . . . In Pennsylvania . . . the regulations of the State Board of Education require that schools' instructional program include intergroup concepts to improve students' understanding and relationships around sex differences, race, national origin, religion, and socio-economic background. . . .
>
> In Hawaii, perhaps the state most conscious and least shy about its diversity, the Legislature called in 1972 for a "more comprehensive program of ethnic studies," listed some of the specific groups to be included (Hawaiian, Chinese, Japanese, Filipino, Samoan, Portuguese, and Caucasian-American), and urged a concentration on their differences and problems as well as their similarities. The Legislature also asked for curriculum to include the pros and cons of the ethnic groups' assimilation into the dominant culture, to focus on the interrelationships among the groups, and to deal with the relationship between ethnicity and the state's labor movement.
>
> California's mandate goes one step further and includes sex along with class and ethnicity. The State law requires "correct

portrayal" of ethnic contributions (Blacks, Mexican-Americans, Indians, and Orientals are listed but "other ethnic groups" are included). It also demands that textbooks "correctly portray" the role and contributions of the entrepreneur and of labor; and, further, that men and women be characterized in textbooks in all types of professional, vocational, and executive roles.

But there are many other laws, too, dealing with textbook selection, teacher training, and the like. The states also have their own bilingual-bicultural programs. In 1971 no state had requirements for school districts to conduct bilingual education. Twenty-two required teaching in English only, except for foreign-language courses. Over the next few years many of these statutes were repealed, so that in 1976 only eleven states still had such a requirement. Ten states had enacted statutes which required bilingual programs under varying circumstances. According to the National Advisory Council on Bilingual Education, *Second Advisory Report* (1976, p. 85):

> In Massachusetts, Michigan, New Jersey and Rhode Island, bilingual education is compulsory when twenty children of the same non-English language are found in a school district. In Texas, the program is required if there are twenty children in a given grade throughout the district. Illinois requires the program for each school which enrolls twenty children of a single non-English language.

It is clear the situation is still in flux. We have a mixed set of programs required, suggested, aided, proposed, with authority and funds flowing from federal, state, and local levels, and divided among legislatures, courts, and education authorities, operating by means of law, order, and regulation. We have in addition a host of voluntary organizations representing distinctive ethnic groups, local alliances of ethnic groups, groups of educators, each proposing programs, developing curricula, bringing pressure on textbook publishers and local school systems. In short, we have a distinctively American buzzing confusion, and it is not easy to describe concretely and realistically what is going on. We have the orders of courts and regulatory agencies which sound severe and sweeping, but we do not know to what extent they are actually carried out, or indeed to what extent they can be carried out with limited school resources. (Federal funds for bilingual education amounted in 1976 to about $100 million, state funds in 1974-1975 to $38 million, local funds to $44 million; but it would be impossible to determine how much was spent for multicultural education generally, since so much of it is incorporated into social studies, English, and civics courses [NAC 1976, pp. 40, 80].)

Voluntary choices, local options, and federal and state requirements are all in play, with what result it would be impossible to say as yet—except for the large result we have already indicated: that some sort of multicultural education seems to be becoming a right, if demanded, and that bilingual education, including a cultural component, is already a right.

ONGOING COMPLEXITIES

A happy ending to a long story of forced assimilation? Perhaps. But there are still some troubling issues, as there always are when the regularities of state requirement enter a subtle and complex area of education, one that must be suited to individual and group needs. There is something ironic about the government mandating responsiveness to individual and group needs—and then issuing rigid guidelines as to how this is to be done. Thus, government specifies how students should be counted, what groups must be counted, what percentage of students from certain groups must be reached before a program must be launched. (As we pointed out, these "must" requirements derive from the extension of the notion of non-discrimination, as provided in Title VI of the Civil Rights Act of 1964, by regulation and court rulings; the federal Bilingual Education Act only provides opportunities and does not mandate programs. But state programs may be mandatory.) The fact that these groups are as various as Navajo Indians and Greek immigrant children, or lower-class Puerto Ricans moving to and fro between island and mainland, or middle-class Cubans committed to making a life in the United States, cannot be taken into account in governmental regulations, and one wonders whether it is taken into account by government compliance review agents.

Ethnicity and race are subtle and complex matters; one doubts there are enough people in the country responsive to this complexity and to the variety of needs of different groups to do more than check whether pro forma requirements—some less than any group needs, some more than a group requires or desires—are being met in the over three hundred school districts investigated for compliance in 1975-1976. This number is up from seventy-four in 1973-1974, and even so is a small fraction of those districts with more than 5 percent linguistic minority children which must provide bilingual/bicultural programs according to the regulations.

In some communities—for example, one with a substantial Greek-origin population in Chicago—there has been resistance to the institution of a bilingual/bicultural program; these parents want their children educated in English. One notes that in Quebec there is severe resistance among immigrants, even among those speaking related languages such as Italian, to a requirement that their children must be educated in French rather than in English. In any group there will be division: there will be assimilationists, those who demand linguistic competence, those who want only maintenance of cultural attachment, those who insist on full education in language and culture. It is hard to see how school districts operating under governmental regulations will satisfy such a variety of interests.

Purely voluntary educational activities, conducted in private schools under only limited public authority, might respond to this variety of needs. In the case of Jewish education, for example, we have seen schools that are religious and secular, Orthodox (of several varieties), Conservative and Reform, all-day, afternoon, and Sunday, variously emphasizing Hebrew, Yiddish, or English, reflecting a history of political tendencies including the anarchist, the socialist, and the communist. One wonders, after this history, what kind of bilingual/bicultural education established under public auspices and common central rules can possibly satisfy or be relevant to—to take one example—the children of Hebrew-speaking Israel immigrants who are now coming to this country in substantial numbers. Or, to take another recent immigrant group, those from India and Pakistan; they speak a dozen languages, are Moslems, Hindus, Sikhs, Jains, and members of other religious groups, and reflect a variety of cultures. Will it now be up to school districts in which their numbers are substantial to provide a program? Particularly since their parents probably insist their education be in English, fully and completely?

The large question that multicultural education has not dealt with as yet is *how* different are the desires and requirements of different groups in the area of bicultural and bilingual education. It is not possible for the state to legislate for each group separately, according to its needs and desires. That would run afoul of the state's need for general legislation, legislation that provides the "equal protection of the laws." Yet blacks, Mexican-Americans, Puerto Ricans, American Indians, Cubans, Portuguese from the islands and the mainland, French-speaking Canadians and Louisiana Cajuns, Jews, Chinese, Japanese, Poles, Italians, etc., etc., all need and require very different things. Some of these groups are concerned primarily with poor educational achievement: they want anything that will work, and if that means multicultural education and black English, so be it, but if it means the exact reverse, they will choose that. Some of these groups have only a transitional language problem and have no desire to maintain in a public school setting education in ancestral languages. Some want only to be recognized: if anything is to be done for any other groups, they want education in their own group's heritage, "equal time," but may not even be sure they want their children to spend time taking it. And we have simplified the complexity, for in each group there are people with very different demands and needs.

Whether it is possible under state auspices to meet all these needs and requirements is a serious question. What tends to happen is that one model is created to deal with the most urgent needs—let us say, black studies for blacks to build up self-respect, and some teaching in Spanish to help bridge the transition to English. But then these initial model programs become models for others, too. They become the most extreme demands for some in each group who bargain for whatever any other group has, even if most people in the group don't recognize the need. The problem with state programs is that they must prescribe the same for everyone, even though the very essence of this situation is that each individual and each group has a rather different set of needs and wants something quite different from multicultural education.

The reason for this complexity derives directly from the American ethnic pattern. It is not a pattern of sharp lines of division between groups. If it were, if each individual were unambiguously a member of one group or another, then perhaps the same program could be prescribed for each. Some people want to see America this way, the way the early cultural pluralists saw it. Indeed, in this perspective, everyone is a member of an ethnic group, including those of Anglo-Saxon origin, and so we have proposals of ethnic studies for those who don't want them and don't need them simply because of someone's ideological commitment to the notion that every American must be a member of an ethnic group and must need the same things. So we have the outlandish discussions in educational journals of "white studies"—if we have black, brown, yellow, and red studies, why not white studies? But in fact some groups in this country are sharply distinguished by color and culture; others are not. Even so, many members of each of the sharply distinguished groups, through cultural change and intermarriage, move toward the boundaries of their group, and perhaps out of their group. And the overall hope for this country—a hope shaken in recent years—is that ultimately no group boundary will be important, that everyone will have the right to accept whatever he or she wants of ancestral culture and ethnic identity, and that this will be a private choice in which government will play no role, whether to encourage it or to discourage it. And it is still, I believe, part of the general expectation that a general American culture will prevail as the dominant one in our country, and one that does create national identity, loyalty, and commitment.

CONCLUSION

John Higham (1975, pp. 242-43) has given to my mind the best characterization of what ideally we should hope for in the way of a relationship between the distinctive ethnic cultures and the general American culture. As against "cultural pluralism" or "assimilation," he proposes "pluralistic intergration":

> Even to consider this possibility will require a conception, clearer than we have yet formulated, of what a system of pluralistic integration might be. In contrast to the integrationist model, it will not eliminate ethnic boundaries. But neither will it maintain them intact. It will uphold the validity of a common culture, to which all individuals have access, while sustaining the efforts of minorities to preserve and enhance their own integrity. In principle this dual commitment can be met by distinguishing between boundaries and nucleus. No ethnic group under these terms may have the support of the general community in strengthening its boundaries. All boundaries are understood to be permeable. Ethnic nuclei, on the other hand, are respected as enduring centers of social action. If self-preservation requires, they may claim exemption from certain universal rules, as the Amish now do from the school laws in some states. Both integration and ethnic cohesion are recognized as worthy goals, which different individuals will accept in different degrees. Ethnicity varies enormously in intensity from one person to another. It will have some meaning for the great majority of Americans, but intense meaning for relatively few. Only minorities of minorities, so to speak, will find in ethnic identity an exclusive loyalty.

The virtues of this approach are first, that it reflects existing social reality, at least as I understand it—this is what ethnic groups want, and it is all that they want—and that second, it does not propose the dismantling of what is after all a great, integrating, culture which, whatever iniquities we may charge it with, has brought within its boundaries more varied groups from more varied origins than any other great culture.

But how does this subtle understanding of the relationship between the American center, ethnic boundaries, and ethnic nuclei get realized through state action? It is not easily done. For state action does not recognize gradations. One either does or does not have the right to bilingual education or to ethnic heritage education. One must get either so much more or so much less, measured in money or time. The fact that many of us want none of it, many a lot of it, many want it for someone else, does not easily get incorporated into state action, though we are trying.

Certainly one easy solution was to create one system for all— the public system—and to let anyone who wanted something special or distinctive find a means for paying for it through private education. We have by now moved far from this model. We have incorporated so many elements responding to needs of distinctive groups into our public education that it is not likely that this neat model, distinguishing between the general and the particular, can be restored. We will have to find new models that respond to the varied needs and desires of various groups, and to the distinctive tastes and desires of the individuals within those groups. One approach is state education vouchers, on the basis of which individual students and their parents can choose whatever type of education and whatever supplement to general education they feel best suits them. Presumably there are other ways of bringing together in all its variety American pluralism with our commitment to a common culture. But it will take a lot of hard work and clear thinking about the nature of American pluralism, and the directions in which we would prefer to see it move.

V

RICHARD E. WAGNER

AMERICAN EDUCATION AND THE ECONOMICS OF CARING

Educational financing and the control of content and quality. The subjective involvement in parental choice. Economic influences on affective and emotional relationships. The effect of choice on strengthening the family. Plato vs. Aristotle. The agent-principal relationship. Government centralization and parental exclusion. The problems of information and parental dependency. Adversary relationships vs. parent-teacher cooperation. Competition and monopoly: the social need for diversity.

Little more than a century ago capital expenditures for education were financed by taxes, but teacher salaries—the primary object of educational expenditure—were financed largely by tuition paid by parents. In the 1830s in New York, for instance, parental tuitions covered 60 percent of teacher salaries. Tax revenues became the sole source of financial support for public schools only in the latter part of the nineteenth century, as the free or public schooling movement took hold.[1] In recent years, moreover, partly because of courtroom challenges to the local property tax, support of public schools has been shifting from local property taxes to statewide taxes.

The history of school finance in America has been one of continuing centralization, moving from parental tuitions to local taxes to state taxes—and even to some national taxes. Nonetheless, decisions about funding education are in principle separate from decisions about who—parents or educators—is ultimately responsible for determining educational content. Public support of education, in short, does not require public provision. There is no reason why taxes cannot continue to finance education, with parents permitted to choose among competing schools. Parents at present possess no such right; educational content is determined instead by politicians and educators. In a system that permitted parental choice, some of the elements of decision that existed when education was subsidized through tuitions would be restored.

The choice between taxes and tuitions or prices has important consequences for educational content. This essay will explore the nature and extent of these consequences, focusing on the manner in which the current means of financing has influenced the present state of American education. The remaining essays in the book will examine the prospects for expanding choice by reforming the way in which education is funded.

THE RELATIONSHIP BETWEEN EDUCATIONAL CONTENT AND FINANCE

Since most discussions about educational finance assume that educational content is independent of the means of finance, questions of funding—and of economics generally—tend to be limited to revenue needs and methods of apportionment. The means of finance, however, can exert an important influence on the substance of education, especially since the source of support determines ultimate authority to control quality. If we were to replace the present system of finance with an entitlement or voucher system permitting parental choice, the character of education in our society would change fundamentally.

There are several reasons why the choice between pricing and taxing—or between choice and no choice—can exert such influence. A system that permits parental choice engages the natural affection that parents have for their own children and cultivates the responsible interest that they normally take in their own child's education. This heightened parental interest can only improve the quality of education as parents become more involved in their children's educational experiences; the quality of products offered in education, as elsewhere, will increase as consumers become more interested in them. In a broader sense, opportunities for choice would surely strengthen the sense of participation in the life of the community by giving expression to the natural sentiments regarding the involvement of one person in the life of another.

Pricing and taxing also produce different information for principals (parents or citizens) about the conduct and actions of their agents (politicians or educators). Pricing or choice generates information about the performance of agents; without choice, such information becomes more difficult to get and less reliable to act upon.

TAXING, PRICING, AND THE ECONOMICS OF CARING

Much of the debate on educational choice has been influenced by economists whose arguments for choice often (especially in the hands of its less sophisticated proponents) seem exclusively to describe rational, individual, self-interested choosers. In this presumed unfeeling world of rational optimizers, the giving, feeling, sacrificing side of man is ignored, and such prerational ties as family seem out of place. Other social scientists thus often dismiss economic analysis for its failure to describe and to account for emotional factors. This problem is particularly evident in education, where strong affective ties of love for children often supersede all other considerations, as they should.

Economists themselves are largely to blame for this mistaken perception of economic analysis which, properly understood and applied, *can* make important contributions to realms of knowledge long thought to be outside the economist's interest or competence. For the fact is that economic relationships—especially in regulating the power to make choices—can exert important and even critical influences on affective ties and emotional relationships. Such influences are particularly evident in education.

The choice among different means of financing education raises important concerns about what may be called the economics of caring. Limiting choice in education lessens emotional commitments nurtured within the family, and therefore probably weakens the importance of the family in our culture. The public school movement socializes parental responsibility, in this case for the future development of children. In its impact on the family, the situation brings to mind the ancient controversy between Aristotle and Plato, a controversy which has important implications for the present.[2] Plato advocated that parents should be prevented from knowing which children biologically were theirs. By doing this, he thought that all parents would come to feel and act parentally toward all children. Speaking of such communized adults, Plato felt that his scheme would

> tend to make them more truly guardians; they will not tear the city in pieces by differing about "mine" and "not mine"; each man dragging any acquisition which he has made into a separate house of his own, where he has a separate wife and children and private pleasures and pains; but all will be affected as far as may be by the same pleasures and pains because they are all of one opinion about what is near and dear to them, and therefore they all tend towards a common end. (Jowett 1892, p. 727)

Aristotle, apparently with better understanding of human nature, noted in his *Politics* that such a practice would merely result in all parents acting with equal indifference toward all children. As he put it:

> The scheme of Plato means that each citizen will have a thousand sons: they will not be the sons of each citizen individually:

and every son will be equally the son of any and every father;
and the result will be that every son will be equally neglected by
every father. (Barker 1946, p. 44)

The responsibility of one parent for all children, and the absence
of particular responsibility for any individual child, would produce universal indifference as Aristotle recognized, not universal love as Plato hoped. Or, as Aristotle put it still more pithily:
"It is better to be own cousin to a man than to be his son after
the Platonic fashion" (Barker 1946, p. 45).

Public education without parental choice injects vestiges of
this Platonic ideal into our social order, eroding the foundations
of family life in the process. Restoring elements of parental
choice would reverse some of these difficulties and thereby
strengthen the sense of caring and community.

THE AGENT-PRINCIPAL RELATIONSHIP

The presence or absence of parental choice affects the character
of the social relations within which education takes place.
Parental choice creates an agent-principal relationship between
parent and teacher; the present system of state choice creates a
paternal relationship, with the state as principal and the parent
as dependent. With the paternal relationship, paternal experts—
educators—are assumed to know what is best; they sense an
obligation to do what they know is best by directing and controlling parents, who are thought incapable of choosing wisely
for themselves and their children. These different relationships
result largely from the differences between pricing and taxing,
which differences determine the identity of the decision-maker.

It is often claimed that, because parents are too uninformed or
ignorant to choose wisely about education, decisions should be
left to professional educators. This problem of ignorance, it is
worth noting, is common to all agent-principal relationships.
The agent with superior knowledge always acts on behalf of a
principal with less knowledge; indeed, this is why the relationship exists in the first place. One person without the time (and
possibly the ability) to undertake an activity himself can have

tasks performed for him in the same manner in which he would perform them for himself, if only he could. Despite this difference in knowledge, the usual presumption is that the principal has the right to choose his agent and to judge his performance. And competition among agents facilitates such choice in a way that would be impossible without freedom to choose.

The problem in such cases is how the principal can monitor his agent, how he can judge his agent's performance. Unable to duplicate the agent's action, he cannot judge it with perfect assurance. But with free choice, the existence of competing agents reduces the ability of the agent to act inimically to the interests of his principal. Should this opportunity for choice be foreclosed—should accountants, lawyers, and physicians simply be assigned to people and financed through taxation—the problem of judging their performance would greatly increase.

Nevertheless, some may still argue that the central social and cultural importance of education makes it unwise to entrust educational choices to uninformed parents. A poor choice of an accountant, lawyer, or physician may cause emotional, monetary, or physical suffering, but this suffering will be largely confined to the principal at that moment in history. Poor educational choices, however, produce consequences borne by one's children and extend over the duration of the child's life. Thus, it is argued, choices about education should be made by experts, by educators.

One wonders about the consistency of this sentiment, which has a certain appeal, with the premises underlying democratic institutions. If parents (citizens) cannot be trusted to make educational choices, one might wonder why they should be trusted to make political choices. After all, choosing a politician is far more complex than choosing a school. In the choice of a politician, a person chooses—at one stage removed—schools, police, fire, and many other services provided by the government.

The real issue here concerns *presumptions*. The current presumption—that no parent is responsible unless he happens to be rich and can opt out of the system—approaches the perverse. It seems much more reasonable that given the parent's special relationship with a child—a relationship no teacher can begin to have—the presumption of responsibility should favor the parent. Cases presenting individual problems can always be dealt with individually, as exceptions.

Without the opportunity for choice, ignorance will increase. There is little reason for people to acquire knowledge on which they cannot act. If a person cannot choose among schools, only curiosity will encourage him to become informed about what is at stake in making a selection. Those who complain about lack of parent knowledge and involvement in the schools overlook the fact that genuine, involved relationships between parents and schools—especially between parents and teachers—become extremely difficult, if not impossible, without choice. The problem extends beyond mere incentives to acquire information. As noted earlier, the right to choose—or its denial—may be the major factor in defining social roles and relationships. Without choice, the state is principal and parents are dependents—at best, they are observers of the educational process. As dependents, parents have no standing to relate to teachers as equals in concern for education of their children. Without choice, therefore, parents not only have no incentive in an economic sense to acquire information about education; their social and psychological roles as dependents further deters them from involving themselves or participating.

These problems of information and dependency go a long way toward answering those critics of choice who argue that the low levels of parent involvement in the present system of public education would make a choice system largely ineffective. By this view, most children would continue to attend the same schools where they would face the same teachers and read the same books. Since choice would only be exercised in marginal cases, it would not affect the majority of the students. It is important here to appreciate the extent to which the problems of information and dependency go to the heart of the manner in which parents of public school children conceive their roles in education. Because of the depth of that influence, as we shall see in a moment, we should expect that these problems will influence parents for some considerable period, even with the introduction of a choice system.

There is a second point here which relates to the claim that, unless large numbers of parents actually exercise their ability to choose, a choice system will be only a marginal phenomenon. This is a mistake. It is not necessary for vast numbers of parents actually to choose differently—say, to change schools—for a system of parental choice to make an important difference. It is necessary only that they have the option to do so. Only a few parents need actually act. This is true whenever service is offered in a market or choice setting. It is sufficient for a few parents to change schools, or even to raise the possibility of doing so, for schools to receive the message that they are not meeting the needs of their clientele as well as they or someone else might fulfil them.

Another group of criticisms is directly encouraged by over-zealous advocates of choice. If some critics say that under a choice system there would be too little choice, other critics—perhaps including most teacher organizations—fear that there would be too much choice. This concern evokes images of legions of parents assaulting principals and teachers with questions and ideas about how to educate their children, thus disrupting the smooth functioning of the schools and jeopardizing the job security of most teachers. This concern was undoubtedly aggravated toward the end of the 1960s, when general tensions in American society greatly influenced the government's early involvement in school voucher experiments: public debates occurred in the intense adversary climate of that period, and it was easy to see how many teachers saw interest in educational choice as a weapon directed at them.

This fear is greatly exaggerated. As noted above, the problems of information and dependency characteristic of the present system have discouraged parents of public school children from serious involvement in education. At several levels, the traditional relationship discourages parents from even thinking they have the *standing* to participate seriously in the educational process—a fact which one would expect is deeply imbedded in parents' conception of themselves and of their proper role in education. Such a conception will not be overturned easily or quickly; we should expect that the introduction of parental choice will encourage a changing attitude only very slowly, in part precisely because most parents will feel they have a lot to learn in order to grow into their new responsibility. This is not a deficiency of choice, however; it is a strength. It would help to ensure considerable institutional continuity, encouraged by the gradual development of strong relationships between parents and teachers as equals in the educational enterprise. One should expect that, with the introduction of a choice system, it may be as long as half a generation before many parents feel fully able to participate.

For those concerned about teachers and their role in a choice system, the brief experience in the Alum Rock voucher experiment should restore some perspective (see Doyle's narrative in Chapter XI). During the first five years of the experiment teachers were the primary beneficiaries—which should come as no surprise, following our discussion here. The fact that parents may gain power and authority in a choice system does not necessarily mean that teachers must lose. In a choice system teachers will cease to be mere employees of a centralized educational bureaucracy and will become professionals, dealing directly with true principals in a relationship of common concern and interest. It will be a relationship which initially finds teachers schooling parents to assume their full responsibility; but once that is achieved, the common commitment of parent and teacher toward the children can develop in a way that has never been possible with the school bureaucracy as principal.

Even with full participation, there is no reason to fear disruptions caused by excessive parental choice. Changes will occur gradually as relationships evolve; changes will not be unimportant because they are marginal. The parent legions will not march on the schools as long as the schools are run reasonably well. Legions of customers do not march on A & P. They well might, of course, should the boneless rump roast purchased on sale turn out to be filled with soybeans. In the absence of such tricks, however, grocers do not have to fear wildly gyrating changes in customer tastes. And the same would be true with choice in education. If anything, precisely because it is education, we would expect great institutional and philosophical continuity.

For overall lessons, we might return to ancient Greece, especially to the interesting contrast in education provided in its city-states. In democratic Athens educational choice was a matter of parent responsibility and was subject to parent control. Schools were private and often owned by the masters. Other than specifying minimal standards, the state's educational activities were limited to military training between the ages of fifteen and twenty. The Athenian system was based on strong recognition of the social value of expressing and nurturing the affective sentiments that are found to be especially intense within families. As one commentator put it: "Rather than to destroy the family, as at Sparta, Athens aimed to preserve it as a means of developing and shaping personality, and upon it placed the burden of responsibility for education" (Monroe 1970, p. 81). The Athenians understood very well how giving expression to these affective sentiments was vital in promoting a healthy sense of personal participation and involvement in the Athenian community.

In Sparta there was no scope for parental choice. There the state's responsibility extended to removing school age children from the home and placing them in schools designed to shape them in the Spartan mold.[3] I think the implications of the two positions speak for themselves.

People generally know more about automobiles than about schooling; it is not because they inherently care more about automobiles, but because at least they can choose among automobiles. For the same reasons, Athenians knew more about education than did Spartans because education was their personal responsibility. The same would be true for American parents of

the future if they were permitted to exercise choice in education.[4]

COMPETITION, MONOPOLY, AND THE
METHOD OF FINANCING EDUCATION

Whether parental choice is permitted or denied can, by affecting
the degree to which affective sentiments can be expressed, influence the nature and sense of community among citizens. The
method of finance—taxes (no choice) or tuitions (choice)—also
raises some more narrowly economic questions concerning
competition and monopoly in the provision of education.
Where education is financed by taxes and parent choice is
denied, public education is a monopoly; with parental choice
comes competition—and active striving to improve educational
quality.[5]

In education, government is the monopolist *par excellence*. A
person can avoid dealing with AT & T by writing letters, buying
a megaphone, or traveling more often. But citizens must pay for
all government services financed by taxes; there is no way they
can opt out. This is the very pinnacle of monopoly power—the
ability to compel purchase. While it is necessary for some services to be financed by taxes without choice, this is certainly not
true of education. This absence of choice when it is feasible
enhances the government's position as monopolist.[6]

The government's monopoly power has several important
consequences for educational content. When schools (or anything else) are financed by taxes without pricing and choice,
there is no efficient way to register information about popular
support. Since parents cannot choose one school over another,
they have no effective way to communicate their desires for
diverse educational programs. And since educators have a captive market, they have little incentive to meet parent needs.
Without choice, education is provided in a *political* as well as a
paternalistic setting.

The ballot box is a poor substitute for conveying information
about parent judgments of different educational programs.

Customers, if they have a choice, will normally find producers who make an effort to tailor products to their differing needs. Thus parents with fundamentalist as well as Sybaritic values will both tend to find schools that satisfy them. In a competitive setting with one vote for each dollar, everyone gets to vote and every dollar counts. In a political setting the majority decides how much diversity will be tolerated, and except for strict constitutional safeguards, minority viewpoints tend to be unprotected and unrepresented. Outcomes in education reflect political power and educator preferences. Educational organizations such as the National Education Association (NEA) and the American Federation of Teachers (AFL-CIO) are quite clear on this, as they have already declared that educational content should be their exclusive preserve. Without choice, control is apportioned only by the relative political power of affected parties.

Without choice, there can be no effective protection of minority interests, and this explains the bitter educational controversies that have erupted in recent years over such things as textbook selection and sex education. In some places controversy has centered around whether or not the so-called "frills" should be replaced by a stronger devotion to the three Rs. And such matters as disciplinary policy and the treatment of religion are also sources of considerable differences of opinion. Any of these dimensions, along with many others, could in a setting of parental choice offer opportunities for variety in educational content among schools.

The opportunities for diversity are indicated, for instance, by the success enjoyed by language and speed-reading schools, as well as by adult education and vocational training. In these instances, such schools as Berlitz have no territorial monopoly; instead, they must succeed in attracting customers by designing programs that satisfy their needs. This is also true now for accountants, lawyers, and physicians—and would be for education under a choice system.

The full implications of monopoly delivery of education may best be demonstrated by an analogy. Consider a situation in which groceries were distributed as education is now distributed.

Instead of being able to select stores and the items in them, we would be assigned to a particular store on the basis of residence. Without prices, and with decisions made by "experts" regarding what groceries to stock, much of the reason for having a place to display groceries (a grocery store) would disappear. To exaggerate the point, we could as easily go to a window and pick up a standardized package of groceries—with everyone being forced to take the same menu. The analogy may be more extreme than the reality, because it is easy to assume more uniformity (less tolerance for diversity) than is realistic, at least in the United States today. In point of fact, it is likely that the experts would permit some choice, just as limited choices are now possible in the public school format. Still, the opportunities are very limited, as they would be in our grocery example. There would always be some tension between professional grocers, experts, and political leaders; but the experience of most other government attempts at regulation suggests that it would not be long before the grocers were making most decisions about what to offer. In a way, the situation is actually worse in our present education system. At least in the grocery situation a resale market in undesired commodities could develop, but with education resale is impossible because the product is not separable from the recipient.

Under these circumstances, without prices, communicating consumer desires becomes extremely difficult even if suppliers wanted to serve them. More likely, suppliers would have their own agenda; and if professional grocers become convinced that their responsibility for the nutrition of their wards requires them to curtail their offerings of foods high in cholesterol, nothing would prevent them short of spirited political opposition—which is difficult and costly to organize. The same would be true if the professionals developed a strong interest in vegetarianism or fructarianism: customers would have to adapt or fight.

With consumer choice, vegetarian and fructarian desires can be satisfied and cultural and social preference respected. When social choices are centralized, diversity and pluralism tend to be discouraged and suppressed—and social tolerance tends not to flourish. On the other hand, a system that gives ready expression to individual, diverse, and pluralistic choices will also encourage the social tolerance essential to a healthy society.

Finally, one would expect that the current monopoly status of schooling reduces efficiency and increases the cost of providing it. Without a residual claimant who can capture the benefits of increased efficiency—or bear the costs of inefficiency—gains or losses are diffused over the entire citizenry. This difference in incentives explains the inefficiency of most government--provided services in other areas, as it does in education.[7] Studies of cost differences that exist between public bureaus and private firms in the provision of fire protection (Ahlbrandt 1973), passenger and freight airline service (Davies 1971), refuse collection (Spann [forthcoming]), and other areas indicate that actual experience supports the theory that public provision, particularly when tax financed, increases inefficiency (Nicols 1967).

CONCLUSION

The choice between pricing and taxing as devices for financing education—the question of whether to permit parental choice and competition among schools—has important implications for both the actual content of education and the character of our social order. Replacing choice with compulsion alters the relations between teachers and parents. In a centralized system the state is principal and the parent is a dependent. In a choice system parents and teachers relate as principal to agent—as equals in concern for education of the child. In the paternal relationship that exists when there is no opportunity for choice, dependent parents are removed from active participation and involvement in education; without choice, and without the ability to participate effectively, they withdraw from a system whose disinterest in them is often quite explicit. They have no incentive to acquire information on which they cannot act—which leaves only the extraordinary few still involved.

The introduction of genuine choice in education would produce fundamental and profound changes in American education—both in content and in the roles of the participants, especially parents and teachers. These changes would be gradual, incremental, and there would be much institutional continuity. The absence of opportunities for genuine relationships inherent in the present centralized system may have hurt teachers most of all, often reducing them to the status of detention officers. Giving parents the right to choose would strengthen the role of teachers as professionals; and even if parental choice did not produce instant educational miracles, permitting parents to participate as equals in the process of education could bring benefits far beyond the classroom.

OPPORTUNITIES FOR CHOICE

VI

JOHN E. COONS   STEPHEN D. SUGARMAN

A CASE FOR CHOICE[1]

Educational controls: government, school personnel, parents, professional lobbies. Freedom of choice: the family obligation; family/child interactions. Present teacher responsibility and free teacher/parent cooperation. Public consensus regarding a child's interests. Variety as a social strength. Racial integration and choice. Elements of free choice: financing, enrollment aspects, teaching contracts, input/output minima. The advantages of free choice.

INTRODUCTION: ON MAKING CASES

Every argument for reform of policy assumes an audience that to some degree shares the advocate's social objectives. It is idle to argue for the eighteen-year-old vote with those preferring a return to monarchy. In arguing for choice in education we run the same risk. Our aims are two. First, education should serve the best interest of the individual child. Second, it should support community in its many aspects; here we will emphasize two of primary importance—public consensus and racial integration. The argument is addressed to readers with similar objectives.

Policy argument also needs two or more alternatives that can be compared for their relative capacity to produce the desired ends. It would be pointless to label the present educational regime good or bad in the absolute. We will, therefore, describe the existing system and, for comparison, a hypothetical system which would increase the authority of families. The descriptions for the moment will be very general; alternative systems of choice will be detailed at the end of the chapter.

THE LEARNING CONNECTION: TWO MODELS

Power over the education of the individual child is currently divided among six forces. There are government institutions; teachers and other school personnel; families of public school pupils; private school families; lobbying professional groups; and a miscellany composed of taxpayers, nonparents, and others we can call the "rest of us." The same individual may appear in a number of these roles.

Government (principally state government), within the limits of state and federal constitutions, creates and empowers school districts. It ordains tax structures that support them and the general rules by which their operations are governed. Districts set the bulk of curriculum policy, establish enrollment rules that determine which school the child attends, and hire the teachers who are assigned there. These processes of decision are abstract and rational. Government does not know individual children.

School personnel, especially teachers, have discretion within broad curricular constraints to affect the child's experience, since the children who are assigned to them are virtually their captive audience for several hours each day. The relation is sometimes fairly personalized, though a class of twenty-five is too large for close involvement of the teacher with more than a few students.

Public school families typically have little influence on their child's formal education. Sophisticated parents with time and interest are a partial exception, but their options are usually limited to whatever variety is available within the assigned school or, at most, the school district. In some cases families discover what they want in other geographic areas and make the sacrifice of moving their residence to obtain it.

Under our national constitution families with money cannot be forced into public schools.[2] Thus those selecting private schools—the well-to-do and those with private subsidies (e.g., parochial school families)—determine more of the basic character of their own children's education.

Professional and commercial organizations affect the individual child by inducing government to employ their members to do things to children that are said to be good for them or society. Thus, construction companies persuade legislatures to require schools to be rebuilt for the purpose of protecting children from earthquakes. Teachers unions obtain laws which limit class size to thirty, and other laws which exclude teachers who lack particular academic credentials.

The "rest of us" vote on taxes and occasionally are aroused by the alarums of special interest groups. The politics of education, however, are dominated by the professionals. This is largely because the class of persons which is the target of education— children—is incapable of representing itself politically. Nor can parents represent children for two reasons. First, individual children's needs and interests are very different from one another. Second, even among those with similar interests it is unlikely that individual families will spend precious time and funds for lobbying. Political scientists and economists call this the "free rider" problem (Olson 1965; Buchanan and Tullock 1962). If others lobby, one does not need to; if others don't, one's own contribution is inconsequential. Under the law, parents cannot coerce the participation of others. Hence they find private uses for their extra money, and the political process is dominated by those organized interests who wish to sell services and in whose interest it is that children remain in need of such services.

Imagine now that this pattern of power over the individual child were altered by providing for each child a full state scholarship plus admission and transport to the school of the family's choice—public or private. There would be several broad effects. School assignments would cease to be orders issued to abstract classes of persons of certain ages and location. They would become personalized decisions about Freddie and Julia, tailored choices that now could be made by the family without having to change its residence.

The power of local authorities to command an audience would terminate; they would, however, retain their right to advise families, to run schools, and to teach those who chose their services. The roles of state government, professional lobbyists, and the general populace would now be limited to the setting and enforcing of guarantees that all schools provide a certain minimum experience or that children achieve a minimum level of competence.

How would a system so dependent upon the family for making assignments and setting minimum standards compare to the present regime in its likely impact upon the interest of the child and of society? By family here we shall mean any adult-child relation, genetic or otherwise, which is expected to be permanent, continous, and intimate at least until the child reaches adulthood.

CHOICE AND THE BEST INTEREST OF THE CHILD

Given the child's interest as our primary concern, and given great differences in the needs and interests of children, we will further assume in this section that the function of society is to choose and empower someone who will make school assignments for the individual child. We suggest three qualities in the ideal chooser. First, he would incorporate the child's own *voice* in the process; he would thus stand as proxy for the child's own perception of his needs and interests. Second, the ideal chooser would *care* for the child in the special sense that the child's interest came ahead of his own. Third, the chooser's welfare would be linked as closely as possible to that of the child; he would be *responsible* for unwise choices in the full sense that they affect the chooser himself adversely. These qualities of voice, caring, and responsibility can be summarized as effective knowledge. How shall we grade the family on this basic standard?

Voice can count within the family in two interrelated ways. First, the child may achieve his own choice. The family normally is a regime flexible enough to give his growing competence increasing scope while yet providing basic protection; the federally sponsored "voucher" experiment in Alum Rock has shown how often the child himself effectively makes the school selection. Second, the family environment encourages the confidentiality and privacy that can be crucial to a child's willingness to reveal his feelings. Moreover, since the parent-child unit is small, enduring, and repetitious, the child's opinions are communicated through nonverbal behavior; the intimacy of the family fosters an effective private language.

Caring is the family function par excellence both in myth and reality; and the reality is importantly enhanced by modern contraceptive culture (Coons 1976b). Adults now must choose to have children, and they must do so in spite of the economic and personal penalty exacted of parents in modern life. Such self-imposed burdens seem to us a convincing measure of devotion.

Responsibility is a primary characteristic of the family, because its happiness is a function of the child's own. The relation imposes the pains of the child vicariously and even directly upon the group, and it will continue to do so throughout life. It is in the objective self-interest of the adults in the family to help the child achieve satisfaction and autonomy.

The sum of the family's qualities is a substantial effective knowledge. It is fallible and varies by families; given broader authority, some families would make grievous errors in educational placement, as perhaps occurs now among private school families. Would those now bound to attend public schools—the non-rich—be less competent? If so, in what degree? The question seems unanswerable without experiment, since these families hitherto have lacked choice. In any case they might grow through the new experience of responsibility. Most people do.

How does the present regime in public education compare for effective knowledge of the individual child? First, the basic system of matching the child to his school experience—neighborhood assignment—is almost wholly abstract;[3] school selection for the child is made by government in total ignorance of the child's wishes or special qualities (unless he is so incapacitated as to be outside the regular system). At the school level, students and teachers are generally assigned to one another in an impersonal process. Individualization that occasionally does occur in teacher-student pairing is necessarily limited—there are only so many third-grade or geometry teachers—and below high school, the child's voice is rarely involved.

Once the child is assigned to a classroom he may achieve some voice. The teacher's ability to hear him is a function of the hours they spend together, the number of students in the class, the child's aggressiveness, and character of his classmates. When heard, the child's desires can receive but limited accommodation. And in reality no child can expect to be heard very clearly unless he is willing to become a deviant, in which case a counselor may spend several hours with him. Were each child to receive substantial time from a psychiatrist, the advantage would be plausible; but experience and social science confirm how little the professional counselor is able to learn and to achieve in the average case beyond relabeling the child. In any event the counselor has few alternative environments to which the child may be sent.[4]

As for caring, most teachers surely do, but their caring by its nature must remain relatively cool and abstract. The teacher who becomes very deeply involved with even one child is likely to be regarded more as neurotic than professional. To the extent that he does so, he is plainly substituting for the parent. It is not a model role for a system of education. This is not a criticism, nor would the degree of affective care by teachers increase under a system of choice. The point is that under the present system, for the child of the non-rich family, there is *no* caring adult who is able to exercise authority over assignment. In our view it is a proper function of the state to provide a competent professional backstop for the occasional child whose parents do not care; but it is not proper to screen out and frustrate the natural care of most parents.

How fares the present system as a focus of responsibility for the individual child's welfare? We cannot here detail the reward system for public educational agents, but two points are plain. First, the systems for purging the classroom of incompetents is of little consequence; virtually no tenured teachers are seriously threatened so long as they show up for work and keep their hands off the children. Second, under the present structure the teacher has no strong natural link of self-interest with the child. He may regret the academic or personal failure of Freddie, but he neither must live with nor even encounter him after June. Freddie is a crisis to be passed, not a cross to be borne—just another forgettable kid. And that is as it should be. Teaching is not parenthood and should not be held accountable in the same manner. It should be responsible only for the reasonable performance of a narrower role. Yet even this will elude us until society supports the child's capacity to transfer to another educator.

It has been convenient to this point to inquire simply whether bureaucracy or the family is by itself the superior decision-maker. Now we should see that this mistakes the real question, for it suggests too broad a conflict of parents and professionals. In a system emphasizing family choice, the fact is that professionals would be likely to play an important role. They have valuable information not available to many parents, and families would come to them for advice. If anything, this should make the professionals' involvement in assignments even more active; since families could reject their advice, professionals would have to depend upon persuasion. The relation would become that of lawyer to client or architect to owner. For the first time public school teaching might become a true profession because its clientele at last was free. That very freedom could well improve the market for professional service. Once the system of expert advice became accountable, families could begin to trust it. It would now be strongly to the family's interest to learn how best to use the available experts—and to use them.

Note that by having the final word the empowered family need no longer fear professional oversight or nonfeasance. Today no one plays this role of backstop, and society knows the consequence both from sad experience and social science.[5] The child once labeled and assigned by bureaucracy is rarely reassigned, however much he needs it. What family choice would give him is an amateur champion—a change agent—to ensure that he is not forgotten by the system. A family which found the professional unresponsive to inquiry could transfer the unhappy child themselves. Such an incentive could in turn have a vitalizing effect on the expert; choice could bring the teaching profession the dignity that has so long eluded it.

GETTING THE QUESTION STRAIGHT

Some would argue that we miss the point. We have compared the efficacy of two regimes for achieving the child's interest as if that interest were currently undefined. Some would argue, however, that it has already been defined by consensus. Our school officials are simply carrying out what the public has agreed *is* good for children; and the public has decided that non-rich children are best off under the present system. This criticism holds good for a certain minimum content of education. However, it fails as a general proposition, for above this narrow minimum the child's interest is a private affair, whether we like it or not.

To have a "public" meaning about the best interest of the individual child there must be a consensus supporting a defined substantive objective embodying the good for children; the consensus should also encompass a specific means to achieve the objective; and there should be a reasonable basis for believing that the means will indeed achieve those ends. At present there are elements of the child's interest (not restricted to education) which are in this sense "public." A consensus, for example, supports positive levels of nutrition and educational curriculum; and that consensus finds negative expression in proscriptions such as curfews and prohibitions upon dangerous labor. In short, there is social agreement concerning a reasonably specific minimum substantive good for children.

However, as in other aspects of his life, the typical child's formal education includes far more than the minimum. Beyond the minimum, it is individuals and subgroups—not the public—whose values and means express the child's welfare. There is no public consensus that the child should become aggressive, a Muslim, a patriot, or a pacifist; these are as much in dissensus as the decision to teach phonics and employ ability grouping. In this immense area beyond consensus, the reality is that government as such has no views (Wolff 1968; Unger 1975; Stewart 1975, p. 1667); the question for government in these circumstances is not the child's interest at all, but rather whom it will authorize to define that interest in his own private terms. Within this domain of dissensus, the state may choose to enforce the decisions of welfare workers, parents, teachers, or family court judges, but in every case these are private judgments that it sanctions. This is in itself no criticism; someone will decide for children and, where it lacks consensus, the most democratic government has no option but to legitimate some micro-sovereignty, allowing it to set the values and means for children. This is, of course, what it has done for education; the school bureaucracy stands, to this extent, not as an implementer of what Americans agree is best, but as sovereign over the interest of the non-rich.

But what is the rationale for society's imposing upon a child it doesn't know the special views of a particular school board, principal, or teacher? Society does not do this to private school users; in justice and common sense, how can it do it to the rest? We know of no principle favoring subordination of low-income children to the peculiar preference of strangers, at least where the family's own choice remains within the range of values and practices legitimate for others. Fair respect for equality of treatment thus reinforces the conclusion of the prior section that beyond the minimum the family is the appropriate sovereign.

There is a final consideration. This is the new humility beginning to pervade the social science of children's welfare. It has in our time become apparent that in many areas the professions know very little of how to intervene successfully in children's lives (Mnookin 1975, p. 226; Coons 1976a). Under conditions of professional dissensus, giving families a broad discretion in education seems little more than common sense.

CHOICE AND SOCIAL GOALS

How would regulated family choice advance the social goals of community and racial integration? These questions are considered by others in this volume, and we will strip our own argument to its essentials.

Community

The social ideal expressed in the concept of community is subtle and somewhat paradoxical. On the one hand it suggests unity and, on the other, variety. This Delphic quality informs the fundamental political dogma—"one out of many." Does it imply that we are many struggling to overcome our differences; or is it, rather, our very differences that make us one? Is human variety a source of order or disorder?

While differences can be risky, we stand with variety as a principle of social strength. As with the genetic order, the least differentiated of human societies may be most vulnerable to environmental change. Variety, to us, is also a social good in itself. It is a source of esthetic fullfillment and intellectual growth. So long as variety remains intact in the distinct cultures and ideologies of our people, it offers to every individual a choice of paths to personal fulfillment. It does so, that is, so long as the law of the society guarantees freedom from discrimination and protects the choice of persons to adopt the life-style they prefer.

When this condition of free choice is fulfilled, variety can also yield peace and cooperation among groups, bedrock social purposes which we share. Nothing conduces more to support of the larger order than for minorities to perceive that their ways are trusted and even valued. Conversely, nothing may so fragment a society as a decision by the majority that minority values deserve nothing better than melting.

A society which trusts its minorities should implement their educational preferences, and family choice is the ideal mechanism for this, since it permits individuals to form educational communities of choice. It is far superior to the direct funding of existing schools, a device which encourages suppliers to fix and limit the forms and ideologies represented in the marketplace of ideas.

A pluralistic strategy in education would respond precisely to the fundamental change in the nature and function of communication since the advent of the melting pot. In a nation of widely scattered farmers and greenhorn immigrants it was at least plausible that coerced aggregation of the unwashed in a common school was a way of instilling the news that we are one people with inseparable destinies. In an age of mass communication the best news that could be leaked to the people is that we are not all slavish consumers of identical products and ideas. Schools of choice could provide this priceless function by giving life to minority ideals, ideas, and culture.

Even the angriest of ideologies can in the long run make its contribution to community. The child who is exposed to one-sided politics and religion at least has no doubt that there is a morality among humans and that morality is important. To see this is to take the first mental step toward brotherhood, a step that must be left unattempted in the neutralist morality of public institutions. Choice would, at its worst, spare us that most grievous sin against community—indifference. It might in the bargain give to minority children that sense of personal distinctness—of "identity"—that seems to underlie the psychology of tolerance. It is those who recognize themselves who are most ready to recognize others.

Racial Integration

If everyone were free to choose his school, what would be the consequence for racial mixing? The question will never be fully answerable. Absolute freedom to choose plainly is impossible to achieve, not only because of finite resources but because of conflicts in preferences; X cannot be free to associate with Y if Y is also to be free to refuse the association. We can, however, approach full freedom for the consumer of education by giving him his choice of school and the right to transfer if later he prefers another. To achieve this much we must in various ways limit the school's (and other patrons') freedom to exclude or discriminate against him. We are content to do so both because we are interested in the child as such (the school is instrumental), and because a rule of associational inclusion can offset the disadvantage of minorities. In a later section we will suggest details of such assignment and protection systems. For the moment we ask the reader to assume success in designing a mechanism that renders the selection process as racially neutral as the ingenuity of man can achieve.

Choice has shown a significantly greater capacity to integrate schools than does a neighborhood system of assignment. It has been tried with varying degrees of sincerity and gusto in a fair number of American cities, several of which we know firsthand. Even many of the narrow and half-hearted programs have produced some increase in physical integration. For the most part, it is blacks who have chosen to attend majority white schools; but in some instances—for example, in Evanston, Illinois, and Redwood City, California—the traffic was heavy in both directions (McAdams 1974, p. 69).[6]

To the extent that integration is voluntary it has several useful qualities. One, its stability is almost a matter of definition; people getting what they want by personal selection tend to stay. In addition, voluntary integration tends to become infectious. It begins with an adventurous few, but others follow. Still another advantage is the capacity of choice to forestall the residential emigration of white families who accept integration but prefer to avoid heavy black majorities.

Chosen integration would be incomplete integration. Very

likely many families would choose to remain in uniracial—principally black—schools. Yet if this choice were truly voluntary we could not consider the outcome to be evil. There is nothing inferior or objectionable in a uniracial school; it would be Olympian arrogance to imagine that black schools could offer nothing in culture or ambience worth choosing.

It would also be political naivete to suppose that society has a more promising option for integration. Those who would escalate compulsion as the hope of physical integration should study both the relevant social science (Orfield 1976; Wolff 1976; Armor 1972, p. 90; Pettigrew, Useem, and Normand 1973; Farley 1975, p. 164)[7] and the recent opinions of the Supreme Court[8] (also Fiss 1975, p.217; Bell 1975, p.341). There is little prospect that the court will order the state to bus the suburban white student back to the city. Indeed, if it did so the exodus to private education could vaporize the very support for education upon which the urban poor must depend.

What hope is there then in a system of choice? A great deal, and now is the time. There is presently a marked surplus of places in suburban public schools which are principally white. There is space in private schools, urban and suburban, and more space and schools would appear if scholarships and transport were available. Perhaps children should be limited to transfers which have an integrating effect, but they should be given the full range of such schools in the metro area to choose from.

MECHANISMS

The administrative and fiscal devices needed for a system of choice can be conveniently considered in their relation to complementary purposes. First, a family's wealth should not affect its capacity to choose whatever is available within a system supported by public funds. Second, barriers to choice should be minimized; these include discrimination against certain types of children by educational suppliers, lack of information among poor families, difficulty in market entry for new schools, and similar impediments. Third, minimums of educational input and/or achievement must be established and supported by alternative forms of administrative control. Obviously the potential forms of intervention for these three general purposes are protean, and we must be content to give but a sense of the richness of fiscal and administrative options (Coons and Sugarman 1971).[9]

Removing Wealth Barriers

Begin with the simplest forms of subsidy in which the family is not permitted to affect the amount. Suppose that each child is supplied a scholarship that is uniform in amount, except perhaps for adjustments representing higher costs of land, goods, and services in certain areas. Then simply add to this a proscription forbidding the charging of tuition beyond the scholarship amount; otherwise wealthier families will add on and income classes will separate themselves into schools of graduated cost; this is intolerable in a publicly financed system (Friedman 1962, pp. 85-107).[10]

A variation of this model would graduate the value of educational grants according to the wealth of the family (Sizer and Whitten 1968, p. 58; Public Policy 1970). Thus schools enrolling large numbers of poor children would have more to spend. There is a certain logic in this if the poor tend to be more costly to educate. It is not easy, however, to focus the actual expenditure of the extra dollars upon the disadvantaged child unless he first be segregated, a practice which seem generally undesirable. The extra dollars could, of course, be directed to after-school opportunities for the child such as private lessons in either academic studies, crafts, or other interests. The latter device is coming to be known as "school stamps" (Sugarman 1974, pp. 513, 546). It could go far toward closing the inevitable gap in the capacities of rich and poor families to provide extra-school opportunities.

If choice in the level of spending is desirable (as we believe), a system of "family power equalizing" may be adopted (Coons and Sugarman 1971). Here each school would charge what it pleased, but the family and the state would share the cost of the tuition. The family's portion of that tuition would increase with its income; a poor family would pay a very small percentage, the rich would pay full cost. The approachable ideal would be a payment formula by which a poor family realistically could "afford" as costly a school as a richer one. Thus family power equalizing lets the non-rich family especially interested in education spend at a higher rate if it is willing to make the extra sacrifice required.

There are other possibilities for financing. Open enrollment in the public system could be supplemented by subsidized private schools started by families. Families could be given credits on federal income tax, with poorer families who pay little or no tax receiving a positive grant for education. The current tax treatment of day-care expenditures is moving in that very direction.[11] The combinations are endless.

Assuring Choice

Enrollment problems are substantial. Here let us start with the assumption that each participating public and private school will determine how many students to enroll, but will not control who is enrolled. For schools with applications equal to or fewer than its enrollment capacity, all would be admitted. For schools in which applications exceed spaces, some random selection method would be employed. A state agency could run the lotteries for admission.

There is a hard policy decision that must precede such a mechanism. Schools wishing to specialize in various ways—ecology, college prep, the arts, dance—seem highly desirable; yet to the extent their students lack the relevant talent, they are affected in their capacity to specialize. For this reason, some supporters of family choice would permit schools to select at least a cadre of their enrollees. Others think it enough that the school can counsel the family against enrolling an untalented child.

It is also necessary to decide whether the selection rule ought to be tilted toward racial integration in order to offset the inertia of history, housing patterns, distance, and habit. It would be our own preference to do so, and we would suggest the wisdom of a regulation of the following sort.

> In cases in which a school has more applicants than places, the [state official] . . . shall first select at random from each racial group which constitutes a minority of the school's applicants a number of students not to exceed fifteen per cent of available places. All applicants not selected in this process shall then be pooled and the remaining places filled by random selection from that pool.

Many variations on this rule can be imagined. It would also be possible to give dollar rewards to schools which successfully integrate.[12] This would stimulate the school to recruit in a manner which produces an integrated pool of applications.

This suggests the importance of an information system which is designed not for the literate and sophisticated but for those who may be used to getting their information by the grapevine. Families must know what kinds of schools exist, and schools that are presently popular may not be motivated to advertise in all neighborhoods. Direct counseling services will be necessary, as well as a right to visit participating schools under certain conditions. It will also be important that the family have access to independent professional counsel concerning the needs and talents of their children. A yearly stipend for this purpose would be ideal both in terms of assisting family choice and in building an independent counseling profession.

Having chosen and been admitted to his first, second, or third choice, how will the child get there? Plainly a system of no-cost transport would be vital. And having arrived, there must be assurance that the school which may not have been eager to have him does not de-select him by discriminatory treatment. In short, we would need a system of due process of the sort already abuilding in the public schools.[13] For the child who is incorrigible or manifestly incapable of benefitting from the school of his choice, a fair system of separation would be necessary. The hope is that it would limit the school's power to behave arbitrarily without destroying efficiency.

To make certain there are new schools to choose from, the state may wish to assist entry by guaranteed building loans and similar devices. Entry costs in the educational business can be kept very low, but it would be well to offset some of the advantage of the public and private institutions already in place. It is also fundamental that public schools—like the rest—be left dependent upon their capacity to attract students. Probably most families would continue in public schools. However, it would be self-defeating for the state to pour in extra money to shore up a school no one wants. A process of dissolution equivalent to bankruptcy should phase out unsuccessful public schools; at the same time, new public entries should be possible, but should be governed by estimates of their ability to survive. This orderly closing of public schools that families shun, and opening of those they prefer, would magnify the importance of even marginal change; if nothing else, existing schools could read the signs and reform.

Public school fatalities suggest the problem of teacher security. If each school rests on its own bottom, the present district and state seniority, transfer, and security systems for public teachers will be replaced in part at least by contracts with individual schools. There are various ways to protect existing staff by "grandfather" provisions without leaving the schools crippled.[14] Teachers may be willing to exchange some of their present perquisites for the prospect of an open and exciting system in which energy and creativity enjoyed some elbowroom. There are risks for teachers, but there are invitations to professionalism that will appeal to many.

Assuring the Minimum

The minimum in education—the public consensus respecting values and means—is today expressed in term of "input"; that is, there are objective experiences required for students. These typically include total hours and days of instruction, coverage of particular subjects, a teacher who has received a degree in education, and instruction in a building of a certain sort. In some states a child may be taught in his own home, but often this is only if the teacher is certified (Sugarman and Kirp 1975, pp. 144, 200, 208-10).

A choice system could include a minimum and might include many of these same input rules. Their observance could be required of any participating institution. We would hope that the teacher certification requirement which has seldom been applied to private schools would be dropped altogether. And a relaxation of parts of the building codes which principally benefit the construction companies would be sensible; likewise we conclude that instruction should be permitted in all sorts of basically safe environments, including private homes. But education in the agreed basics for, say, 175 days a year could well remain compulsory. So long as flexible schedules and environments were accommodated, the bulk of present requirements could survive in a choice system. That is not to say that it should.

One broad alternative is to move toward output minimums—that is, to standards based upon the actual development of the individual child. One model is the neglect laws by which children are removed from families; if the child falls below a certain standard of educational achievement the family would lose its authority to direct his placement in formal education. There are several variations on the input/output theme. The state could view input as sufficient; families would retain choice so long as they met an input minimum, regardless of output. Another would view input merely as necessary; families would lose choice unless the child met both the input and the achievement standard. Still another variation would disregard the character of the educational experience so long as the output were sufficient.

What devices would be used to establish output criteria? No doubt tests, interviews, and observation would be suggested. One difficult question is whether to establish a uniform minimum or to vary it according to some prediction of how the individual child "ought" to be doing given his natural gifts as measured by the professionals. Allowing families to offer their own objectives and programs for approval by an independent inspectorate seems an appealing part of any package.

Whatever form of output minimum were adopted we would expect systems of choice to increase the percentage of children who achieve it. Among today's population of habitual truants and dropouts alone there must be many who would today be in formal education had they not been driven from pursuit of the minimum by assignment to a school experience they could not accept. Given their choice of schools they might still have dropped out or failed, but if any at all were saved it would amount to a net gain.

Those who have not yet dropped out but are merely failing could also benefit. Once freed to seek another educational environment, at least some families of children now failing in compulsory assignments would look for a solution. Of course there is a risk that those now succeeding under coercion would be corrupted by choice. We would be willing to see that possibility tested.

CONCLUSION

Many assert that choice can never come, that the political impediments are structural and beyond redemption. This may be, but our present observation is that the old structure of educational finance and governance is quaking. The forces are not merely a popular discontent, though that is real. In some states, including California, there is an opening of the political process by constitutional fiat. The legislative renaissance provoked by *Serrano* v. *Priest*[15] is the first since the imposition of public compulsion a century ago. It is impossible to predict its outcome, but there are signs that those who prefer choice, including minorities, will have a voice in the final solution. It could include substantial experiments with choice as a part of the *Serrano* package.

Some warn us that choice, if it does come, will cause disorder and cultural discontinuity—that it will bring too much change. Others fear the opposite: that essential change is beyond the power of social mechanisms and that choice would bring little more than marginal variations on the present themes. Pessimism, it seems, can make the most of anything. We have already answered the fear of social disruption. In concluding, we would answer the alternative fear of inadequate change by suggesting that marginal differences in observable behavior can count in a deep and powerful manner. A large measure of institutional continuity is exactly what one would expect; the race is not programmed for anarchy. Nevertheless freedom to select one's own way could have profound psychological significance, even if only the few employ it to alter their external experience in substantial respects. To choose what has previously been compelled is choosing nonetheless. Perhaps the difference is only a matter of human dignity and our view of one another. To us that seems enough.

VII

WILLIAM H. CORNOG

THE OPTIONS MARKET
IN EDUCATION

**Variations in educational opportunity, and how to equalize them.
Consumer assumptions. Proliferating courses. Geographical predestination and transfer. Criteria of public choice. Admissions standards and parent sensitivity. Inequalities in other professions.
Differences in teacher motivation. Professional opposition to competition. Organized teachers and their political strength. Tenure as
shelter for mediocrity vs. merit pay for competence. Master teachers.**

Anyone who still cherishes the illusion of a present or future
free economy in postindustrial America will doubtless support
the concept of an open market in educational opportunities. But
an economy energized and sustained by the twin drives of privilege and profit—while asserting faith in free enterprise and
equal opportunity—can scarely afford to jeopardize privilege by
fostering equality of opportunity, or risk profit in a totally free

and unmanaged market. This is somewhat the case with education in America. For more than a century the nation has pointed with pride to its free schools. But though they are free through the secondary level to all but taxpayers, they have not yet seen such tax-supported freeness mature into equality. Inner-city schools and suburban schools may be equally free to their clientele, as are rural schools in poor states and rural schools in affluent states, but they are as unequal as they are separate. Geographical predestination operates in our educational system as it does in the systems of other countries; that is to say, where you are born and raised, and in what socioeconomic environment, has much to do with the quality and extent of the schooling you receive, if for one reason or another you stay put and the schools stay put.

This disturbing fact of geographical or environmental predestination, offering a range of educational opportunities from the most nurturing and nourishing to the most deprived or debilitating, has had in several states the attention and lately the mandated remedies of the courts, notably the *Serrano* decision in California. Anyone who has studied the disparateness of educational opportunity in slum and suburb or among states must be persuaded by now that equality of educational opportunity can scarcely be accomplished without the employment of massive political, economic, and social makeweights or counterbalances amounting to a radical redistribution of human, financial, and technical resources in our schools and colleges.

Nevertheless, like Vachel Lindsay's mouse who gnawed the oak tree down, advocates do exist for modest measures of equalizing educational opportunities and opening options in the educational marketplace.

These advocates, usually of a voucher plan or a tax credit compensation, base their case on several assumptions. At least I would argue on the basis of such assumptions if I were to advocate such remedies, because I know these are the positions I would have to defend against the direct attack of the major party at interest, namely the teachers.

When consumerism raised its many-tongued head and a few

tongues lashed at schools and teachers, it became and possibly remains an open question as to whether curricular and educational options in general should be designed on the basis of market research, on the theory that the customers are always right or have to be pleased; or whether the teachers, professors of special knowledge and skills, know best and should stick to schoolmastering rather than turn to course-merchandising, credit-mongering, and the wiles of consumer-oriented educational shopkeeping.

Those who speak for the consumers of education seem to the producers of it to make the following assumptions about the state of education, elementary and secondary, and chiefly public:

1. More educational options must be made more widely available, either by vouchers or tax credits, or by some form of subsidy of competition for students and patrons.

2. At present, choices among a wide variety of schools and kinds of educational programs seem to be possible, but are quickly recognized as in fact limited by district policies on boundaries, transfers of students and teachers, monies allocated to transportation, and so forth.

3. The present choosers or determiners of educational offerings, the professionals, are not good—or good enough—at either pleasing or edifying customers.

4. The consumers themselves would make wiser, or at least more self-satisfying, choices than the present producers and electors.

5. The challenge of increased choice and consequent competition would benefit both consumers and producers and would improve the product universally.

Underlying these assumptions are some broad-based propositions highly critical of the present dispensation of the educational establishment, as follows:

1. Educational designs and performance criteria are too vital
   to students, parents, and the public at large to be left to the
   teaching profession.

2. Father and/or mother knows best or better than most other
   education decision-makers.

3. Students should have a say in what they are taught and how.

4. The public schools especially need further spur to reform,
   and compensation is that spur.

5. The teaching profession, the whole pedagogical *apparatchik,*
   will never seek, let alone accomplish, self-examination and
   improvement.

6. *Ergo,* the patrons and consumers must cause to be organized
   alternative structures and operations.

The most radical or deep-lying assumption of all is that by
some kind of enlargement of opportunity to pick curricula or
specific courses, or innovative educational programs, or a
different climate of learning or school pattern of organization,
Johnny will compensate for his present circumstances' deficiencies and be launched into a gratifying learning experience accommodated to his gifts, style, limitations and aspirations.

As one who has worked both sides of the street—twenty years
as a buyer or at least a consumer of teaching and forty years as a
seller of it—I must express on the basis of my direct experience
and without polls, opinion sampling, or what passes for educational research, a series of doubts and reservations engendered
by the positions taken by advocates of consumerism, competition, and compensatory mechanisms to make unevenness even.

If one could clear out of the way the grave political or constitutional obstacles to vouchers or other option-opening devices,
what are the realities of wide choice in a free educational
market?

In what segment of American education are the choices now
too narrow or restricted? It has been the peculiar characteristic

of American schools and colleges to manufacture courses with assembly-line speed. My experience has been that whenever or wherever educators have been given a chance, or have seized it, to proliferate courses, courses have bred like rabbits. Few of us would want to evaluate the quality of American education on the basis of the variety and sheer quantity of goods offered by our present educational supermarkets. The merchandising needs-meeting orientation of our educational enterprise has been full of bustle and hustle for years. Some carefree evangels encourage schools to take not only all learning but all living for their province, and to accept a kind of messianic responsibility to teach with high seriousness and equal zeal both trivial and essential knowledge and skills. What is needed, it seems to me, is not greater freedom of choice among such a tasteless smorgasbord, but a greater economy of choice among reasonably nutritious, well-prepared victuals. It is a legitimate criticism of American education that many designers of curricula haven't known Spinoza from ravioli. We have suffered a surfeit of pablum and pasties. There seems to me to be small need to enlarge the delicatessen of mediocrity.

The exponents of wider choice via vouchers, however, espouse for the most part freer choice among schools or total educational environments.

Here I have difficulty accepting the general feasibility of this solution. The reality of geographical predestination, the confined bounds of privileged enclaves and provinces vis-a-vis the spacious domain of public apathy and the private poor, make me dubious about a plan to move students by voucher and parental option to the greener pastures. If the choice lies between moving students to a better environment or improving the present environment, the latter would seem the more defensible. Moving them out, the argument goes, would improve the deficient environment, presumably through the shock of awakening to its transgressions and responding manfully to competition. This is to say that the morale of losers can be uplifted by yet another sound thrashing and yet another dose of the bracing tonic of public disfavor.

The option of a move to a "better" educational environment is hedged about with the thorniest questions of 1) how to evaluate "better," the evaluating to be done by parents and students where less than angelic experts have long feared to tread; and 2) how to make educational choices for truly intrinsic educational values.

I taught in the liberal arts colleges of two of the "better" universities, and I was the chief administrator of two of the "better"—some would say two of the best—high schools in the country. The two universities were considered among the better ones, I suppose, because of the eminence of their faculties and the distinctions achieved by their alumni. The same was largely true of the two high schools, although the quality of secondary schools of their particular clientele—in high proportion college-bound—was and is subject to almost immediate judgment on the basis of the achievement records of the schools' graduates in colleges and universities.

The criteria in the public mind for judging the excellence of an educational institution are, in the case of high schools, associated with college board scores, number of National Merit finalists and scholars, and other visible presumed measures of academic performance. In addition there is the competition for admission to the so-called prestigious colleges which are popularly regarded as "better" or "the best" for anyone who can get in. As a result many students and parents seek admission to colleges and universities which may well not be the best or even the better choices for the individual students concerned.

Picking an educational institution at any level as the best, i.e., the most appropriate, environment for an individual is clearly not simple even for the most well-meaning and well-informed among students and their parents. It has been my experience that most who have a choice of school or college make that choice very commonly on emotional, non-educational grounds. It is a very large assumption that students and parents can be better trained in the decision-making process and made more skillful analysts of individual cultural and intellectual needs. It is hard enough to find a means of broad objective judgment of excellence or even unique strengths among institutions. It would take a rare power of discrimination to sort out an available "better" school environment for the the kid who has voucher and will travel.

But given the choice, the ticket, and given insight into—broadly speaking—a "better" environment, will the student, and especially will the parent, make the choice resolutely and purely on the basis of perceived intrinsic educational values?

Taking again college choice as a model, where the options—through state-supported low-fee institutions and through a considerable if not lavish supply of scholarships, loans, student aid and work plans—are already as open as voucher-aided programs can in the long term hope to be, I see no reason to believe that choices will soon be purified of snobbism, sexism, family prejudice or prudence, or the bartering of talent, athletic or otherwise. An American's selection of a "preferred" or "proper" higher education is likely to be a far less rational process than the way he picks a horse. This may well be because the form books on racehorses are more reliable than a lot of college catalogs or school press notices.

I have seen students and parents with all sorts of information, with sufficient funds, with high hopes and purest motives, opt for the wrong colleges and make quite unrealistic choices of careers. Witness the floating college population drifting about the country. Witness the pinball knockabout careening among career choices. For most of my time in teaching and administration, the academic procession has been in a revolving door. That's better, perhaps, than serving time in a single cell-block academe, but it doesn't encourage a faith that younger students and parents, in the pre-college or even in pre-high school years, will be able to make wise choices on the basis of intrinsic educational values and well-formed career interests.

It is at least conceivable that some voucher options would be exercised to escape not only educational deprivation, but distasteful association with minority groups other than one's own. Certainly the burgeoning of private schools offering such escapes to respectability or a putative and often actual gentility indicates one of the popular options taken by parents oppressed by the social disadvantages of free public schools.

Even the best public schools academically are not always or to all eligible a viable option. The high school I administered in Philadelphia was open on a selective admission basis, taking ninth-grade boys of high IQ and strong scholastic records from all over the city. It offered an excellent, rigorous, academic option to the able, ambitious, academically talented boys, as a sister school did for girls. We obviously did not get all who could qualify. The option was refused by some parents for various reasons, good, bad, and false. Too far to travel—maybe. Too tough on kids—very likely. Too undemocratic—false. Too many Jews. Sure. I had some parents who directly asked how many Jews. But there was one prevailing reason for rejecting an otherwise excellent option, and that was the binding tie to the neighborhood school, out of a fear of possible ostracism, which is still occasionally suffered in this country by conspicuous high intelligence and an appetite for learning.

Departure from the norm, except in terms of fast muscular reflexes, is hard enough for the guiltily gifted to live with; departure from one's home turf to get an educational advantage becomes a burden not easily accepted by those most likely to benefit from the option. If one thinks of where a voucher plan would be most useful, it is certainly not inevitable that it will there be most used. It was not easy, for example, in my old school in Philadelphia for boys of early adolescence from poor neighborhoods who were the sons of tradesmen, plasterers, carpenters, i.e., of the so-called less privileged social and economic background, to come to what many regarded as an elite school, associate with the sons of the professional classes, and return to share evenings and weekends with non-elect kids of the neighborhood school.

If the elect beneficiaries of vouchers or tax credits or whatever are reluctant to move to what one assumes can be described as a better educational environment, how can the local school or school system be made better? If consumerism, with all its power to evaluate and enlighten; and competition with all its power to raise not only living but teaching standards; and compensating mechanisms, including ordinary buses, cannot equalize opportunites and make unevenness even, who or what can?

There is a touching naivete, an almost childlike faith, among our technocrats and social engineers in a systems or things approach to redeeming democracy's pledge of liberty and justice for all. The route to equality of educational opportunity is thought to be through the orchestrated manipulation of things—money, institutional structures, transportation, curricula, facilities, schedules, and other material variables lying within reach.

The variations in quality of services of all kinds in our country are often wide and sometimes polar. On a scale of values it is clear that there are in our midst excellent, good, fair, and poor institutions, including institutions of learning, just as there is a spectrum of competence, dedication, and integrity among the operators and managers of these institutions, lawyers, judges, doctors, hospital administrators, teachers, principals, provosts, deans, engineers, etc. Health care is superb in some places and mediocre or absent elsewhere; evenhanded justice in the nation's courts is hardly a *fait accompli*. Our schools are by no means unique in their unequal progress toward perfection.

I cannot say how health care might be more equitably distributed and medical fraud and incompetence dealt with, any more than I can suggest remedies for the law's delays, and corruption high and low in the legal profession. I see little evidence to date that a systems or things approach has yielded significant social benefits in these fields. The AMA and the ABA have somewhat modest records in self-correction, considering the abundant excesses of identifiable cheats and connivers.

The teaching profession, which has come only lately to recognize the power of union organization to achieve privilege and profit, also faces a moral dilemma as it attempts to command, in its turn, the sophisticated professional and political clout it must have either to answer or harmlessly to turn aside public dissatisfaction with schools and teachers. The dilemma lies in the choice between loyalty to colleagues, sometimes called professional courtesy, and a commitment to upgrade teaching, improve the schools, and hold oneself *and* one's colleagues accountable for a performance worthy of one's hire.

In the national educational lottery you win or lose depending on the teachers you get. Why else the differences in educational opportunities, why else the disparity among schools? Geography, social and economic status of parents, financial resources— all contribute to the inequalities. But I have seen superb teaching in inner-city schools, and mediocre teaching in well-heeled suburbia. I have seen dedicated teachers triumph over severe handicaps of every kind, and I have seen timeservers relax in the luxury of high salaries, motivated students, and the ineffable security of tenure.

I am for a voucher plan for teachers. There could be two kinds: one a merit recognition expressed in salary or paid vacation or honorarium for extraordinary teaching service; the other a voucher for the incompetent, or slovenly, or disenchanted, to get some training in another trade.

Teacher organizations have from the beginning been vehemently against the proposed voucher plan. Small wonder. The profession at large, but especially its public school teaching division and thus the teachers' unions, the NEA and the AFT, have denounced vouchers as an attack not only on the professional qualifications and quality of performance of teachers, but upon the root principle of public education as nurturer of democratic government, brotherhood, and the common weal.

At the heart of the issue of vouchers or free market competition as a spur to improvement of teaching lies the 1) alleged inviolability of tenure, and the 2) alleged impossibility and sheer immorality of merit pay.

I am aware of the compelling arguments for tenure, the right of job security after demonstrated professional competence; tenure, the ward and shield of academic freedom, the baffle against administrative malice or malign whim. I am also aware of the case constantly made against merit salary plans which are said to be everywhere based on questionable, invalid, or loaded schemes of teacher evaluation. In the college ranks, tenure election and recognition of high professional merit by promotion are favorably regarded by the winners and possibly only by them, and not unanimously there. In the old Baconian phrase, the "bias on the bowl" in college teacher evaluation is the inclusion of scholarly production in judging a faculty member's entitlements. If all the winners were scholars who could teach, undergraduate life would be happier and more intellectually rewarding than it presently is. There might be fewer dropouts and nomadic samplers of options.

While a scholarly attitude and habit are important in school teaching, school teachers are evaluated, when they are, almost wholly on the quality of their teaching. It is a pity that the critical evaluation, the go or no-go one, usually happens only once in a teacher's career. It seems to me irrational and indefensible for a profession to assert that its practitioners, once evaluated and found acceptable, should be forever safe from further examination of merit; and that all, once admitted to the fraternity of licensed pros, are equally worthy and competent forever, and forever should be equally compensated, varying only on the scale of length of servitude.

The profession of teaching, certainly public school teaching, needs more than the spur of voucher-inspired competition. The voucher plan has no chance against the opposition of organized teacher-labor. Indeed the implied threat will only cause teacher organizations to close ranks, sheltering ever more valiantly the mediocrities and even the total misfits among them.

The salvation of the profession and thus of its schools lies in the profession's growing concern about the quality of its services, and in the competency and selfless devotion of those who serve. Such concern can grow to a mature self-examination and self-improvement only if society at large and its several school communities press for better schooling, not via transport but *in situ*. Good schools are where good teachers and adequate services are; the best schools are where the best teachers and abundant services are in conspicuous and powerful majority.

I think that the voucher mice are gnawing at the wrong oak tree. The fault, dear Brutuses, lies not in our systems but in ourselves. It is a popular idea among the fortunate and therefore self-admittedly deserving communities in our country that cities and suburbs, upstate and downstate villages, all get the schools they deserve. This is analoguous to the conscience-easing social theory that the poor are poor because they choose to be poor. The poor are with us because we, American society, have not cared enough, or, caring, have not been smart and unselfish enough to help them out of their poverty. Poor schools are with us also not so much because people in their communities deserve them, through indifference or willful neglect, but because we, the American people, haven't cared enough about improving education, which means in the end *upgrading the teaching profession.*

Not that we haven't tried here and there. Indeed on a national scale we have had large foundation grants and extraordinary government largesse—federal aid poured into the troughs of learning's feedlots—without much demonstrable improvement in the quality of teaching and some measurable deterioration in the general performance of students.

Clearly once again we have found that throwing money doesn't do much more than overnourish the most aggressive grant-and-aid swillers. The educational establishment on the whole has often been embarrassed by the challenge of spending funds unless it's done for gymnasiums or stadia or other crowd-pleasers like marching bands. If the millenium arrived tomorrow and educators received all the money they've been asking for, consternation would reign. I doubt that the profession would show any more imagination in planning and allotting resources than the military-industrial complex has shown. Pay scales would go up, costs would rise universally, the local and state bureaucracy would double or triple, and the call would soon go out for more money.

"My poverty but not my will consents"—for years teachers have exhibited publicly and privately this apothecary's syndrome. And society's reply in these recent years is Romeo's, "I pay thy poverty and not thy will." Most teachers in most parts of the country hardly suffer poverty any longer, but the will to teach well apparently cannot be purchased.

Again, I do not believe that competition induced by the voucher plan will be an effective currency.

The basic lack is a shortage of first-rate teaching talent. It was never abundant. Neither is talent, nor has it been, in other professions, trades, occupations, or uses of the mind and spirit.

But for the simpler tasks of public education first-rate teachers in moderate numbers and good teachers in good supply can do the job; and these I believe we can and must find if we are to move at all toward equalizing educational opportunities and upgrading teaching everywhere.

The right oak tree to nibble at, in my opinion, is the hollow one of teacher recruitment and training. I am for vouchers or passes to get persons of good intelligence and goodwill into teaching, uninspected by government bureaucracies and uninstructed by educationists. How many able teachers have public schools lost to private schools and colleges because of the intellectually disreputable status of "education" courses? Why are private schools, untrammeled by certification requirements and automatic tenure and salary scales, flourishing and strengthening their teaching year by year? More power to them. They will continue to thrive until public schools can give them some competition for teaching talent.

If public teaching can throw off the bondage to a training and certifying cabal of politico-educationists and we are able to attract good teachers, what then? How can we accomplish a continuous upgrading?

I believe we cannot abandon the hope that the powerful teacher organizations, Washington's most active lobby, will soon in pure self-interest realize that tenure must go and some form of merit pay must come. No profession can attain or hold public respect and be honored which seeks only its own good (though "we're thinking always of the children"), does nothing about its clods and clowns (indeed harbors them), and denies to its stars and exemplars the recognition a true profession would joyfully accord—including recognition paid in the coin of the realm.

The teaching profession was right to be alarmed by vouchers or other threats to open the competition for public esteem. If it has wise leadership it will not merely reject vouchers, but will divert some of its energies from political pressure for economic advantage to professional critiques and a candid appraisal of the grosser defects staining its advertised professionalism. The teacher organizations, in a new spirit of universal service, may even recognize that they too bear some responsibility in the struggle to make unevenness even. They might, for example, mitigate their stand on teacher transfers and the sanctity of seniority. They might see to it that no longer shall most "difficult" schools of an inner city receive the least experienced teachers. They might even help a school district to saturate a ghetto with an abundance of teachers and services, with or without combat pay, for the cause, for the profession, for the children!

Give me voucher money, X dollars worth, to spend to help kids to a better school environment. I'd spend it not to send kids out to another school, but to send teachers in. I think more kids would get more for the money.

I worry less about the poverty of circumstances in American education than the poverty of aim, the poverty of imagination, the poverty of faith and daring, and the wealth of temerity, status-quoism, self-defensiveness, cynicism, and ungodly lust for security and no fuss.

Perhaps society does get the education it deserves. America will have better schools when it wants them. The system of public education is a good deal younger than the republic, and remains as subject to error, inefficiency and disorder, unevenness, as any other institution of democratic government. Yet—it seems to me—the schools, if American teaching is a profession worthy of an ancient heritage, cannot excuse shortcomings as youthful misdemeanors, growing pains of an adolescent culture, or the natural corruptions and inequities of a free and free-wheeling society. The teaching profession cannot excuse the schools' defects by pointing to the cultural and political biases or the economic deprivations which always frustrate good teaching. The generation of the 1960s, which sent thousands of youth into the Peace Corps and Vista, into civil rights and anti-Vietnam protest marches, seemed to be a new breed capable of supplying the teaching profession with dedicated men and women. Many did become teachers, and it is possible that their influence upon the moral commitment of the profession will yet gain ascendancy over the apologists of accommodation to public apathy and professional sloth.

I must add in all candor, however, that my experience with and general observation of the militants of teacher unionism lead me to conclude that the day of mature, enlightened, bighearted embracing of professional obligations transcending self-interest remains remote. When a profession unionizes and establishes a piecework rate scale for every small duty of service— so much for staying after sessions, so much for any obligation assigned outside of classroom teaching—it should abandon its yen to be considered a profession.

Fortunately there are still many public school teachers, and a very high proportion of private school teachers, who regard themselves as sovereign masters of their trade and serve selflessly, honoring an ancient and noble calling. Such men and women will never need the challenge and competition of a voucher plan. The challenge, to them, lies within, and competition for excellence is a way of life. Such teachers will be unconcerned about tenure, and though always pleased with recognition, won't teach any better if they get merit raises.

As for evaluating such, it will be done and their excellence will be celebrated. I have never known a master teacher the competence and humanity of whose teaching did not reverberate through a school. His or her love of teaching took the terrain like an army with banners.

Equal education for all depends upon a teaching profession willing to stand up and be a profession on a more valid basis than being certified and delivered by a self-praising, self-perpetuating in-group dedicated chiefly to its own survival.

Equal education for all depends also on a profession free enough of its own organization leadership to give individual teachers a chance to become independent, self-determining professionals.

Equal education, or excellent education everywhere, is possibly a wholly impractical ideal, only arduously approachable like others of democracy's impossible dreams; but if we one day find ourselves somewhat nearer its fulfillment it will be because we the people have finally developed an obtrusive, insistent, deep-rooted respect for learning, for the creative imagination, for man's heritage and still untried missions. It will be because there has been a warming of the moral and intellectual climate of America favorable to the cultivation of free minds and whole persons.

One's capacity and will to learn are in part functions of the ambient society and culture, and the teaching to which one has been exposed. Often when home environment, social status, even the power of a strong cultural heritage, fail to support one's capacity and will, teaching—the gifted teacher, patient, zealous and clear—will do it. But then great teaching has changed not only personal lives, but whole societies and cultures.

What has the profession, with such a tradition, to do with public relations, market research, shopkeeping, self-salesmanship, and self-defense?

One great teacher, who himself was taught by a great teacher, gave the challenge to the rest of us:

> Nowhere must we hold education in dishonor, for with the noblest of men it ranks foremost among blessings. If ever it leaves its proper path and can be restored to it again, to this end everyone should always labor throughout life with all his powers.
>
> Plato, *Laws*, 644

VIII

THOMAS SOWELL

CHOICE IN EDUCATION AND PARENTAL RESPONSIBILITY*

Professional educators and the low-income child. Free black determination in the antebellum South. Parental responsibility vs. educator resistance. Examining successful black education and the reasons for its success. The history of six black high schools: plant facilities, student body, teacher quality and continuity, parent support, present-day decline. Pedagogic theory vs. educational experience.

Educational "experts" often proceed on the implicit assumption that low-income parents are not competent to make decisions about their children's education. Compulsory attendance laws and the compulsory assignment of children to particular public schools are among the heavy-handed procedures justified by the

*Portions of this chapter are adapted from articles published in *The Public Interest* 35 (Spring 1974) and 43 (Spring 1976).

belief that low-income parents either do not know or do not care about what is good for their own children. Because such a belief is obviously self-serving for the educational "experts" whose services are thus made to seem more needed, it is well worth considering the *factual* evidence on this crucial point.

The pervasiveness of the public school system's control of low-income children makes it difficult to see what would happen in the absence of such control. Fortunately, however, there are, or have been, situations in which low-income parents have been able to exercise decision-making responsibilities for their children; and the results suggest that the need for professional educators' paternalism is not nearly so urgent as those educators like to believe. For example, the half-million "free persons of color" in the United States before the Civil War were not subject to compulsory attendance laws, were usually not even permitted in the public schools in most parts of the country, and were expressly forbidden to attend or conduct any schools (public or private) under penalty of law in a number of Southern states—and yet more than half of them were literate in 1850! Clandestine private schools for blacks existed throughout the South. In Sherman's march through Georgia, he uncovered a black school that had been operating underground for thirty years. The Census of 1850 found 90 percent of the free black population of Savannah literate, even though *officially* not a single black child in the city was reported as attending school. In some cities, notably New Orleans and Charleston, violations of the compulsory *non*attendance laws were so widespread that there was little pretense of enforcing the law. In other cities the law was enforced—a black man was publicly whipped for running an unauthorized school in the nation's capitol in 1855—but the education of black children continued anyway.

The historical record of the antebellum "free persons of color" in sending their children to school under very adverse circumstances suggests that parental responsibility is not something to be casually written off by educational "experts" who may have had an overdose of sociology. Undoubtedly the record of parental responsibility is far from perfect in low-income neighborhoods—or even in high-income neighborhoods, for that matter. But the relevant comparison is not with perfection, but with the far more modest record of education "experts"—those same experts who have given us years of rising costs and declining achievement scores. The zeal with which public school officials, teachers, and teachers' unions have fought against vouchers, "open enrollment," and other methods of permitting parental choice suggest that they know all too well that parental responsibility *would* be exercised—and that a lot of teachers and bureaucrats would find themselves without pupils and without jobs as a result.

Today, in urban ghettoes around the country, black Protestant parents are sending their children to Catholic schools. These are often schools in low-income neighborhoods once inhabited by European immigrant groups of the Catholic religion. But the black parents today send their children there for educational rather than religious reasons. Even the modest tuitions of these schools are a burden to many low-income families, but it is a burden that a significant number choose to bear. For example, it is estimated that about 10 percent of the ghetto children in Chicago go to Catholic schools. Yet this national phenomenon is passed over in almost total silence by the education "experts" and by intellectuals generally. To acknowledge it would undermine a whole vision of themselves as indispensable caretakers for the poor and minorities.

The preoccupation of educators and educational researchers with the social pathology of black education has been accompanied by virtually no concern whatsoever with successful black education or outstanding black education. Indeed, it is often implicitly assumed that (1) such things do not now exist, (2) have not ever existed, and (3) can possibly exist in the future only as a result of exotic new approaches to education. "Innovation" is an appropriate watchword for those who refuse to study history. The plain fact, however, is that quality education for black youngsters existed in some schools more than half a century ago and exists in some at this very moment. In 1954 the Supreme Court of the United States declared that separate schools for blacks were inherently inferior, but fifteen years earlier there was an average IQ of 111 in an all-black school within walking distance of the Supreme Court. The very lawyer who argued for the NAACP in the 1954 case was a graduate of a similar all-black high school in Baltimore. Legal minds can also overdose on sociology and fail to recognize what is happening immediately around them.

Successful black education is worth examining, not merely in order to document its existence, but in order to consider what elements have gone into it, what educational "prerequisites" it does and does *not* contain, and what are its broader implications for social policy. It offers further insight into the role of parental responsibility in the educational process—not only its general importance, but the specific forms in which it is important. For example, parental responsibility might mean parental involvement in the school's internal decision-making process, or in the internal values the children bring to school with them, or in the back-up support the school can expect from the home in dealing with the children's problems. There is no *a priori* way to decide which is more fruitful, and which perhaps counterproductive, though there are plenty of fashions and catchwords afloat. The facts tell a very different story from the educational fads.

One of the few scholars to attempt to analyze the sources of black success, rather than failure or pathology, was the late Horace Mann Bond. He compiled a list of those black high schools with the most Ph.D.s awarded to their alumni in 1957-1962. Six high schools from that list have subsequently been researched by the present writer and assistants. In addition, two elementary schools for black children have been selected for study because of their outstanding performances on academic achievement tests. These schools were researched not only in terms of such "hard" data as test scores, but also in terms of such intangibles as atmosphere and school/community relations as these could be either observed or reconstructed from documents and from interviews with alumni, former teachers, and others. On basis of this research, several questions were raised:

.1. Is black "success" largely an individual phenomenon—simply "cream rising to the top"—or are the successes produced in such isolated concentrations as to suggest powerful forces at work in special social or institutional settings? Strong and clear patterns would indicate that there are things that can be done through social policy to create or enhance the prospect of individual development.

2. Does the environment for successful black education have to be a special "black" environment—either culturally, or in terms of the race of the principals and teachers, or in terms of the particular teaching methods used? Are such conventional indices as test scores more or less relevant to black students? For example, do these top black schools have average IQ scores higher than the average (around 85) for black youngsters in the country as a whole? Are their IQ scores as high as white schools of comparable performance by other criteria?

3. How much of the academic success of these schools can be explained as a product of the "middle-class" origins of its students? Have most of the children taught in these schools been the sons and daughters of doctors and lawyers, or have they represented a cross section of the black community?

4. How important was the surrounding community as an influence on the quality of education in these schools? Did this influence come through involvement in school decision-making or through moral support in other ways?

5. How many of the assumed "prerequisites" of quality education actually existed in these outstanding schools? Did they have good facilities, an adequate budget, innovative programs, internal harmony, etc?

6. What kind of individual was shaped by these institutions? More bluntly, was black excellence of the past an accommodationist or "Uncle Tom" success molded by meek or cautious educators, or the product of bold individuals with high personal and racial pride?

Although these questions will be treated in the course of this article, the first question is perhaps the easiest to answer immediately. Black successes, whether measured by academic degrees or by career achievement, have not occurred at random among the millions of black people scattered across the United States, as might be expected if individual natural ability were the major factor. On the contrary, a very few institutions in a few urban centers with a special history have produced a disproportionate share of black pioneers and high achievers. In Horace Mann Bond's study, 5 percent of the top black high schools produced 21 percent of all black Ph.D.s.

Four of the six high schools mentioned below produced a long list of black "firsts"; ranging from the first black state superintendent of schools to the first black general, the first black Cabinet member, the first black Supreme Court justice, a Nobel prize winner, the discoverer of blood plasma, and the first black senator in this century.

All of this from just four schools suggests some systematic social process at work, rather than anything as geographically random as outstanding individual ability—though these particular individuals had to be personally outstanding, besides being the products of special conditions.

The locations of these four schools are suggestive: Washington, D.C., Baltimore, New Orleans, and Atlanta. Baltimore, New Orleans, and Washington were the three largest communities of "free persons of color" in the Southern or border states in 1850. None of these schools goes back to 1850, and some of them are relatively new; but the communities in which they developed had long traditions among the old families, and historical head starts apparently have enduring consequences. New Orleans had the most prosperous and culturally advanced community of "free persons of color" and the largest number of high schools on H. M. Bond's list, all three of which are still outstanding high schools today.

FREDERICK DOUGLASS HIGH SCHOOL IN BALTIMORE

There were no public high schools for black children in most

American cities at the turn of the century. It was 1918 before the first such school appeared in New Orleans, and 1924 in Atlanta. Baltimore was more fortunate. Its first high schoool for black youngsters was established in 1892, one of the earliest in the nation. In many ways, the early history of Frederick Douglass High School was typical of the early history of black high schools elsewhere: (1) it was located in a hand-me-down school building discarded by whites; (2) for years thereafter its black students received only books, desks, and sports equipment already used and discarded by white pupils elsewhere in the dual (segregated) school system; (3) financial support was chronically inadequate, leading to large classes; and (4) the general attitude of the all-white school board could most charitably be described as "benign neglect." The "benign" might be questioned, but the neglect is well documented.

Clearly these are not the kinds of conditions that educational sociology or psychology would consider promising, but the actual results belie the theories. The average IQ of youngsters in the academic program at Frederick Douglass for a twenty-year period prior to the 1954 Supreme Court decision was around the national average IQ of 100. The school average IQ ranged from 93 to 105 during this period, compared to a national average of about 85 for blacks in general. What are today euphemistically called "discipline problems"—including felonies—were virtually unheard of at Douglass in that era. With so much that was wrong, what was the school doing right that could offset it?

The teachers of that day included men and women educated in intellectual content at the leading colleges and universities in the country—not people trained in "methods" at teachers' colleges. One of the principals in the 1930s had a Ph.D. from the University of Pennsylvania, and some of his teachers had degrees from Harvard, Brown, Smith, and Cornell. They were, by all accounts, dedicated teachers who worked with youngsters after school, voluntarily assumed counseling functions (the budget provided for no official counselor), and in general were an inspiration. Though they had compassion for their students, this took the form of helping them to reach toward standards, not bringing the standards down to them. As one teacher and administrator at Douglass for forty years said: "Even though you are pushing for them, and dying inside for them, you have to let them know that they have to produce."

Parents reciprocated the dedication of the teachers with their moral support. The school "could do no wrong" as far as parents were concerned, and the students were well aware of this attitude. There was no parent "control," "involvement," or "power" in the school decision-making process. Yet parents were a major factor in the success of the school, because of the attitudes with which they sent their children to school.

Continuity was another element of Douglass High School's pattern. Principals and teachers served for many years, sometimes decades, in contrast to the virtual revolving door among today's teachers and pupils in ghetto schools. There was also community continuity in an historical sense. The Negro community in Baltimore goes back well before the Civil War. It was the largest community of "free persons of color" in the nation in 1850. Internal color and class differences existed in this community and in the school, but there was unity on the importance of supporting the school.

The school's days of glory are now past. Its decline is perhaps as instructive as its earlier success. Today it has many of the things it lacked in the past and which are considered important in educational literature: better physical facilities, some integration of the faculty, more parental input into the decision-making process, as well as a school system now dominated by black officials. The most precipitous period of Douglass's academic decline was immediately after the Supreme Court decision of 1954—ironically, a case won by its alumnus Thurgood Marshall, himself later destined to sit on the Supreme Court. The average IQ of the school plummetted into the 80s in 1955, as the ablest black youngsters went to formerly all-white schools. Today it is just another ghetto school plagued with the usual problems: a researcher gathering data there had her purse snatched in the school building itself, and a few weeks before that there had been a shooting on campus.

Some of the reasons for Douglass's decline are natural, and even desirable. Able black graduates from good colleges now have many better options than teaching in the public schools. Social progress also cost Douglass its position as one of the few black high schools in the country and the only black high school in the Baltimore area—positions which gave it a monopolistic position as regards both students and faculty. Racial integration sped it on a downward course. None of this need be lamented in itself, but the era of success is more than an historical curiosity. It provides an experimental test as to what is and is not necessary to produce good education for black youngsters. It shows the presence and importance of black parental responsibility— and how unnecessary so-called "community control" and "student rights" are to the educational process. Indeed, some knowledgeable people in the Baltimore school system attribute much of the decline in discipline in the schools precisely to such trends and to the "leaders" who promote them.

DUNBAR HIGH SCHOOL IN WASHINGTON

The oldest and most illustrious of the black high schools was Dunbar. Its alumni were the most numerous among black Ph.D.s; its IQs the highest; its list of "firsts" among black achievers the most striking. For the eighty-five years of its academic success—from 1870 to 1955—more than half of all its graduates went on to college at a time when most white Americans did not go to college, and extremely few blacks. As early as 1899, Dunbar scored higher in city-wide tests than any white high school in the District of Columbia. In the 1918-1923 period, Dunbar graduates earned twenty-five degrees in the Ivy League or from Amherst, Williams, and Wesleyan. For a period of about thirty years it was a tradition that a Dunbar graduate annually received a scholarship to Amherst—and more than 20 percent of these young men were subsequently Phi Beta Kappa at Amherst. During World War II, Dunbar alumni in the army included "nearly a score of Majors, nine Colonels and Lieutenant Colonels, and a Brigadier General"—a substantial percentage of all high-ranking black officers at that time.

You might think that there would be some interest in educational circles in how Dunbar did all that—but you would be wrong. It has been impossible to find a single article on the subject in the educational journals, and the only book on Dunbar is an obscure little volume whose publication was financed by its author, a former Dunbar teacher.

How *did* Dunbar do it? Many of the same factors found at Douglass are found in the history of Dunbar. This includes the negative as well as the positive factors. The physical plant was inadequate; budgets skimped, and classes large. The city's all-white school board was also insensitive: its members refused parents' requests for calculus to be taught in the school in the 1940s, and in 1955 they did not even discuss the possible effect on Dunbar of the reorganization plan which virtually destroyed the school's academic standards overnight. On the positive side, we again find no "innovations" in methods, no mystique of "blackness," and no white liberals involved in any capacity. Instead, highly educated teachers—some with Ph.D.s from leading universities—and dedicated people of great personal character. The first black woman to receive a college degree in the United States (Oberlin, 1862) was an early principal in the school's formative years. Of its first nine principals, seven had degrees from Harvard, Oberlin, Dartmouth, or Amherst; another was educated in British universities, and the other was a Phi Beta Kappa from Western Reserve. These had to be remarkable people even to attempt what they did when they did, and they brought these indomitable qualities to their work at Dunbar.

Again, parental support of the school was virtually absolute, as was their exclusion from any role in internal school policy. In some cases their concern was also shown by the fact that they sent their children to Dunbar *illegally* from surrounding communities in nearby Maryland and Virginia. This pattern was also common to Douglass High School in Baltimore and Booker T. Washington High School in Atlanta, among others. Another pattern common among these schools was continuity: teachers and principals remained at Dunbar for decades. Some families sent generations of their children there. The Washington Negro community went well back into the 19th century, as did its concern for education. The "free persons of color" in the District of Columbia built the first school for their children in 1807. Despite a persistent myth of "middle-class" parents, a survey of parental occupations for 1938 through 1955 shows that white collar and professional occupations together added up to only 17 percent of the total. The related myth of mulatto families is equally easily disproved by looking through old yearbook photographs. As in the case of Douglass, Dunbar has had much more physical and financial resources in its decline than in its ascendancy, and its all-white school board officials have been replaced by black officials. It seems to make little difference. Dunbar is today a typical slum school.

McDONOUGH 35 HIGH SCHOOL IN NEW ORLEANS

McDonough 35 High School repeats many of the patterns already noted with other successful black schools: physical plant inadequacies, general neglect by an all-white school board, and yet successful academic functioning due to dedicated teachers, supportive parents, and continuity of school leadership.

The first building in which the school was housed was already thirty years old when the school opened. It was the first hand-me-down from the white school system, and it continued to house McDonough 35 for almost fifty additional years. As late as the 1950s the building lacked central heating and was heated by potbellied stoves in classrooms, tended by the students themselves. The building collapsed during a hurricane in 1965.

As far as the role of the all-white board of education in the educational program at McDonough 35, according to a former principal, they "did not give a damn—and we took *advantage* of that to build academic excellence." The school board was apparently as willing to casually destroy the school as similar school boards were in Washington and other cities. After the ancient building collapsed during a hurricane, they decided simply to disband the school and scatter the students and teachers among other schools in the system. Only a politically savvy principal blocked this action by holding community rallies and seeking political help in various quarters. As a result the school was kept intact, temporarily housed in an unused courthouse, and finally given a new building years later.

The community to which the principal appealed was neither middle class nor mulatto, but it was a very old community in a city with a unique history in the evolution of black Americans. The antebellum "free persons of color" were more financially successful in New Orleans than in any other city, largely for reasons connected with its Latin past before the Louisiana Purchase. Quality education for Negroes existed in New Orleans long before the first public school was built. The enduring effect of this history may be reflected in the fact that New Orleans today has at least three successful schools for blacks still functioning successfully.

Like other black high schools that once had a monopoly, McDonough 35 suffered a decline, with average IQs falling into the low 80s. But IQs rose again in the 1960s under an imaginative principal and have remained in the normal range by national standards—which is to say substantially higher than the average for Southern black schools and above the citywide average for New Orleans public school students, black or white.

ST. AUGUSTINE HIGH SCHOOL IN NEW ORLEANS

Unlike the other schools already discussed, St. Augustine was begun by whites—the Josephite Fathers, a Catholic order with a long history of work among blacks. However, the first principal and his faculty had no personal fund of experience to draw on. They were young priests with little or no training or experience in education. This may have been their salvation and the school's, for they had no education doctrines or fashions to unlearn.

Founded in the early 1950s, by the mid-1960s St. Augustine consistently had an IQ at or above the national average. The first Southern black youngster to win a National Merit Scholarship came from St. Augustine. So did the first Presidential Scholar of any race from the State of Louisiana—and, over the next decade, 20 percent of all Presidental Scholars from the state.

Although a private school, St. Augustine's students were by no means "middle class." Its tuition is modest ($645 per year) and about 15 percent of the students pay no tuition at all, while others pay reduced rates based on their parents' low income.

St. Augustine's was an educational success and a political failure. The same principal who brought it to its educational peak came under fire from community activists—*not* parents—during the late 1960s' "blackness" mystique and community "involvement" syndrome, which he resisted letting into the school. Although from a religious order long devoted to the service of blacks, his next assignment was in Switzerland and, after that, as a parish priest in Idaho. His successor was no success; still another principal has assumed leadership, trying to restore the earlier spirit and achievements.

XAVIER PREP IN NEW ORLEANS

Xavier Prep is an all-girl Catholic school founded in 1915 by the Sisters of the Blessed Sacrament. The mean IQ of the school ranged from 96 to 108 during the 1960s and has been at or above 100 during the 1970s. The outstanding educational results reflect hard work by the school with students who often enter with serious educational deficiencies. Like St. Augustine, Xavier's private school status does not mean that its students are middle class. Parents with professional and white collar occupations together add up to only 7 percent of the total. The tuition is only $35 a month.

Parents are strong supporters of the school, but refrain from "participation" in school decision-making processes even to the extent that they are invited to do so. Alumnae of the school give a similar vote of confidence to the school and to its dedicated teachers. That the principal and at least half the teachers are white seems to make as little difference as the fact that teachers and principals were all black in the heyday of Douglass, Dunbar, and other successful black schools.

BOOKER T. WASHINGTON HIGH SCHOOL IN ATLANTA

The very idea of a high school for black youngsters was considered outrageous by many whites—including school board members—when Booker T. Washington was founded in 1924 as the first such school in the state of Georgia. A bitter political fight was necessary to get the high school. Black voters turned out—at the height of Ku Klux Klan terrorism—in sufficient numbers to repeatedly defeat bond issues until an agreement was finally reached to build a high school for their children. But the board of education did not go one step beyond its grudging agreement: the school building alone was built on bare land. The same community effort which was responsible for the building had to be invoked again to raise money among black Atlantans to pay for landscaping and for supporting many school activities such as sports, which the board of education refused to finance in the early years of the school.

Parental and community support were strongly in evidence in the early decades of the school's existence. Racial pride was evidenced in the teachers' attitudes and actions rather than in the curriculum, which was highly traditional, including Latin. Many teachers refused the indignity of riding in the back of segregated buses, which meant that most of them walked in an era when cars were rare. This was the school that Martin Luther King attended.

Hard data are unavailable for the early period during which the Ph.D.s on H.M. Bond's list would have been students at Washington High School. Data which has become available only in the past five years reveal that a familiar pattern had emerged: a loss of the school's monopoly of students and teachers in the area, and the erosion of parental *support* despite rising parental "involvement" in school decisions. Today's test scores show Booker T. Washington ranking below the average of other Atlanta schools, black and white. There is today far more financial support, smaller classes, better equipment, and a school board headed by a black superintendent in a city run by a black mayor. As elsewhere, these things are apparently of little avail.

What it once had were the things other successful black schools had—outstanding leadership and continuity. There were only two principals in the first quarter-century of the school's existence. The first was the son of poor sharecroppers. As a child he walked ten miles to the nearest school, which held classes only three months a year. Somehow he managed to go to college, and then on to graduate work at Columbia and the University of Chicago. He was also a courageous civil rights leader in a period when such activity invited retaliation from whites. As an educator, his long hours and extracurricular efforts on behalf of students were a legend—and an inspiration to teachers, who carried on the tradition with unpaid work with youngsters after school or during "vacation."

P.S. 91 IN BROOKLYN

Perhaps the most remarkable of the schools studied is P.S. 91, an elementary school in a run-down ghetto neighborhood in Brooklyn. Here, where over half the students are eligible for the free lunch program and many are on welfare, every grade approximates or exceeds the national norms in reading! Students work quietly and intently under the direction of teachers and teacher aides who represent a wide range of ages, races, and personal styles, but a common dedication.

As in other cases, the remarkable results go with remarkable leadership—in this case, a white principal "left over" from an earlier period when the school and the neighborhood were white. As the neighborhood's racial composition changed, its socioeconomic level fell, but not its school's performance. Indeed, the proportions of students exceeding the national average has been *rising.* This is all the more remarkable in view of the high student turnover characteristic of many ghetto schools, but which some successful black schools escaped in past days of high achievement.

The teaching methods used in the school depend heavily on the students knowing how to read, and a large part of the school's resources go into producing that basic skill in the first grade or even in kindergarten. But even more important than the particular methods is the drive and resourcefulness of a principal who is confident that it *can* be done and who refuses to be stopped by so-called "cultural deprivation." Instead of watering down the curriculum to the children's level, the classes use materials that are a year or more *ahead* of what is "normal."

ST. PAUL OF THE CROSS IN ATLANTA

A sharper contrast could hardly be imagined than that between P.S. 91 in Brooklyn and St. Paul's in Atlanta: one in a run-down urban ghetto, the other in a lovely middle-class suburban area of Atlanta. Yet they share outstanding educational results with black youngsters. The average IQ at St. Paul's has ranged from 99 to 107 in the 1960s and 1970s. Although St. Paul's is a Catholic school run by nuns, about 70 percent of the children are *non-*Catholic. Like black youngsters in other Catholic schools around the country, they are sent there primarily for educational reasons.

St. Paul's comes closer than any of the other schools in this survey to being "middle class." But even it does not fully merit this fatal label. Only about 40 percent of its parents are in either white collar or professional occupations. Of these, many are public school teachers. Ironically, the latter are more likely than most parents to fear that the school is *too* intellectually advanced. The modest tuition ($450 per year) keeps the school within reach of a wide range of families.

SUMMARY AND CONCLUSIONS

The history of black education—and especially of the *successful* education of black youngsters—refutes almost every fashionable assumption about the education of minorities. The popular litany of small classes, good facilities, "innovative" teaching methods, racial integration, and community control, lists what most of these schools never had in the days of their greatest success. As for "role models" with which the students can "identify": the teachers and principals of these schools have been black and white, men and women, lay and clerical, disciplinarians and warm mothering figures. In short, there is no formula, but there is a pattern: hard work, mutual respect, and leadership holding the conviction that it can and must be done at whatever political cost.

Historically, differences between students and their teacher role-models have been a common experience among American ethnic groups. The children of the first low-income Irish Catholic immigrants were taught by upper-income Protestant teachers. Two generations later, Jewish immigrant children were being taught by Irish Catholic teachers in New York. Two generations after that, black youngsters in New York were being taught by Jewish teachers. The same pattern carried over into other institutions: it was common in cities around the country for Italian immigrant neighborhoods to be represented by Irish politicians; in the civil rights area today, "minority" organizations and programs typically means black-run operations, often to the discontent of other ethnic minorities. All this simply reflects the fact that head starts in any area are not lost overnight. But the long-term advancement of all these groups also suggests that the narrow provincialism or tribalism implied in the ideology of identical "role-models" need not be accepted, much less promoted.

While few have mastered all the ingredients of the successful education of disadvantaged youngsters, many are well able to recognize a good end product. Parents have sought out these schools—sometimes illegally, from out of the district in the case of the public schools, and assuming a financial burden in the case of private schools. The history of black schools before the Civil War and in the decades following Emancipation likewise shows parental responsibility exercised under very trying conditions. The wholesale disasters of ghetto schools today are a product of modern fashions, promoted by the education "experts" who express fears that *parents'* decisions would not be good for the children's education. Parents' decisions will certainly not be perfect; but if the alternative is not perfection but

what the education establishment is likely to do, the parents
have by far the better track record.

IX

ANDREW M. GREELEY

FREEDOM OF CHOICE: "OUR COMMITMENT TO INTEGRATION"

Educational choice and racial integration. Two models of public reaction to integrated schools. Detailed changes in attitude 1963-1976: by region, age, education, community, religion. Integration and busing. The effect of integration on education. Court decisions and "white flight." The effects of free choice. Assumptions concerning American attitudes. Using a choice or voucher system to encourage integration.

Various plans to increase choice in education, including voucher plans, are often criticized as "racist" or as backing away from our national commitment to integrate education. Some critics give the impression that they think voucher plans are the ultimate act in the campaign to repeal *Brown vs. Board of Education*—the last sneaky attempt of a white racist society to resegregate public education. Like the racist, the hard-line integrationist ideologue has a strong strain of paranoia. Both see conspiracy lurking behind every bush.

Apart from such conspiratorial perspectives, one may still legitimately wonder whether an educational reform that has other goals in mind—such as breaking up the public school monopoly—might diminish racial integration without its proponents intending such a result.

We do not know what effect freedom of educational choice would have on racial integration. We will not know until careful and elaborate social experiments are attempted to measure the results of some kind of voucher system. The California social experiment (Alum Rock) is hardly a useful guideline because, while it did not increase segregation as some predicted, it still occurred within the public school monopoly, and one simply cannot visualize what would happen in a voucher system operating without a public school monopoly.

So one must speculate.

And one might do well to speculate under the following assumptions:

1. It is possible (though not inevitable) that increasing educational choice might lead to a decline in what Thomas Sowell called "body count" integration;

2. but a voucher system need not lead to an increase in the number of all-white schools...

3. nor inhibit the educational opportunities available to black parents who want their children to attend integrated schools . . .

4. so that most of the increased segregation will result from black parents choosing to organize schools of "their own" that are predominantly if not exclusively black.

PUBLIC ATTITUDES TOWARD INTEGRATED SCHOOLS

Two alternative models are available to describe the reaction of the American public to the prospect of racially integrated schools. According to the first model—fashionable to certain

left-wing liberal integrationist ideologues and university professors (many of whose children are already in private schools)—
the American public is essentially racist. Indeed it is steeped in a
profound and pervasive racism. Only the most herculean efforts
by an enlightened elite, combining force and endless moralistic
preaching, can even begin to redeem the American public from
its racism. Judicial decision and bureaucratic rule, fashioned and
enforced by the elites, are the principal strategies of their unend-
ing battle for integration. This struggle simply cannot be submitted to any kind of vote for popular approval either in the Congress or among the public because the racists would easily win
any clear-cut electoral confrontation. The battle for racial integration in the schools is a desperate fight for the soul of
America.

The other model pictures the American public as accepting
the need for racial integration in schools and in the rest of the
society; indeed they accept it overwhelmingly if not always
enthusiastically. Such an attitude, it is argued, represents a major
change of dramatic importance in the space of two decades, so
that of the large multiracial societies of the world, the United
States is probably more committed to racial integration than any
other.

The evidence available in the survey research which has
monitored racial attitudes in the United States over the last
several decades strongly supports the latter model. What follows
here is a brief discussion of the data from the National Opinion
Research Center's (NORC) ongoing studies of American racial
attitudes.

The first table presents the proportion taking prointegration
positions in 1963, 1970, 1972, and 1976. There have been very
substantial changes in American attitudes toward integration in
these thirteen years. The proportion opposing laws against racial
intermarriage has gone up 29 percentage points; the proportion
ready to bring black friends home to dinner has gone up 23 percentage points; and those rejecting the right to keep blacks out
of the neighborhood has gone up 15 percentage points. The final
item in the scale has only increased 2 percentage points since

Table 1

Attitudes on Integration 1963, 1970, 1972, and 1976
(percent prointegration)

Item	1963	1970	1972	1976
"Do you think White students and Negro students should go to the same schools, or to separate schools?" ("Same schools")	63	74	86	85
"How strongly would you object if a member of your family wanted to bring a Negro friend home to dinner?" ("Not at all")	49	63	70	72
"White people have a right to keep Negroes out of their neighborhoods if they want to, and Negroes should respect that right" ("Disagree slightly" or "Disagree strongly")	44	49	56	61
"Do you think there should be laws against marriages between Negroes and Whites?" ("No")	36	48	59	67
"Negroes shouldn't push themselves where they're not wanted" ("Disagree slightly" or "Disagree strongly")	27	16	22	29

1963, but measuring from the 1970 dip, the proportion of those who disagree that Negroes shouldn't push themselves where they're not wanted has risen 13 percentage points. While there was a change between 1972 and 1976, the change for the first four items on Table 1 was greater in the years from 1970 to 1972.

Between 1963 and 1976 the magnitude of change in the South (Table 2) was one-third larger than that of the change in the North, though even in 1976 the South is still a full point lower than the North on the integration scale. However, while the change was greater in the North than in the South in the first half of the thirteen-year period (1963-1970), in the second half (1970-1976) the change was almost twice as large in the South.

Table 2

Prointegration Scale by Region
(black respondents excluded)

	1963	1970	1976	Change 1963–1970	Change 1970–1976	Change 1963–1976
Non-South	2.45 (887)	2.88 (911)	3.46 (875)	.43	.58	1.01
South	1.11 (331)	1.47 (352)	2.46 (356)	.36	.99	1.35

Table 3

Prointegration Scale by Age in 1963

Cohort	1963	1976	Change 1963–1976
Under 21 in 1963	—	3.72 (439)	Not comparable
21-24 in 1963	2.38 (218)	3.28 (96)	.90
25-44 in 1963	2.32 (545)	3.01 (353)	.69
45-64 in 1963	1.93 (400)	2.63 (276)	.70
65+ in 1963	1.53 (184)	2.45 (67)	.92

Younger people continue to be more prointegration than older people (Table 3). But the changing attitudes of the American people regarding racial integration are not limited to the young. All four of the age cohorts interviewed in 1963 have become notably more prointegration in the last thirteen years, with both the oldest and youngest groups (those presently between 34 and 37 and those over 78) indicating the largest change in the direction of more favorable integration attitudes. Thus we have a clear and indisputable case of attitude change throughout the population.

Among Northerners, in fact, the largest change in integration attitudes has occurred among those who were over 65 in 1963 and are not over 78 (Table 4). Older people still are much less sympathetic to integration than younger people but, unlike those who have not graduated from high school, the older Northerners have actually closed the gap somewhat with their younger coregionalists.

In the South the greatest change is among the two younger cohorts, although it should be noted that they are still substantially behind their Northern counterparts, however much the gap is closing. Another way to put it is that in the first two cohorts the South is catching up with the North; but in the two older cohorts (admittedly a population over 58 years old now), the South is lagging further behind the North.

Over the entire thirteen years the magnitude of the change is about the same for each of the educational groups (Table 5), but in the second half of the period the change was considerably higher from high school graduates and over, indicating that in the last seven years the difference between those who had not graduated from high school and those who had was actually increased on the integration scale. Thus in 1970 the high school graduates were .34 above those who attended high school and did not graduate, while seven years later they were .60 higher. The less well educated, in other words, continued to become more prointegration, but the gap between them and those with better education has increased in the last seven years.

In the North there does not seem to be a correlation between

Table 4

Prointegration Scale by Region and Age in 1963

	Non-South		
Cohort	1963	1976	Change 1963–1976
Under 21 in 1963	—	3.98 (313)	Not applicable
21-24	2.93 (80)	3.61 (67)	.68
25-44	2.66 (401)	3.27 (244)	.61
45-64	2.26 (283)	2.98 (201)	.72
65+	1.90 (120)	2.78 (50)	.88

	South		
Under 21 in 1963	—	3.06 (126)	Not applicable
21-24	1.37 (37)	2.52 (29)	1.15
25-44	1.19 (131)	2.44 (109)	1.25
45-64	1.06 (107)	1.71 (75)	.65
65+	.82 (56)	1.47 (17)	.65

Table 5

Prointegration Scale by Education

	1963	1970	1976	Change 1963-1970	Change 1970-1976	Change 1963-1976
Grammar school	1.32 (335)	1.69 (281)	2.18 (188)	.37	.49	.86
Some high school	1.88 (315)	2.23 (242)	2.61 (205)	.35	.38	.73
High school graduate	2.32 (376)	2.57 (413)	3.21 (442)	.25	.64	.89
Some college	2.73 (193)	3.06 (189)	3.69 (195)	.33	.63	.96
College graduate.	3.15 (130)	3.48 (135)	4.10 (198)	.33	.62	.95

education and the size of change between 1963 and 1976. Those who only attended grammar school have become .80 more sympathetic to racial integration, and those who have graduated from college have become .73 more sympathetic to integration. Furthermore, both of these groups have gone up by exactly the same amounts in the second half of the period—.44. The larger increases in sympathy among the high school graduates and those who have had some college, however, can be accounted for mostly by changes that have occurred in the second half of the period (.59, .56 respectively). In the South there is a strong correlation between educational attainment and attitude shift in favor of integration, and most of this correlation is the result of change that has occurred since 1970—in the case of college graduates, an increase of 1.43 since 1970. The "catching up of the South" is something that is occurring especially among the young and among college graduates. Virtually all of this "catch-up" has occurred since 1970, much of that since 1972 (Table 6).

Table 6

Prointegration Scale by Region and Education

Non-South

	1963	1970	1976	Change 1963-1970	Change 1970-1976	Change 1963-1976
Grammar school	1.73 (207)	2.09 (176)	2.53 (117)	.36	.44	.80
Some high school	2.27 (208)	2.74 (164)	2.99 (136)	.47	.25	.72
High school graduate	2.60 (263)	2.85 (311)	3.44 (330)	.25	.59	.84
Some college	2.99 (121)	3.36 (149)	3.92 (143)	.37	.56	.93
College graduate	3.48 (86)	3.77 (108)	4.21 (148)	.29	.44	.73

South

	1963	1970	1976	Change 1963-1970	Change 1970-1976	Change 1963-1976
Grammar school	.68 (112)	1.03 (105)	1.61 (71)	.35	.58	.93
Some high school	1.01 (84)	1.17 (78)	1.87 (69)	.16	.70	.86
High school graduate	1.36 (72)	1.75 (102)	2.55 (112)	.39	.80	1.19
Some college	1.42 (33)	1.95 (40)	3.06 (52)	.53	1.11	1.64
College graduate	2.00 (30)	2.33 (27)	3.76 (50)	.33	1.43	1.76

The problems of racial integration, of course, affect city dwellers more than those outside the metropolitan areas. Over the thirteen-year period those who live in metropolitan areas other than the twelve largest (those who presumably have less serious integration problems) show the greatest change in sympathy toward racial integration (1.37). However, they still lag behind those who live in the twelve largest metropolitan regions, even though the gap has been closed somewhat. In the second half, the largest changes in attitudes of sympathy for integration occurred in the metropolitan areas (.70 for those in the twelve largest and .95 for those in other metropolitan areas). Thus, since 1970, metropolitan area dwellers have increased their lead in sympathy for racial integration over the rest of the country, and the gap between them and nonmetropolitanites in the last seven years has grown larger (Table 7).

Table 7

Prointegration Scale by City Size

	1963	1970	1976	Change 1963-1970	Change 1970-1976	Change 1963-1976
10 (12) largest metropolitan areas*	2.73 (269)	3.06 (270)	3.76 (229)	.33	.70	1.03
Metropolitan areas under 2 million	2.05 (475)	2.47 (493)	3.42 (290)	.42	.95	1.37
Urban county	1.94 (217)	2.47 (216)	3.01 (500)	.53	.54	1.07
Rural county	1.63 (257)	1.98 (284)	2.57 (212)	.35	.59	.94

*In 1976, the General Social Survey was changed to include the twelve largest metropolitan areas in its sample.

In the thirteen-year period, the largest change in attitudes toward racial integration has occurred among American Protestants (Table 8), the second largest among Catholics, and the third largest among Jews. I would note, of course, that the Jews had the highest scores to begin with. The differences among the three religious groups have narrowed, as Protestants have cut in half the difference between themselves and Jews. In the more recent half of the period, the largest change has occurred among Catholics, so that the gap between them and Jews in racial integration attitudes is narrowing while the gap between Protestants and Catholics has increased somewhat in the last six years. This despite the fact that Catholics are urban dwellers and more likely to face problems of racial integration than Protestants; they are also not as affluent as the urban dwelling Jews, and are perhaps not so able to flee from urban problems into the suburbs.

We cannot measure the 1963-1976 change in religioethnic groups because the NORC researchers in 1963 were not persuaded that ethnicity was a variable worth looking at. However, in the last six years, the largest changes in support of racial integration have occurred among Italian Catholics, Scandinavian Protestants, and "Slavic" Catholics. Irish Catholics continue to be the most prointegration of all non-South gentiles, though in the last seven years Scandinavian Protestants and German Catholics are narrowing the gap somewhat (Table 9).

The most resistant to racial integration of the northern religioethnics are the German Protestants, who have both the lowest score and the lowest increase over the six-year period. Since the group is disproportionately rural, one can hardly attribute to them unpleasant racial experiences in recent years. The reason why the gap is widening between them and other northern whites is not easy to ascertain—save for the possibility that they may have less contact with blacks and less reason to think about racial integration.

Despite the conflict over various new racial issues of busing and positive discrimination, the attitudes of Americans on the more traditional issues of racial integration continued to change

Table 8

Prointegration Scale by Religion

	1963	1970	1976	Change 1963-1970	Change 1970-1976	Change 1963-1976
Protestant	1.81 (878)	2.28 (783)	2.91 (748)	.47	.63	1.10
Catholic	2.58 (344)	2.75 (335)	3.46 (346)	.17	.71	.88
Jew	3.61 (36)	3.79 (24)	4.15 (26)	.18	.36	.54

Table 9

Prointegration Scale by Ethnicity
(Non-South only)

	1970	1976	Change 1970-1976
All Northerners	2.88	3.46	.58
Anglo-Saxons	2.80 (220)	3.42 (125)	.62
German Protestants	2.81 (137)	3.07 (116)	.26
Scandinavian Protestants	2.82 (29)	3.55 (40)	.73
Irish Catholics	3.06 (48)	3.59 (37)	.53
German Catholics	2.97 (41)	3.52 (33)	.55
Italian Catholics	2.65 (38)	3.42 (65)	.77
Slavic Catholics	2.45 (53)	3.12 (41)	.67
Jews	3.79 (24)	4.15 (26)	.36

during the last six years at an accelerated rate. A majority of Americans now think it is wrong to try to keep blacks out of their neighborhood and to support laws against intermarriage, a majority of three-fifths and two-thirds respectively. Granting all the appropriate qualifications about the relationship between attitudes and behavior, one must still say that in the last seven years there has been a notable change among Americans in what they think are the acceptable answers to give on matters of racial integration. Furthermore, this change has gone on at all age levels and all education groups regardless of the influx of younger and better educated citizens into the adult population. The change is especially large in the South (which we might have taken for granted) and in the big cities among Catholics and older people (which we would not have taken for granted at all). While these substantive findings are by no means the whole picture of race relations in the United States, they are, it seems to me, a not unimportant part of the picture either.

There are two arguments cited against the data I have described. It is said that the responses are simply not to be believed. The interviewees are giving what they consider to be the "right answers" and not those they would follow in practice. Secondly, the overwhelming opposition to compulsory school busing is evidence that the American public is not as integrationist as it claims to be.

One wonders how those who raise the first objection can be so confident that they know what the American public really thinks. They must have some special insight or private revelation that enables them not merely to see through the falsehood perpetrated upon national survey interviewers but also to get at "the real truth" about what the American public "really feels." But if the public is lying on the answers to other questions of racial integration, then why does it not also lie in answers to questions on busing? Why be inconsistent and pretend to be integrationist on the one hand and reject that form of integration that has recently acquired a special fashion among the cultural and intellectual elites on the other?

According to the second model presented here, the public sees no inconsistency in accepting racial integration while rejecting busing. For unlike the U.S. Supreme Court, its thinking has not blurred the distinction between de jure and de facto segregation; or, to put the matter more bluntly, the public does not seem inclined to believe that you overcome the difficulties of segregated housing by eliminating the neighborhood schools. It would make far more sense, so the public seems to think, to deal directly with the problem of racially segregated neighborhoods.

The argument assumed in the second model should not be exaggerated. A fair segment of the American population, a decided minority now, is racist in the traditional sense of the word. It doesn't like people of other races and would sooner not associate with them. (And there are black racists as well as white racists.) A much larger segment of the society—probably a majority—accepts the need for racial integration but is ill at ease with the awkwardness and the conflict that frequently arises because of the cultural differences between and among various groups. (And these groups are not always racial by any means.) This segment of the society would doubtless prefer to keep integration at a minimum simply because it is disturbed by cultural differentiation. Finally a very large group, probably the majority of urban Americans, not only accepts racial integration but also believes in it in principle and to some extent in practice. But they are frightened by the de facto threats to their property values, the continuation of the neighborhood, the quality of education their children receive, and the physical safety of their children in schools—all of which are inherent in the racial situation in many large American cities.

Unfortunately most discussion of the popular reaction to various integration schemes such as busing makes no distinction among the three types of reaction described above. This failure is bound to lead to analysis and policy decisions that are inadequate at best and often counterproductive because they do not account for the complexities of the social reality of large urban centers.

The first group mentioned above, the racists, would surely seize upon a voucher plan as a pretext for avoiding all contact with other races. There are, it will be argued here, ways of preventing them from doing so. The second group, those who dislike culturally pluralistic social contexts, can easily be inhibited from crawling back to the confines of their own comfortable one-class, one-religion, one-culture ghettos. The right to minimize cross-culture, cross-racial contacts cannot be denied so long as the exercise of it does not interfere with the constitutional rights of others. Those who are uneasy, threatened, or frightened by the current racial situation in big cities could find in a voucher plan methods for achieving racial integration in education in which both educational quality and the safety of their children could be preserved.

Mind you, the voucher system could not solve the fundamental racial problems in large cities, but it might separate to some extent the questions of integrated education from the more basic and fundamental racial problems of the city. But these problems, one must agree, cannot be notably influenced by the way the educational enterprise is organized.

It is doubtless clear to the reader that I subscribe to the second model as being the more accurate and more useful way to think about the American public. It is, I have argued, supported overwhelmingly by the empirical evidence and also by the experience of anyone who gets out of the university faculty club and governmental bureaucratic agencies. I would not deny that there is room for court decisions, bureaucratic rulings, and moralistic hasseling in the accomplishment of social change—all have their role to play; I simply question the accuracy of many of the assumptions that seem to underpin the approach of many of those whose basic strategy in approaching the racial problems of America seems to be confined to decisions, regulations, and sermons. And the nicely balanced body counts and racial quotas have rather little to do with effecting social change either. The world just doesn't work that way.

Furthermore, it should be clear from the beginning that the purpose of the racial integration of the school is *not* to improve the quality of education. Despite the extravagant claims made by social scientists, it is now evident that the Kenneth Clark research did not play a controlling part in the *Brown vs. Board of Education* decision (for which we should be grateful because the Clark research does not stand up to subsequent standards of scholarship). The fundamental arguments in *Brown vs. Board of Education* were constitutional and legal, not social scientific. Even if there were complete equality of educational outcomes, separate but equal schools would still not be acceptable to the American creed or the American Constitution. Undoubtedly, later court decisions began to rely on social science evidence to prove that racial integration did indeed enhance the equality of the educational outcome for blacks; but the use of social science evidence can have dangerous boomerang effects, and the canny if narrow-minded Mr. Justice Powell quickly saw that. In a later decision he turned the argument against the integrationists: since social scientists couldn't agree on the educational outcome, he argued, there seemed no reason to believe that there was any difference and therefore no need for the relief sought by the plaintiff. So from a question of high principle and constitutional law, the argument became twisted to questions of social science fact. Heaven help a plaintiff whose case rests on something as thin as social science data.

INTEGRATION AND EDUCATIONAL OUTCOME

It is fashionable to say that it is still too early to tell what impact racial integration will have on educational outcome. All this argument means is that the research done so far finds little if any effects. It is not too early to say, however, that we can have no reasonable expectation of great differences in educational outcome in integrated schools from those previously observed in segregated schools. James Coleman and his colleagues did find that under certain sets of circumstance, black children in integrated schools did better than their counterparts in segregated schools. But the situation where this improvement occurred was highly specific; that is, a rather small number of lower class students integrated into a predominantly middle to upper class educational environment. It goes without saying that such a specific condition can hardly be expected to occur in most big city school systems. In the classic South Boston situation, for example, we see the integration of poor blacks with poor whites in a school where the scores were already beneath the city system's average. It is not seriously argued that anyone gets much of an education in South Boston's schools whether they be blacks bused in or white children who live in the neighborhood.

Thus, I take it for the purpose of this article, that the issue is integration as such, that integration is a civil and constitutional desirable and necessary end for the society and not a technique for enhancing educational outcomes.[1]

I also take it that the integration to which we are committed is such that there will be few if any all-white schools but not necessarily a situation in which every child is in an integrated school. This is, I am convinced, the integration to which the American public is committed; it is not, however, the integration to which the ideological elites are committed. At least some of them seem to believe that every free school must mirror more or less the racial mathematics of the larger environment. The courts are still confused on this subject, partly because the issue is complicated and partly because the legal reasoning by which the shift was made from de jure to de facto segregation was incredibly sloppy. The shift of the burden of proof onto the defendant to show that he was not deliberately segregating the schools has created a host of problems with which the courts have not yet been able to cope. Indeed, in some instances the courts do not even seem to be aware that they are caught in a legal and logical mess (Graglia 1976).

In any event, the courts have *not* endorsed the notion that the school must reflect the racial proportions of the society, and now they do not seem likely to do so. Thus, however desirable it is as a moral goal to have every child in an integrated school, the national consensus, insofar as it exists, is rather more limited. There shall be in the society, at least in those areas where there are large numbers of different racial groups, no public school which by deliberate design is all white or almost all white.[2]

It has even been argued that the ultimate solution to school integration is the abolition of all private education and the assignment of students by the state to schools that reflect the racial composition of a given metropolitan area. I would not exclude the possibility that there is somewhere in the country a federal judge who would take such draconian steps to achieve racial integration, but it does not seem likely that such a decision would be upheld on appeal. Too many judges, congressmen, university professors, and newspaper people have children in private and white suburban schools.

Hence the principal goal for the proponents of free choice in education is to organize their schemes to avoid the reappearance of lily-white schools. The most powerful force at work in America toward the resegregation of schools is the phenomenon of "white flight"—the migration of whites out of urban public school systems and out of the central city. There is some debate about how integration of the schools and white flight from the central city are related. The evidence gathered by James Coleman suggests that court-ordered integration accelerates white flight from the public schools. On balance, Coleman has the better of the argument, I think.

There is no particular reason to believe that free choice in education would reduce the white flight from the central city, though it would add great variety to the American educational enterprise and might change substantially the racial picture in public schools. But there is absolutely no reason to believe that a choice system would increase white flight either. Those critics who claim that increasing choice would lead to resegregation often pay little attention to the much more powerful resegregating dynamics of white flight. Following Amy Carter's enrollment in a public school near the White House, an enterprising Washington reporter concluded that the children of all but two congressmen—one a conservative and one a radical—had fled the Washington public school system. It is not necessarily hypocritical to support racial integration and to withdraw one's own children from urban public schools, but to flee the public schools and at the same time extol racial integration and pretend the white flight phenomenon is not important, the judgment may legitimately be different. How can they seek for their own children both quality and safety in education and condemn the same behavior by others?

The most that can be said, then, about the enhancement of freedom of choice in urban education is that it would create a totally new situation for schools in the cities: decisions about where children go to school would be made by parents, who would then not be completely at the mercy of the impersonal dynamics of urban change and succession. When one looks at the public schools in Washington, for example, which have become almost solidly black and where the quality of education is recognized as extremely low, one has to say that almost any change would be an improvement.

These preliminary clarifications obviously form much of the argument about integration and educational choice; but since they are rarely made explicit in the argument, those engaged in explicit discussion frequently talk at cross purposes. The issue in such controversy is not really choice in education, but something more fundamental. Those who oppose freedom of choice because it would impede integration in fact assume at least one of the following things about American attitudes: (1) Most Americans are racists; (2) the school should mirror the racial composition of the society; (3) racial integration improves the quality of educational outcome; and (4) private schools ought to be abolished. These are judgments of ethical value and of philosophical faith; they are not supported either by empirical evidence or by clearcut decisions in constitutional law. About matters of faith it does little good to argue; nor is any useful purpose served by arguing about matters of basic and fundamental ethical value. The choices one makes in either direction are beyond intellectual discussion.

But if one believes that racial segregation is bad for society and particularly bad when it takes place in the public school system, yet is not committed to one of the four propositions cited above, one can imagine a choice system with reasonable guarantees against major resegregation. It seems to me that the only kind of resegregation or continuing segregation one could anticipate from greatly expanded educational choice would be the self-segregation of black parents who elect to establish their own schools, and either deliberately or not, organize or choose schools that are overwhelmingly black. One can anticipate, for example, that many black religious groups would organize their own denominational schools and that few whites would elect to attend them. These schools would be all black in the same sense that most Roman Catholic parochial schools are all Catholic. Some ideologues would deny black parents the right to make such a choice, arguing in effect that they know better what black parents want or should want. Most Americans, however, would not object to some blacks wanting schools that were "their own" any more than they objected to some Catholics wanting schools of "their own."

The problem of preventing white parents from choosing schools in which blacks were deliberately excluded is the critical—perhaps the only really important—question that the advocates of expanded educational freedom of choice must answer on the subject of racial integration.

INTEGRATING MECHANISMS; OR PREVENTING RESEGREGATION

It should be relatively simple (admittedly with some administrative and legal complications) to insist that every school receiving funds under a choice system be required to admit minority members who apply and who have the proper religious and/or educational qualifications up to that proportion of the minority group which is found in the total related metropolitan region. Such a requirement would be imposed on all "choice schools" in the whole metropolitan region, thus taking pressures off schools that happen to be in the central city and permitting no one to escape from integration simply by moving across the artificial city boundaries.

It might even be required that any school receiving funds under a choice system actually recruit a certain number of minority students (perhaps somewhere between one-quarter and one-half of the proportion of the minority in the metropolitan region). Under this system tax funds would be available only to schools willing to admit minorities. Under such circumstances it seems very likely that virtually all black parents who actively wanted their children in integrated environments could obtain them for their children. Indeed under such circumstances of educational integration, one might reasonably expect modest improvement of educational output.

It is not my purpose to describe here how such a program should be practically administered, but it seems unlikely that there exist any insurmountable difficulties.

A more serious problem for the advocates of a voucher scheme would be those black parents who for one reason or another do not choose to exercise freedom of choice and who continue to enroll their children in the existing public school system. This might be an especially serious difficulty for families that are already socially or economically disadvantaged—precisely those, it will be said, to whom the schools have the greatest obligation. (Though it must be added, I think, it is also precisely those for whom the schools seem ill equipped to do anything at all.)

It would be a mistake to underestimate the number of disadvantaged black and white parents (or "the welfare poor" or whatever other name one might want to give them) who would prove quite capable of exercising educational freedom of choice wisely, if they were given the opportunity to do so. However, even for those who choose to remain in the public school setting, there is no reason to think that their situation would be any worse under a voucher system than it is now. Indeed, since under a voucher plan much of the administrative overhead of the public school monopoly could be eliminated, there would be more money available for intensive educational efforts toward those who remained in the public schools.

But more than this could be done. The public school authority could be empowered with the right to contract with voucher-receiving private schools for the enrollment of black students up to the metropolitan quota for those schools. The public educational authority, in other words, would exercise the parents' freedom of choice for them—though only for those who did not object. Under these circumstances virtually all of the children who remained in segregated, all-black public schools would be children of those parents who wanted them to be there.

The integration that would occur within such a version of freedom of choice would be entirely voluntary in the sense that no parent would be compelled to send his child to a school where he was a member of a racial minority. Yet every black parent who wanted to send his child to an integrated school would find one available. Similarly, no white parent would be compelled to send his child to a school where the proportion of blacks was higher than that of the total metropolitan region. The only segregated schools, then, would be those schools where black parents exercised their own freedom to choose self-segregation either in private voucher-funded or traditional public schools.[3]

Funds for transporting children enrolled in the public educational authority to voucher schools would be provided by that authority.

The plan described is essentially a modification of proposals for metropolitan-wide, voluntary but subsidized quota integration made by such writers as Anthony Downs and Theodore Lowi. There are four components to any such plan: (1) Integration becomes voluntary in that no child is sent to a school without his parents' consent. (2) Integration is subsidized in that the receiving schools are powerfully motivated to accept if not to recruit minority students. (In the voucher plan this is done by the requirement that minorities be recruited to be eligible for vouchers.) (3) Quotas of minorities that a school will be held to accept (or recruit) are based on metropolitan proportions and not on central city proportions. (4) All the schools in the metropolitan region are eligible to be "receiving" schools— under penalty of losing their subsidy. Obviously the fourth condition is the most important; without that, the other three become irrelevant.

There are doubtless other ways of harmonizing freedom of

educational choice and substantial school integration. I have described one specific way in which it might be done simply to illustrate that there is no necessary conflict between the two highly desirable goals for American society. Indeed, only if one is caught up in a rigid public educational ideology or a rigid integrationist ideology will one find such harmony inconceivable; but by definition proponents of either ideology reject freedom of choice in principle, and will reject any enhancement of it as intolerable. The best that the supporters of freedom of educational choice can do is to agree to disagree with them and hope that in a free society each side has the right to try to gain allies for its position.

X

R. KENT GREENAWALT

VOUCHER PLANS AND SECTARIAN SCHOOLS: THE CONSTITUTIONAL PROBLEM

The Establishment Clause and religious schools: Supreme Court decisions before and after 1970—sectarian schools and busing, book loans, tax exemption, reimbursement for instructional expense, state surveillance. The question of "entanglement." Diversity of views among the justices. Aid to higher education. The changing climate. Prospects for vouchers.

The Constitution forbids the government from giving financial aid to religious bodies including—according to the Supreme Court—sectarian schools. The question whether a voucher program that included attendance at sectarian elementary and secondary schools would survive a constitutional challenge is uncertain. This essay summarizes the bases on which a lawyer would try to estimate the likely decision of that question.

Existing decisions do not give clear guidance on crucial issues; the present Supreme Court justices are divided over both doctrine and the constitutionality of particular practices. One could not predict with confidence the outcome, should a voucher program including sectarian schools be presented to the present Supreme Court in the near future; and one can be even less confident about the outcome in a different court some years hence.

If one looks only at recent majority opinions and at the forms of aid declared invalid, one would not be very optimistic about the prospects of a voucher program. But the language of majority opinions does leave the issue open, and some justices would almost certainly approve vouchers. An extensive voucher program is likely to be enacted only if there is a substantial shift of thought about primary and secondary education, and such a shift would probably reach some or all of the justices then sitting. Other relevant factors might be the contending political forces over the issue of vouchers when the first case arose, how high a percentage of the schools benefiting were sectarian, and how sectarian were the sectarian schools. With so many possibly relevant and unpredictable variables, sure prognosis is impossible.

Because the relevant constitutional doctrines are complex and because they shift subtly over time, in exploring these summary conclusions it will be necessary to begin by considering the historical background underlying the present state of the law. In analyzing recent decisions, I will indicate as much as one can the views of each present justice, and consider some factors that might influence the outcome of a constitutional test over vouchers.

For purposes of this essay, a voucher program is taken to mean a system in which government makes payments to parents of school-age children, which payments the parents can spend on schools of their choice, including existing public schools. In such a system, parent vouchers would be the sole source of funding for public education. We shall consider briefly whether it would make a constitutional difference if the same effect were accomplished through the income tax system.

THE SUPREME COURT AND AID TO SECTARIAN SCHOOLS BEFORE 1970

The First Amendment to the Constitution provides that "Congress shall make no law respecting the establishment of religion, or prohibiting the free exercise therof." Originally this limitation—the so-called "Establishment Clause"—applied only to the federal government, and states were left free to have established churches if they wished. But the Supreme Court has decided that the post-Civil War Fourteenth Amendment, which protects persons against deprivations of "life, liberty or property without due process of law," makes the religious guarantees also applicable against states and their local subdivisions. Any state law or practice thus is invalid if it is inconsistent with the Establishment Clause. Since many state constitutions are more specific about prohibiting state support of religion, it is possible that state law may prohibit a practice permitted under the Establishment Clause. In some states, therefore, state constitutions may be an added barrier to voucher plans. Our concern here is federal constitutional law, which has national application and which influences state court decisions even where the precise constitutional language may be different.

The Supreme Court's first major decision concerning the Establishment Clause did not occur until 1947. In *Everson v. Board of Education* it held by a 5-4 margin that a state could authorize school districts to pay for the bus transportation of pupils attending private schools, including parochial schools. Justice Black wrote for the majority: "No tax in any amount, large or small, can be levied to support any religious activities or institutions, whatever they may be called, or whatever form they may adopt to teach or practice religion." The opinion, however, held that since bus transportation was like general government services such as police and fire protection, state payment for fares did not constitute forbidden support of parochial schools. The court noted, "[W]e must not strike that state statute down if it is within the State's constitutional power even though it approaches the verge of the power." Four dissenters, largely subscribing to the majority's general theory of the Establishment Clause, thought New Jersey's statute had overstepped constitutional boundaries.

Two decades elapsed before the court's next financial aid case. During that time debate raged among interested groups over the true meaning of *Everson* and the proper constitutional approach to financial assistance. Four major alternative theories were developed, three of which purported to find support in the language of the *Everson* opinion. The theory most consonant with the language of *Everson* taken as a whole was that the Constitution proclaimed absolute separation of church and state and did not permit aid in any form to benefit sectarian schools. Under this theory, the only task was to distinguish impermissible aid from permissible general services provided by the state to all institutions, including sectarian ones. The second theory was that direct aid to parochial schools was forbidden; but that benefits given to children, or to parents on their behalf, was all right. The third theory was that since sectarian schools perform the important secular function of providing children with a general education, they may be directly aided, but only to the extent of their secular services. The fourth was that the state might aid religious schools to promote the free exercise of religion of families who desired sectarian schools (some also suggested that such aid would prevent the "establishment" of a "religion" of "secularism" through the public schools). This theory found little support in *Everson,* but it was a striking way to articulate what many people perceived as unfairness to parents who were required by the state to pay public school taxes and required by religious conscience to pay parochial school tuition.

In *Abington School District v. Schempp* (1963), the Supreme Court held that prayers in public school classrooms were unconstitutional. Though the decision did not directly touch aid to sectarian schools, the majority announced a test of forbidden establishments that has subsequently been developed and applied to school aid cases. Under the *Schempp* test, a statute is unconstitutional if its purpose or primary effect is the advancement or inhibition of religion.

Five years later the Supreme Court decided its next school aid case, *Board of Education v. Allen* (1968). By New York law, local school boards were permitted to loan secular school "textbooks" to children in parochial schools. Justices Black and Douglas, the only remaining members of the *Everson* majority, thought that books, "the heart of any school," would inevitably be used to propagate religious views and that they could not be provided at state expense. The majority of the court disagreed, holding that the purpose and primary effect of the statute were secular, to further educational opportunities. Justice White's majority opinion noted that the books were provided to children rather than to schools, but its major emphasis was on the secular educational function performed by sectarian schools. The opinion appeared to open up the possibility of considerably more generous treatment than *Everson* had countenanced, perhaps even direct aid for secular functions.

In fact, if one goes by the language of majority opinions, *Board of Education v. Allen* has been the high-water mark thus far for proponents of aid. The reason for this is instructive. The Chief Justice assigns the majority opinion in cases in which he votes with the majority. In this case the opinion was assigned to Justice White. As subsequent cases have demonstrated, he does endorse the broader implications of that opinion, but subsequent cases have also demonstrated that other justices who joined the opinion viewed the ground of decision as much narrower. The wider lesson is this: in a complex area of law such as that of religious establishments, one should not rely too heavily on the particular language of any majority opinion, because each reflects the special stamp of its particular author and may not faithfully reflect the views of every justice willing to join the opinion.

SUPREME COURT DECISIONS SINCE 1970:
IMPLICATIONS FOR VOUCHERS

In the 1960s public concern over education grew, and federal and state aid to education increased. It seemed unfair to many to exclude sectarian schools from increased benefits, and political reality often dictated some aid to sectarian institutions to gain approval for grants to public schools. Moreover, the increasing financial plight of many sectarian schools, as well as distress over the quality of public schools in many areas, contributed to greater pressures for public aid to sectarian schools.

Responding to these conditions and pressures, both the federal Congress and many state legislatures approved various forms of assistance, many of which have been tested in the courts. These cases did not reach the Supreme Court until the tenure of Chief Justice Burger had begun in autumn of 1969. In less than three years four new members of the court replaced justices who had decided *Board of Education v. Allen,* and Justice Stevens subsequently replaced Justice Douglas. Since 1970 there have been a number of important decisions on school aid, involving review of a variety of techniques of assistance. The opinions in these cases provide the main source for estimates about the constitutionality of a voucher program.

The first establishment decision under Chief Justice Burger did not involve school aid, but tax exemptions for churches. For our purposes, the decision in *Walz v. Tax Commissioner* (1970) is important for two reasons. The first is that the court, with only one dissenter, approved a property tax exemption that saved a great deal of money for the most completely sectarian institutions. That result raises the possibility that the government may be able to accomplish some educational purposes through exemptions from taxes that it could not accomplish by direct financial grants. The case is also important because Chief Justice Burger's majority opinion emphasizes the question whether a challenged practice unduly entangles the government with religion. The inquiry into entanglement has since become a standard part of the relevant test in school aid cases.

During the next year the Burger court decided its first round of financial aid cases. In two cases decided under the name of *Lemon v. Kurtzman* (1971), the court reviewed a Rhode Island program to supplement salaries of teachers of secular subjects in private schools, and a Pensylvania program to purchase "secular educational services" by state reimbursements to private schools for teachers' salaries, textbooks, and instructional materials. Both programs failed by a decisive 8-1 margin, with the Chief Justice writing the majority opinion.

From the earlier cases, the court gleaned a three-fold test to determine if the programs violated the Establishment Clause:

> First, the statute must have a secular legislative purpose; second, its principal or primary effect must be one that neither advances nor inhibits religion; finally, the statute must not foster "an excessive government entanglement with religion."

Both states had made strenuous efforts to separate the secular activities of private schools, to which aid was to be given, from religious activities, to which aid was not to be given. No doubt the opinion in *Board of Education v. Allen* had been carefully read and the states had attempted to apply its apparent lessons. Rhode Island's salary supplements were given only to teachers who taught secular subjects with teaching materials used in public schools and who agreed in writing not to teach any religious subjects while receiving salary supplements. Pennsylvania limited reimbursement to courses in designated secular subjects given with materials approved by the Superintendent of Public Instruction. No reimbursement was to be allowed for any course containing "subject matter expressing religious teaching, or the morals or forms of worship of any sect." These restrictions made the court's inquiry into purpose a simple one; it quickly accepted the stated secular purposes of the programs. It found it unnecessary to discuss effect, because it determined that the very efforts to distinguish secular from sectarian contributed to an unacceptable entanglement of the states with religion.

Having already noted that all teachers who applied for supplements in Rhode Island taught in Roman Catholic schools and that 96 percent of the pupils in Pennsylvania schools receiving aid were attending church-related, mostly Roman Catholic, schools, the court stressed that teachers in religious organizations would "inevitably experience great difficulty in remaining religiously neutral" even when teaching secular subjects. Only a comprehensive and continuing state surveillance could enforce the legislative attempts to preclude aid to religious instruction; unlike a textbook, a single inspection of a particular teacher could not suffice. Such surveillance would entwine the states too far in the affairs of sectarian schools, resulting in unconstitutional entanglement. The Pennsylvania law, in the majority's view, had "the further defect of providing state financial aid directly to the church related school."

The court also relied on another sort of entanglement with divisive political potential. Once the principle of aid to sectarian schools was admitted, there would be continuing controversy over the amount of aid to be given, with contending forces dividing largely on religious lines. Since "political division along religious lines was one of the principal evils against which the First Amendment was intended to protect," this potentially divisive entanglement of religious issues in the political process was an added reason for holding the programs unconstitutional.

Only Justice White, the author of *Board of Education v. Allen,* dissented, saying "It is enough for me that the . . . [public is] financing a separable function of overriding importance in order to sustain the legislation here challenged."

The decision in *Lemon v. Kurtzman* set the stage for the next round of school aid litigation, including the case that is most directly relevant for voucher programs. In 1973 the court considered programs involving reimbursements and tax relief for parents. By a 6-3 vote, it declared these unconstitutional in *Committee for Public Education and Religious Liberty v. Nyquist* (1973), with Justice Powell, who had not been on the court in 1971, writing the majority opinion.

The case involved three New York aid programs. The first provided direct money grants for "maintenance and repair of . . .

school facilities and equipment to assure the health, welfare and safety of enrolled pupils." The second program granted modest tuition reimbursement to indigent parents, those with less than $5,000 annual income, who sent their children to private schools. The third involved relief from state income tax for more affluent parents. The tax benefit for parents with incomes of less than $9,000 was equivalent to the tuition reimbursement given to indigent parents; the benefit declined as income increased.

In evaluating the programs, the court employed the three-fold test from *Lemon v. Kurtzman,* with one important clarification or modification to be discussed below. It first asked if the New York statute authorizing these programs had a clearly secular purpose. It quickly accepted as valid secular purposes the preservation of a healthy and safe educational environment for all school children, the interest in diversity and pluralism among public and nonpublic schools, and the desire to keep nonpublic funds afloat so that further burdens would not be cast on the public schools. Given the ease with which the court accepted stated legislative purposes in both *Lemon* and *Nyquist* and its broad interpretation of permissible secular purposes, including the promotion of pluralism in schooling, it seems clear that a voucher program adopted to promote excellence and diversity in education would have little difficulty passing the purpose part of the prevailing three-pronged test.

The part of the test that proved fatal in *Nyquist* was effect. In asking whether each program had a primary effect of advancing religion, the court explicitly eschewed determination of any single predominant effect. It indicated that if one "direct and immediate" effect was to advance religion, other secular primary effects would not save a statute, but a statute could be valid if an "indirect and incidental" effect was to benefit religious institutions.

The court first dealt with the maintenance and repair provisions, finding a primary effect to advance religion. Since payments were not to be limited to secular facilities and activities, they would subsidize "directly the religious activities of sectarian elementary and secondary schools." New York had argued that support would not go beyond the secular functions of sectarian schools, since the statute provided that payments for maintenance and repair could not exceed 50 percent of normal public school requirements. The court noted, however, that payments to a particular private school might still cover all its maintenance and repair needs. More fundamentally, the court rejected that idea that funds could be given to sectarian schools without separation of sectarian and secular functions so long as the total amount of funds was not greater than required for secular functions. Citing the invalidation of Rhode Island's salary supplements in *Lemon,* it said, "our cases make clear that a mere statistical judgment will not suffice as a guarantee that state funds will not be used to finance religious education."

The court next considered the tuition reimbursement program. Starting from the premise that direct grants to sectarian schools would be invalid "[i]n the absence of an effective means of guaranteeing that the state aid derived from public funds will be used exclusively for secular, neutral, and nonideological purposes," the opinion put the "controlling question" as "whether the fact that the grants are delivered to parents rather than schools is of such significance as to compel a contrary result." The court's answer was no. That aid was given to parents rather than to schools was only one factor to be considered. In contrast to the practices approved in *Everson* and *Allen,* there was no restriction on tuition grants to see that they went for secular purposes; and the very purpose of the statute was to relieve the financial burdens on parents so they might continue to send children to private schools, about 85 percent of which were church-related. The effect of the aid "is unmistakably to provide desired financial support for nonpublic, sectarian institutions."

The opinion did not find it relevant that the money was given to parents in the form of reimbursements for tuition already paid, rather than as grants to pay tuition. The state had urged that since parents were free to spend the state's money in any way they chose, it would not necessarily be used to support sectarian schools. The court answered that since the grants were "offered as an incentive to parents to send their children to sectarian schools by making unrestricted cash payments to them, the Establishment Clause is violated whether or not the actual dollars given eventually find their way into the sectarian institutions."

Since voucher programs would give money to parents to spend on schools of their choice, the court's discussion of tuition reimbursement is particularly relevant. Much of the language of *Nyquist* suggests that money given to parents to enable them to send children to sectarian schools is unconstitutional, at least absent a clear separation of secular and sectarian functions. Whether such a separation is realistically possible in the context of tuition grants may be in doubt, and in any event, the "entanglement" problems discussed in *Lemon* might undermine an attempt to compartmentalize secular function.

Taken at face value, most of the majority opinion in *Nyquist* is discouraging in regard to the prospects for a voucher program that includes sectarian schools; but in one footnote the court does express some important reservations about what it has held. The footnote is an answer to argument in the Chief Justice's dissent. He suggests that the tuition reimbursement program was an attempt to give parents of all school children equal benefits. The majority responds that parents of private school children are given benefits in addition to their right to send their children without cost to public school. The opinion went on to say:

> Because of the manner in which we have resolved the tuition-grant issue, we need not decide whether the significantly religious character of the statute's beneficiaries might differentiate the present case from a case involving some form of public assistance (e. g., scholarships) made available generally without regard to the sectarian-nonsectarian, or public-nonpublic nature of the institution benefitted.

What the court apparently had in mind were programs like the GI Bill, but the sort of assistance about which it says it is not deciding would also include many voucher proposals.

The court in *Nyquist* last considered the tax relief program. It found it difficult to characterize the relief, which in form was a deduction but which had the effect of a credit, since it was designed to yield a predetermined amount of tax forgiveness for the specific act of sending a child to private school. In practical terms, the tax relief was not significantly different from tuition reimbursement and had a similarly impermissible primary effect. The opinion then rejected the argument that if the property tax exemption approved in *Walz v. Tax Commission* was constitutional, so also must be New York's tax relief program. It said that the property tax exemption was distinguishable because it had enjoyed long historical acceptance and, even more important, because it decreased government involvement with religion rather than increasing it.

The opinion also noted that the property tax exemption covered all property devoted to religious, educational, or charitable purposes whereas the "tax reductions authorized by this law flow primarily to the parents of children attending sectarian, nonpublic schools." The court went on to say, without intimating how important this factor alone might be, that "it should be apparent that in terms of the potential divisiveness of any legislative measure the narrowness of the benefitted class would be an important factor." Like the footnote already discussed, this language leaves some room for argument that a voucher program including sectarian schools would be significantly different from the problems addressed by the court in *Nyquist*.

Having already struck down each of the challenged programs, the court found it unnecessary to decide how they would fare under the "entanglement" portion of the *Lemon* test.

Though of all the relevant cases *Nyquist* comes closest to the issues of a voucher program, we can get some further guidance on the views of the five present justices who were in its majority from opinions in other cases. Before turning to those cases, however, we shall look at the three dissents in *Nyquist*. Only Justice White would have sustained the maintenance and repair program; but Chief Justice Burger and Justice Rehnquist agreed with him that the tuition reimbursement and tax relief programs were constitutional. Each dissenter wrote an opinion of his own, and each joined the opinions of the two others as they related to reimbursement and tax relief.

Chief Justice Burger thought that *Everson* and *Allen* were the relevant precedents; in his view, "government aid to individuals generally stands on an entirely different footing from direct aid to religious institutions." In *Everson* and *Allen,* state aid might have encouraged parents to send their children to parochial schools, so that effect did not distinguish New York's reimbursement and tax relief programs from the practices approved there. Nor was it relevant, he thought, that aid was not apportioned between secular and religious functions. In his view, aid to individuals to exercise their recognized right to send their children to private schools is not prohibited by the Establishment Clause even though the exercise of the right has both secular and religious consequences.

Justice White emphasized that the "effect" test was one of "primary" effect, not of any effect. For him, "preserving the secular functions of these schools is the overriding consequence of these laws and the resulting, but incidental, benefit to religion should not invalidate them." Justice Rehnquist believed the property tax exemption approved in *Walz* was not distinguishable in principle from New York's tax relief program, and that both that and tuition reimbursement were appropriate means of keeping pluralism in education alive.

From these opinions, it is highly probable that each of the dissenters would approve a voucher program including sectarian schools. One or more of them might have difficulty if the total aid from the state covered that part of a school's activities that were exclusively or primarily religious (e.g., upkeep of the chapel); but so long as state payments did not exceed what was necessary to support the secular aspects of a school's program, it would be acceptable if secular and religious elements were mixed and if the state's money, given to parents and then paid by them to the school, were not narrowly allocated to specific secular functions.

Two other school aid cases were decided the same day as *Ny-*

quist, but neither gives us further insight into the likely fate of a voucher program. *Soan v. Lemon* (1973) involved a tuition reimbursement program that was broader in its application than New York's analogue but indistinguishable in its essential features. The other case, *Levitt v. Committee for Public Education* (1973), concerned state payments to private schools for testing and record-keeping. With only Justice White dissenting, the court held such payments invalid because testing was an integral part of the teaching process, and internal tests might reflect religious perspective.

In *Meek v. Pittinger* (1975) the court reviewed three kinds of aid provided by Pennsylvania. The state loaned textbooks, at least in form, to children; it loaned instructional materials such as maps, and instructional equipment such as that for laboratories, to nonpublic schools; and it provided auxiliary services such as remedial reading instruction performed by publicly paid personnel in the private schools. The dissenters from *Nyquist* would have upheld all three kinds of aid. Justices Brennan, Douglas, and Marshall would have held each unconstitutional. Justice Brennan's opinion placed great weight on the politically divisive effect of continuing battles over the amount of aid to sectarian schools, whatever form that aid might take. Viewing the textbook loans as practically indistinguishable from the loans to the schools of instructional materials, he would have held them unconstitutional despite the court's approval of similar loans in *Board of Education v. Allen.* The determinative plurality, Justices Stewart, Blackmun, and Powell, sustained the textbook program on the basis of *Allen.* But they decided that loans of instructional materials and equipment to the schools themselves were unconstitutional because they would be used as part of a teaching process largely concerned with the inculcation of religious values. The teachers providing auxiliary services might also mix religious and secular values, and the state supervision necessary to prevent that would improperly entangle the state with religion. Justice Stewart's plurality opinion mentions the potential for religious divisiveness in struggles over appropriations, though the point is less central in his analysis than it is in Justice Brennan's opinion.

Meek v. Pittinger reveals that all five remaining members of the *Nyquist* majority are wary even of peripheral aids to sectarian schools, with two of them ready to draw back from the *Allen* holding which permits textbook loans.

SUPREME COURT DECISIONS ON AID TO HIGHER EDUCATION

Some of the Supreme Court's aid cases have concerned higher education rather than primary and secondary school education. The opinions in these cases are helpful in indicating what altered circumstances in school aid might alter the perspectives of justices on school aid cases. The same day *Lemon v. Kurtzman* was decided, the court, in *Tilton v. Richardson* (1971), upheld the constitutionality of federal grants to church-related colleges and universities for buildings used exclusively for secular-educational purposes. Justice Stewart and Justice Blackmun joined Chief Justice Burger's plurality opinion, which distinguished the federal grants from the state grants declared invalid in *Lemon* for several reasons. College students are less susceptible to indoctrination than younger students, and "religious indoctrination was not a substantial purpose or activity of [the] church-related colleges and universities" involved in the case. For this reason, and because a one-time grant for a building rather than a yearly payment for teachers was involved, less continual surveillance would be necessary to assure secular use, and entanglement of government with religion would be reduced. Moreover, the opinion asserts, the dangers of political divisiveness were not as great as in connection with lower schools, whose constituency and support is more exclusively local. Among the four dissenters were Justices Brennan and Marshall, who found the plurality's distinctions factually specious or constitutionally irrelevant.

In *Hunt v. McNair* (1973) the court upheld a complicated state program to assist sectarian colleges, among others, by revenue bonds which effectively allowed colleges to borrow money for purely secular facilities at a reduced rate of interest. Justice Powell, who wrote for the majority, followed *Tilton* and concluded that, since the college involved had not been shown to be "pervasively sectarian," the assistance did not have a primary effect of aiding religion and was therefore not barred by the "effect" prong of the test used the same day in *Nyquist.*

By a 5-4 margin, the court in 1976 upheld grants by Maryland to sectarian colleges within the state for secular purposes. The state program differed from the federal statue involved in *Tilton* in that grants were made annually to eligible institutions for purposes determined by the institutions themselves. In 1971 only five of seventeen eligible institutions were church-related and they received less than one-third of funds spent. The plurality opinion of Justice Blackmun, joined by the Chief Justice and Justice Powell, acknowledged that limited yearly supervision was necessary concerning use of the grants. But since the colleges in question did not attempt to indoctrinate students in their teaching of ordinary academic subjects, the supervision would not have to be nearly as detailed as that required to assure secular use of funds in elementary and secondary parochial schools. The opinion noted that the potential for political divisiveness was substantially diminished by the fact that two-thirds of the colleges receiving money had no religious affiliations. Justice White, joined by Justice Rehnquist, concurred in the result, continuing to dissociate himself from the result in *Lemon* and the entanglement branch of the *Lemon* test.

Justices Brennan, Marshall, Stewart, and Stevens dissented. For Justice Stewart, the crucial distinction between this case and *Tilton* was the district court's inability to find that mandatory theology courses were taught in an academic manner rather than to inculcate particular religious views. Justice Stevens, in the only words he has written as a justice on aid questions, agreed with Justice Brennan that the state should not be permitted to provide funds to sectarian universities, adding his own emphasis on the danger that state subsidies will "tempt religious schools to compromise their religious mission without wholly abandoning it."

THE CONSTITUTIONAL PROSPECTS FOR VOUCHER PROGRAMS INCLUDING SECTARIAN SCHOOLS

Of the present members of the court, the Chief Justice, Justice White, and Justice Rehnquist are the three most sympathetic to aid to parents of children in sectarian schools, and their opinions leave little doubt they would view voucher programs with favor. Justices Brennan and Marshall are the most uncompromising in their resistance to all forms of aid. It is still too early to tell, but Justice Steven's one brief opinion may indicate that he is of similar view. Justices Stewart, Blackmun, and Powell take the middle position, and therefore it is they who would determine the validity of vouchers used for sectarian schools. The language of opinions they have written and joined does not give a clear indication how each of them would react to a voucher program.

Beyond the doctrinal tests that have been used in various cases and their particular applications, it is possible to generalize about some matters that obviously concern these members of the court who have disapproved virtually every form of aid to primary and secondary private schools, but have accepted direct grants to church-related colleges. It is fair to assume, I think, that these matters will continue to be of concern even if the court's composition changes substantially.

Aid to private schools has always been overwhelmingly aid to sectarian schools, and more particularly, aid to Roman Catholic schools. Despite the court's repeated assertions of the values of pluralism in education, one is doubtful whether the failure of virtually all private schools seems nearly as "unthinkable" as the failure of virtually all private colleges and universities. Aid to private schools seems less to be assistance to a generally valued social resource than a concession to the needs of a particular sectarian group.

The court has in its mind a model of the church-related school which is pervasively sectarian, in which teachers are typically responsible to religious superiors, regard the inculcation of particular religious values as an important part of their function, and permeate their teaching with instruction in those values. That may well still be an accurate picture of most Roman Catholic schools, but whether it is or not, it undoubtedly influences the court to be skeptical that the secular functions of sectarian schools can be separated from their religious ones.

The court believes that struggles over the amount of aid for private schools will cause people to line up largely along religious lines. Roman Catholics, with limited support from other groups, will push very strongly for increasing aid. Enthusiasts for public education and believers in church-state separation will resist strongly. Although this concern has never surfaced in opinions, some members of the court may believe that increased aid to private schools will, in many areas, be at the expense of public education and, therefore, will be largely at the expense of the poor and of members of racial minorities who constitute such a large component of the public school population in large industrial cities.

What this discussion is meant to suggest is that the fate of voucher programs, if they are ever instituted, may well depend on how far these disturbing perceptions about aid to sectarian schools have been altered.

If voucher aid, or reimbursement, were given to all parents of school children, it is unlikely that most parents in most states would choose pervasively sectarian schools, so that such schools would not, as now, receive the preponderate share of funds. Aid would no longer be seen as "really" to sectarian schools, and with large numbers of other sorts of nonpublic schools participating, it might seem unfair to exclude sectarian schools. Their position would then more closely approximate the present position of sectarian colleges, a significant but not predominant part of a larger class of nonpublic colleges. Just the fact that many nonsectarian schools would benefit could reduce the danger of political divisiveness along religious lines. It might also matter whether a voucher program at its adoption was seen as largely a covert attempt to channel funds to those already sending children to sectarian schools, or was seen as having broad-based support and was widely believed to increase educational choices for low income and minority students.

Finally, the growing secularization of society, the spirit of ecumenicity, and the decline of religious vocations have almost certainly made denominational schools less fiercely sectarian than they once were. If these trends continue, aid to sectarian schools may appear to be more like aid to sectarian colleges than it now appears, and thus may seem more acceptable.

It will take a substantial change in popular views of primary and secondary education to produce a voucher program. These changed views would be sure to influence perceptions of the difficult constitutional questions concerning aid to sectarian schools. In the period between the present and the adoption of a voucher program, other institutional changes would also influence consitutional perceptions in unforeseeable or only partially foreseeable ways. And there is sure to be some alteration in the composition of a court that is now divided over many of the major constitutional issues. Thus it is much too early to predict the outcome of a challenge to state vouchers redeemed by parents in sectarian schools. At the least, such a program, in Justice Black's language, would approach the verge of the constitutionally permissible; whether the court would decide that it oversteps the verge is uncertain.

XI

DENIS P. DOYLE

THE POLITICS OF CHOICE: A VIEW FROM THE BRIDGE

Education vouchers: Friedman, OEO, Jencks. The political nature of education. "Educational choice" as a reform strategy. OEO and the Jencks plan. The Friedman plan in New Hampshire and Connecticut. NIE and declining federal support. The role of parochial schools. Opposition: Catholic, civil rights, liberal, conservative, teacher organizations. Alum Rock and "teacher power." The implications of choice. Decentralization and uniformity of American education. Current trends. Prospects for choice.

The politics surrounding the movement for increasing choice in public education is best revealed by the federal government's experience with education vouchers over the past decade. The history of school vouchers is, in fact, remarkable, for they have captured the attention of a widely diverse group of intellectuals, critics, and reformers, and they continue to be the subject of intense interest.

The program was the brainchild of President Johnson's policy planners in OEO (Office of Economic Opportunity), but was taken to the bosom of the Nixon administration. Vouchers first attained prominence in this century when Milton Friedman proposed them in *Capitalism and Freedom*; yet Christopher Jencks, a democratic socialist, put forward the first concrete model for testing vouchers.

Although vouchers never developed a strong constituency, rarely has an innovation been so written and talked about: one partial bibliography now runs to twelve pages, and vouchers have been the subject of serious discussion at the federal level since 1968. In the early 1970s the Office of Management and Budget allocated tens of millions of dollars for voucher demonstrations, and the federal government has spent over $12 million on vouchers over a period of seven years. Yet to date, no real voucher demonstration has succeeded.

The purpose of this essay is to sketch out some of the reasons that vouchers have been the subject of such intense interest, in what ways they have failed, and what promise remains. As I will try to suggest, the significance of vouchers lies not in what they did, but in what they reveal about American education. As with no other reform effort of the past decade, vouchers speak to the political nature of education.

A BRIEF HISTORY OF VOUCHER DEMONSTRATION PROJECTS

For the better part of this century and the last, the nonpolitical nature of public education has been an article of faith. The conventional wisdom—carefully nurtured by generations of educators—views education as the domain of experts and professionals, a system susceptible to technical management and organization. Despite its nonpolitical tradition, as education has commanded an increasing share of the gross national product it has come under increasingly close public scrutiny. Moreover, apart from concern about spiraling costs, in the emerging American meritocracy the public has become convinced that education and its concomitant credentials are the passport to both personal fulfillment and economic security.

At the federal level, vouchers had been presented as part of a dispassionate education research agenda; but it was clear from the beginning that vouchers were politically charged and reflected the most strongly held views of how society in general and education in particular should be organized. The first claim made in favor of vouchers is precisely that education is too important to be left to educators. Vouchers then raised the education debate from one of technical procedures to fundamental political questions of power, authority, and legitimacy.

Even without the benefits of hindsight, however, the question must be raised: did the federal government really propose radically to redistribute educational power and influence without expecting to encounter overwhelming resistance from those it proposed to disenfranchise? Did the planners really believe that wrapping vouchers in a research cloak would deflect the opposition? If not, did they actually think that school superintendents, teacher associations, and school committees would participate in the unmaking of the public school system of which they were not only a part, but the actual embodiment?

To answer these questions, and the more recent question about why vouchers have so far failed, we must return to Washington in 1969.

The history of federal interest in vouchers is the history of interest in "educational choice" as a primary strategy to reform education. It is a story of a diverse group of intellectuals and reformers intent on "improving" education through increasing "diversity," "accountability," and "local control." Conceived in OEO, vouchers were viewed as the answer to the problems of the powerless, inner-city, disadvantaged. In the halcyon days of the 1960s education was still the solution, not the problem. OEO planners saw education as the way up and out of poverty.

Coleman's famous report had indicated that schools were more nearly similar than dissimilar in plant, spending, curriculum, and staff, and dissimilar primarily in students served. Federal reformers thus concluded that the key to the problem lay in the expectations schools and students have for each other. One way to improve the relationship of poor children to their schools was to provide families with economic and political leverage on the system. The nearly simultaneous appearance of an article by Jencks on private schools for black children, a piece by Henry Levin (a radical Stanford economist) on vouchers, and Coleman's report precipitated a meeting in Washington to see "what could be done." The result was an OEO grant to Jencks to design a voucher system that would maximize benefits and minimize liabilities.[1]

Vouchers of course had enjoyed periodic vogues among intellectuals. Adam Smith was apparently the first serious supporter in the 18th century; in the 19th John Stuart Mill wrote persuasively about such a scheme; and Milton Friedman reopened the discussion in the 20th with *Capitalism and Freedom.*

To OEO planners, the Jencks scheme was simplicity itself, even if it seemed a bureaucratic nightmare to *laissez faire* economists. Jencks's purpose was to serve the disadvantaged, those most in need of help. His interest, to exaggerate only slightly, was egalitarian rather than libertarian. When tension between these goals existed, Jencks tilted toward equality. He self-consciously designed a "regulated, compensatory" plan to help the poor to help themselves. They enjoyed unlimited choice, subject to certain "necessary" controls:

> No participating school could charge more than the value of the voucher;
>
> Any participating school must accept all applicants, eliminating racial or social class discrimination;
>
> Over-applied schools could select (and de-select) only by lot;
>
> While all children received basic vouchers, poor children were to be given a "bonus" or compensatory voucher, both to make them "attractive" to schools and to provide additional resources for their education;

A parent/student information system was to be established;

A school evaluation system was also required, a "truth in packaging" device for the participants.

The Jencks plan called for a variety of other features, but these were central.

After the decision to support Jencks in the design of a voucher scheme, much of what followed was preordained. Given his interest in equality, his mandate to serve the poor, and his mistrust of the unregulated market as an appropriate mechanism for distributing goods and services, Jencks's "regulated, compensatory" voucher model emerged quite naturally. The regulations were designed to protect the poor from the vagaries of the market, from their inability to compete with their more skillful middle class brethren, and from the depredations of the expert professional educators who had played an important role in corrupting the existing system.

The compensatory feature of the Jencks model was of special interest from a political perspective. Ostensibly it was designed to provide extra resources for poor children, to permit the provision of extra services, and at the same time to make poor children "attractive" to schools. Placing the compensatory funds in the form of compensatory vouchers, rather than block grants to schools as is the case with Title I, was a carefully thought-out tactic; compensatory vouchers in the possession of children in an open enrollment system gave real financial meaning to choice.

At the same time, in the aggregate the compensatory vouchers represented a substantial financial incentive to the school district. The money was to be unfettered; unlike any other federal program, the compensatory vouchers were to be controlled by student enrollment choices. After selecting a school, the money could be used for virtually any category of expenditure. Because the compensatory vouchers would be given to large numbers of children and because the individual voucher value was high, the prospect of district enrichment was high indeed. In the case of

Alum Rock, California, for instance—OEO's one operational
site—over half the children were eligible for compensatory
vouchers worth $250 each in the first year. A teacher who at-
tracted fifteen to twenty compensatory voucher children found
herself presiding over an educational gold mine. (In fact, the
Alum Rock teachers were so overwhelmed with the generosity
of the compensatory vouchers that they could not spend the
money as rapidly as it poured in.)

At both the practical and theoretical level, the Jencks voucher
model was greeted with alarm by conservatives as another example of needless and meddlesome bureaucratic interference.
On the other hand, liberals were not fooled by Jencks's attempt
to defang Friedman's *laissez faire* affront to the liberal
bureaucracy. As one prominent liberal attorney observed,
"safeguards don't." In sum, the Jencks voucher scheme satisfied
a small coterie of intellectuals, bureaucrats, and reformers with
the patience to understand it, but few others.

It is ironic that the task of designing an operational model of a
voucher scheme was given to Jencks, as far left on the political
spectrum as Friedman is on the right. It is doubly ironic that
Jencks never escaped the conservative association of vouchers,
for he found his report the object of as much liberal criticism as
Friedman had before; and he gained little or no conservative
support.

Friedman vouchers, however, were to have their day as well,
in part because of a bizarre final act played out in OEO's last
days.

New Hampshire and Connecticut

Shortly after Nixon's landslide victory in 1972, his new director
of OEO was instructed to dismantle the agency. One of his first
acts as director was to institute an agency-wide review of all
OEO programs, which led to a decision to abandon the voucher
project that was underway in Alum Rock, California, and to
begin a "proper" Friedman voucher scheme in New England.

The governor of New Hampshire and his newly selected chairman of the State Board of Education expressed strong interest in a feasibility study for a voucher model designed around Friedman's essay on the subject, and funds for the study were soon provided.

By that time, however, the California project had attained enough bureaucratic momentum to keep going in spite of the new OEO director's decision to terminate. The prolonged negotiations and the grant instrument establishing the project both promised five-year funding, and termination proved as difficult to accomplish as starting the project had been in the first instance. Within a matter of months, however, as OEO began to fold, the New Hampshire feasibility study and the California project were transferred to the newly formed National Institute of Education (NIE).

At the same time, the federal government's last voucher feasibility study was begun in East Hartford, Connecticut. Bolstered by strong support from a variety of sources, the project was clearly the most promising of all feasibility studies attempted. Strong legislative interest had produced enabling legislation; the two major metropolitan newspapers supported the project; the superintendent was a vocal and effective supporter; the school committee chairman and several key members found the idea promising; and the teachers and parents, if not supporters, were not opposed. The project failed to move from a feasibility study to operational status because of a strong antipathy to it on the part of the building principals, to whom a serious voucher program spelled intolerable diminution of their role. But more important, East Hartford's reluctance to go forward was caused by NIE's failure to provide vigorous support.

DECLINING SUPPORT AT NIE

In the transfer of authority from OEO to NIE, the federal government's voucher strategy was significantly altered. Vouchers now were no longer solely a reform strategy to improve the education of the poor, but a reform strategy to improve education in general. The transfer of vouchers to NIE in August 1973 was accompanied by a president's budget "mark" of $20 million; but within two years the program was dead. Interest in the idea waned, and vouchers became a casualty of bureaucratic indifference and hostility. At OEO a narrowly defined voucher program had enjoyed strong support; at NIE the wider-based voucher program was scarcely tolerated. A hothouse exotic like vouchers wilted and died in such an environment.

What accounted for such a remarkable reversal of voucher fortunes? External opposition had not increased, but internal support had evaporated. In part, the explanation is to be found in the holding power of the idea. As the novelty of vouchers dimmed, the idea lost its appeal. In part this reflected the desire among NIE senior staff to initiate new programs: reputations are not made on inherited programs. But more important, vouchers were a casualty of larger budgetary and political problems at the agency.

As a new entity, NIE expected gentle treatment from Congress. There had been enough votes to establish NIE, although congressional interest outside of the authorizing committee had been lukewarm. However, disaster followed that fall. For reasons that may never be understood, Senator Warren Magnuson of Washington, chairman of the Appropriations Committee, took a strong interest in the institute and did not like what he saw. Instead of appropriating the $120 million NIE had requested, the first-year budget was cut from $104 million to $60 million. Neither the institute as an organization nor its top leadership have fully recovered from that blow. More than three years later, after resignations by the first director and the first chairman of the NIE policy board and the dismissal of the second director by Secretary Califano, the institute is still in bureaucratic distress.

A sort of institutional paranoia descended on NIE, and radical, potentially explosive research schemes were greeted without enthusiasm. Although no evidence was ever presented, several ranking agency staff members were convinced that vouchers were the cause of NIE's misfortune. No member of Congress ever reported displeasure with vouchers, and since Congressmen are not noted for their general shyness or disinclination to express themselves, the theory that Congress secretly disliked vouchers was hardly convincing. Nevertheless, NIE withdrew from vouchers as rapidly as possible. At OEO vouchers had commanded sizable budgets; at NIE they had no "line item." When asked by East Hartford or New Hampshire officials about the budget for voucher operations, the NIE response was that if the money were to be found at all it would come from the director's reserve.

Even if NIE had been more eager and responsive, however, it is doubtful that vouchers would have gone much further. It is possible that East Hartford might have undertaken a demonstration project, but almost certain that New Hampshire would not. There never was strong interest on the part of superintendents and school committees in vouchers, and East Hartford might have turned out as an exciting but idiosyncratic project.

SEARCHING FOR A CONSTITUENCY

As I have tried to suggest, the story of vouchers is the history of an idea in search of a constituency. The appeal of vouchers has been magnetic as a concept by elites for elites, and it continues to attract interest. The support of the rank and file, whether teachers or parents, unfortunately has been modest.

In no community did vouchers receive more than lukewarm support from a small minority; their movement to an operational project in Alum Rock, California, was due not to community support, but to lack of community opposition and to active support by the superintendent. The president of the local teachers association explained his position by observing that "anything the Superintendent wants to do can't be all wrong." The teachers association, then, was willing to reserve judgment, even though the state association was bitterly opposed—so opposed, in fact, that the local broke away for a year until the state organization reluctantly endorsed a compromise "open enrollment, choice scheme."

The OEO vouchers, by attempting to satisfy everyone, satisfied almost no one. Jencks's safeguards perplexed rather than illuminated; observers wondered, rightly, that if a system needed so many bureaucratic protections, what would happen when these protections began to break down? The very constituency OEO was seeking to help refused to support vouchers.

THE CATHOLIC MODEL

The intellectual history of vouchers is all the more interesting in light of this. Jencks's interest in the idea was an outgrowth of his interest in Catholic schools. After examining the American experience with Catholic immigrants and parochial schools, he proposed that this model be used for inner-city black children. He argued that what the inner-city poor needed was some measure of cultural and social identity; improved education would flow naturally from such an arrangement. Any misgivings that Jencks may have had about the appropriateness of Catholic schools as a proper model for egalitarian and democratic society were dispelled by studies which showed that graduates of Catholic schools were as tolerant as their coreligionists who attended non-Catholic schools. This, it should be noted, symbolizes a turning point, for it signaled an ebbing of the powerful anti-Catholic prejudices of the WASP establishment; using Catholic accomplishment as something worth emulating was rather a novel idea to emerge from Harvard Yard.

In addition to using the Catholic parochial school experience as an abstract model, it became apparent to anyone who thought about the matter that the biggest provider of nonpublic education was the church. Exeter and Dalton, Miss Porter's and Choate, might still school the nation's elite; but insofar as numbers counted, it was the parish school of the inner city that was important. Thus, early on, voucher planners had to confront the Catholic question directly. For the liberal intellectuals and bureaucrats associated with the project this presented a profound dilemma; many had been raised on a vaguely anti-Catholic rhetoric—or to be more generous, they believed in separation of church and state. The dilemma, of course, was this: if one believed in choice, one believed in choice; or were some choices worse than others? After working through this problem by the time-honored device of compromise and strategic ambiguities (OEO supported the inclusion of Catholic schools insofar as such "inclusion was consistent with the Constitution"), there was some surprise when it was discovered that Catholics themselves had reservations about vouchers.

Catholic Ambivalence

The Catholic reluctance to embrace vouchers was the reciprocal of the church-state separatists' aversion to vouchers: public control cannot be far behind public support. It had been assumed that a natural "parochaid" constituency was waiting to be rallied, so there was some surprise when many Catholics, both laymen and clerics, approached vouchers with some serious misgivings.

Ironically, vouchers were not the "answer" that "parochaid" supporters sought, however, for vouchers promised to deliver too much. A voucher worth the amount spent in a typical public school—$1,000 to $2,000—was simply too rich for parochial blood. The parochial schools, used to older plants, a decreasing but still substantial supply of "free" teachers, larger classes, and less lavish administration and support, needed relatively little in the way of public support; $100 to $300 per child was typically the most proposed by even the most ardent supporters of "parochaid."

The issue was further complicated by a variety of confusing and ambiguous legal questions: with some optimism and perseverance, many voucher supporters could convince themselves that vouchers would be upheld by the court. Using variations of "child benefit" theory, voucher supporters were at least prepared to move to the technical questions about how a voucher scheme could best be designed to pass legal muster. To the surprise of many, the best legal advice suggested the fundamental correctness of the "parochaid" supporters: less is more. A discounted or reduced-value voucher for parochial schools was proposed as the preferred way to avoid the charge that vouchers would advance religion as distinct from education. Accordingly, the grand voucher scheme supported by OEO was more than "parochaid" supporters wanted.

Given the ambiguous role vouchers might play vis-a-vis church schools, it should have come as no surprise that Catholics, too, were lukewarm about vouchers. Thus, a small portion of vouchers' "natural" constituency was itself not overly enthusiastic. The decision to include Catholics, then, brought little support, but it brought down the wrath of those committed to separation of church and state. In this case, as in others, a strategy designed to gain constituents gained relatively few; rather, it guaranteed an alert, active opposition.

VOUCHER OPPOSITION

Civil Rights

Civil rights groups were opposed to vouchers from the start. They remembered vividly the attempt by a number of Southern school systems to use "vouchers" to frustrate court-ordered integration, and the elaborate protections designed by Jencks simply were not convincing. Many civil rights activists believed that vouchers were part of a Nixon-Agnew-Reagan axis and no guarantees could have been presented to persuade them otherwise.

In addition to this profound political antipathy, a number of civil rights groups—most notably the ACLU local in California—were absolutely convinced that vouchers would be found unconstitutional if church-related schools were permitted to participate. (Southern "segregation" vouchers had already been found unconstitutional.) Thus, while the ACLU was strongly opposed to vouchers, they were so confident of the strength of their legal position that their opposition was never more than *pro forma*. Before the California legislature the ACLU argued, simply, that it was a waste of time to pass unconstitutional legislation.

Liberals

Although broad political categorizations often obscure as much as they reveal, the group popularly thought of as liberals—the spiritual inheritors of the New Deal—found vouchers an odd and slightly distasteful proposal. Most liberals knew that Jencks's credentials were in order; accordingly, his reform proposal should be treated with some respect. But they could not bring themselves to support a notion which legitimized private schools. In some cases their investment in bureaucracy and the public sector was too high to reverse fields; others were infused with an egalitarian passion for public schools. In either case, they could never see vouchers as a solution to their understanding of the problem. The schools needed reform, but it should be evolutionary reform from within, guided in part by interested citizens. They saw no reason to contest the established order.

Voucher supporters on the left were young or radical or both. The virtues of choice were self-evident, the protections designed by Jencks necessary and useful, and the romantic appeal of giving power to ghetto dwellers was enough to enthuse most poverty fighters.

Conservatives

Many conservatives found the idea of vouchers attractive. The rhetoric of the market place—competition, accountability, rewarding success and punishing failure—was congenial. Their ardor dimmed, however, when they discovered what Jencks and OEO proposed to do with vouchers: bureaucratize and sanitize them beyond recognition. Although a number of conservatives were able to swallow their distaste for Jencks-style vouchers— they reasoned that something was better than nothing—the extent to which the OEO plan was acceptable in fact became a sort of conservative litmus test. The "real" conservatives, like President Nixon's selection to dismantle OEO, refused to support the Jencks scheme at all.

Thus, conservatives broke as did liberals, with a small number of conservative centrists, young liberals, and radicals supporting vouchers, but with the larger number indifferent or hostile.

Labor

Organizational labor—except, of course, teacher unions—was silent on vouchers. Whether the issues raised by vouchers were simply too removed for consideration, or whether the large number of Catholic union members inhibited any statement of opposition, is pure speculation. The teacher associations were another matter, however. The AFT and the NEA took strong stands in opposition.

The rhetoric of opposition was reasonably straightforward: Albert Shanker, for example, argued that vouchers *per se* were noxious. Vouchers as disinterested research, said Shanker, were analogous to making an omelette: if it doesn't work, it can't be unscrambled. Shanker's view appeared to reflect accurately the feelings of teacher organizations across the country. In each of eight feasibility studies, teachers were inclined to view vouchers as an assault on the established order. Teachers saw vouchers as a malign attempt to redistribute power and authority, an affront to professional educators.

It goes without saying that there was a good deal of truth in the teacher reactions. After all, vouchers were viewed as a strategy to completely reform a corrupt institution, and the inheritors of that institution were not keen to be labeled as corruptors. Jencks and his supporters at OEO really believed that education might be improved by taking the existing system apart and starting again. While the view may have much to recommend it, it is hardly calculated to gain the support of professional educators.

THE RESULTS FROM ALUM ROCK

It would be unfortunate to leave the impression that vouchers represented an altogether anomalous bureaucratic and intellectual event. The project in Alum Rock, California—while in many respects limited—did provide some important information. In response to Jencks's regulated, compensatory voucher scheme, Alum Rock proposed to launch a "transition" voucher model, complete in all respects except for one crucial variable: no private schools were included in the first year.

Alum Rock is a K-8 district in a lower income, bedroom community within the city limits of San Jose; the population is about 55 percent Mexican-American, 12 percent black, and the balance Anglo. The Alum Rock program began in September 1972 and involved 4,000 students in six of the district's twenty-two schools. Each year the project was expanded to include either or both more students and schools. In this, the last year, the full district is involved, including nearly 14,000 students in twenty-one schools (one school building closed since the project began). The district's annual operating budget and the OEO/NIE support for the five years of the project appear in Table 1.

Table 1

Alum Rock Annual Budget and OEO/NIE Support
(all figures in thousands)

| | | OEO/NIE Voucher Funding | | |
Year	State and Local Alum Rock Operating Budget	Operational Support	Rand Evaluation	CMLA Data Management
Pre-demon.		$ 107	$ 409	$116
1972-1973	$16,325	1,586	851	286
1973-1974	18,552	2,925	1,139	264
1974-1975	20,206	2,368	412	273
1975-1976	20,892	1,510	365	207
1976-1977	22,027	140 [a]	399	228
Total	$98,002	$8,636	$3,575	$1,374

[a]Estimated award.

The most important "finding" remains to be made: whether or not Alum Rock will continue in a "transition voucher" mode absent federal support. All indications suggest that most of the voucher mechanisms put in place there will remain; as the new status quo, open enrollment and program differentiation are likely to continue. A unique per-pupil building budget system may revert to centralized budgeting, as may some other aspects of the project. The district will also have to decide whether it can continue to afford to offer free transportation to non-neighborhood schools. Even though we are not sure of the final outlines, we can at least assert the following:

—Vouchers are administratively feasible: they do not overburden our administrative and institutional capacities.

—All things being equal, parents strongly prefer neighborhood schools. Vouchers or choice systems, however, can tip that balance by offering alternatives more attractive than neighborhood schools. Parents will send their children out of the neighborhood in search of a program of studies more to their liking.

—School evaluations and community information systems can be designed in a way that will be useful to the community and non-threatening to teachers.

—Vouchers did not (and need not) lead to greater segregation. To the contrary, vouchers can be used to insure racial balance.

—Teachers—the professionals with the most at stake in the demonstration project—have gained the most. Although many commented on the extra work required by vouchers in the beginning, they have clearly increased their authority and power in the district. In short, teachers find the project very much to their liking and their advantage.

—Preliminary analyses of reading and affective test scores reveal an interesting trend which, while not conclusive, is provocative. In "traditional" classrooms reading scores are increasing at a faster pace than in less traditional classrooms, while at the same time students in less traditional classrooms exhibit higher results on affective tests than do students in traditional classrooms. While it is premature to conclude that this suggests a dichotomy of "happy and stupid" vs. "smart but unhappy," it is an indicator that we intend to watch closely as the program draws to a conclusion.

—Only one moderately serious spontaneous effort was made to include nonpublic schools in the project. Although such an effort was difficult to mount, its isolated character and attentuated nature suggest a much weaker market response than some voucher theorists had predicted.

—Vouchers in Alum Rock were not used by parents as economic instruments to influence the behavior of professional educators. On a few isolated occasions, voucher parents changed the course of events, but the threat of withholding vouchers was never used. The convention of PTA meetings survived as the forum for airing grievances.

—The major "lesson" of the federal voucher programs is that no serious constituency could be developed. Beyond a limited circle of intellectuals and reformers, vouchers were viewed as a remedy to a nonexistent problem. While this may have been as much a reaction to the sponsor as to the idea, we have no way of knowing.

Until the Alum Rock project, however, voucher debates were unencumbered by facts. Proponents and opponents could freely soar on rhetorical thermals. Yet we now have a limited body of empirical evidence, and it is about the teacher responses to a "transition" voucher scheme that we have learned the most. The teachers' role in the Alum Rock project has gone largely unreported, which is remarkable, for they enjoyed a rapid and irreversible gain of power. Long a centralized district, Alum Rock adopted vouchers as part of a program to decentralize. The superintendent was convinced that transfer of power and decision-making authority to the building level would be beneficial to the community. Underlying this assumption was the belief that power would devolve from the superintendent to the principals: although most voucher theorists predicted the emergence of powerful parent groups, the superintendent saw that as a risk worth running. Neither principals nor parents, however, emerged as central forces to be reckoned with. Instead, teachers, with well developed organizational skills and high levels of personal motivation, emerged as the big winners. What had begun as the last OEO "power to the people" program ended as a "teacher power" program.

There is irony in this development, since most reformers assume that successful educational reform requires transfer of authority from the powers in public education to parents. At the same time, it is probably important to distinguish between the administrative bureaucracy of public schools and their teachers; it is certainly true that successful institutional reform requires the support and goodwill of teachers, just as their support and cooperation are essential to educational reform.

It is important to remember that the conclusions drawn from Alum Rock are tentative, and based on the experience in one idiosyncratic school district. It may well be that the citizens, students, and teachers of other communities would have behaved differently; given the decreased level of interest in vouchers at the federal level, however, this hypothesis is not likely to be tested soon.

AN ANSWER IN SEARCH OF A QUESTION:
RETURNING TO FIRST PRINCIPLES

What are we to make of the dismal suggestion that vouchers are an answer in search of a question? Are vouchers another painful example of good theory and bad practice? Were the political stars not in conjuction? Would different actors or different times have made a critical difference? There are, of course, no final and totally persuasive answers to these questions, but they do suggest that it would be useful to return to vouchers' first principles to see if vouchers were the appropriate mechanism to successfully advance those principles.

As I have suggested, the guiding spirit behind vouchers—whether Friedman or Jencks—was a commitment to diversity, responsiveness, and accountability. To secure these objectives, the key word to voucher supporters is choice.

The emphasis on accountability and diversity was critical in shaping perceptions about the implications of choice in education. To both Friedman and Jencks, choice was a device to reconnect students and schooling, to make each more accountable to the other. For many voucher supporters, choice was the reciprocal of diversity and diversity was the key to successful matching of students and schooling. Middle class white education was not what poor blacks needed, but it was what they would get so long as they were unable to select the schools they attended. Vouchers would give real educational power to parents, just as food stamps provided the resources to secure sustenance. Choice, then, was a form of leverage which would yield diversity and accountability.

The insight in this conception was also its fatal flaw, for it surfaced the political tensions inherent in the educational process. It cast educator against client; its claim was that the consumer had a better sense of his own self-interest than the provider. No stance could be better calculated to trigger the defenses of monopolists: the Jencks formulation, in particular, cast in the general adversary climate of its time, was clearly a battling of education windmills.

Recognizing the futility of confrontation politics, the OEO voucher office and its supporters attempted to domesticate vouchers and to present them as benign and beneficent. Instead of casting diversity as a reflection of political difference and tension, diversity was presented in the terms of technical and professional configurations. Different teachers and different students had differing learning and teaching styles. Vouchers, then, would simply legitimize and make possible a kind of educational musical chairs. This mechanistic view of diversity does not, of course, require vouchers to be realized, although choice would almost certainly improve the clarity of communications regarding both teacher and student interests and needs.

The marriage of vouchers and diversity was exaggerated, despite its relation to America's unique historical and cultural experience. American society is composed of widely diverse ethnic, racial, and religious groups, suggesting, theoretically, the probability of a wide variety of educational offerings—especially in light of the decentralized political structure of American education which, with notable exceptions, is decentralized to the local level.[2] There are, in fact, nearly 18,000 independent school districts across the country (only Hawaii has a unitary statewide system), and each district receives its policy guidance from a lay board or committee. Given this organizational structure and the heterogeneity of the American population, outside observers are surprised to discover that American education is as homogeneous as though it were centralized.

In fact, critics are fond of pointing out that American schools are more similar than dissimilar; and the remarkable thing is that this similarity has been essentially spontaneous and voluntary. The institutions which encourage uniformity—or which, perhaps, reflect it—are almost exclusively private, such as regional and national accrediting associations, nationwide publishing houses, and nationally based college entrance testing organizations, i.e., the Education Testing Service (ETS) and American College Test (ACT).

This educational uniformity extends to the private as well as the public sector. It is true, of course, that religiously affiliated schools offered a sharply different educational program than the secular public schools, but most observers agree that this distinction has diminished significantly over the past four decades. The major difference between public and private is qualitative rather than quantitative; private schools, including many with religious affiliations, exist not so much as "different" schools but "better" schools—"lighthouses" or examples of best practice. Although the true extremes in American education—hippie free schools or military academies—do exist in the private sector, they are so few as to be anomalous. The distinction between private and public that remains, and is likely to remain, is between good and better rather than differences in kind.

Despite the political and functional potential for diversity, American education remains remarkably uniform, demonstrating again the remarkable power of Tocqueville's insights into America's passion for equality; in the contemporary world "this passion for equality" assumes its operational expression in uniformity.

Although the line separating public and private is fine, and although private education is itself a reflection of the same model which inspires public education, there are several interesting trends which may provide some indications about the future of choice.

CURRENT TRENDS

Except for inner-city Catholic parish schools, boarding schools, and military academies, there is a steady and continued growth in nonpublic school enrollment. "Academic" secular and non-secular day schools have increased their enrollments at about 2 percent a year for the last six years. And that enrollment growth has three important components: middle class blacks are overrepresented in private schools; the big growth in private school enrollment is occurring in the suburbs; and the major new school entry in the private school market is "Christian" schools, those that are organized around a "value-centered" curriculum.

The trend lines, then, suggest that American education is moving much the same today as yesterday. Opinion polls show that the public wants not different schools, but better schools. Satisfaction with the basic structure and form of American education appears to be pervasive. There is no evidence that the vast majority finds outlying schools either interesting or attractive. While those on the margins will continue to look to radical alternatives as the answer, the mass of the American public is likely to prefer evolutionary reform of our homogeneous system.

But it was precisely this qualitative question that OEO and NIE voucher supporters found most difficult to deal with. If parents would actually choose among good, better, and best schooling, the most dangerous aspect of the market economy would be introduced to education: for every winner there could be a loser. Teachers and principals were particularly sensitive to this implicit threat, and OEO labored heroically to develop a persuasive rhetoric to soften it. In this domesticated version, as I suggested earlier, vouchers permit choice among "different" kinds rather than different qualities of education. This logic leads to the conclusion that the main function of choice is to match students and children; the probability of fundamental mismatch between the interest of consumers and providers as a monopoly was never vigorously scrutinized. And so diversity— as a harmless, technical, and mechanistic set of curriculum or classroom differences—became inextricably bound to choice. Essentially, to "sell" vouchers, it had become necessary to propose that there were no fundamental choices to be made, because real "choices" would have real consequences, affecting the jobs and lives of real people.

Choice, then, of the kind that made its appearance at Alum Rock, and the kind the education establishment finds palatable, is not central to vouchers. What roles, then, might "choice" systems play in the future?

CHOICE AND DIVERSITY IN EDUCATION

There are three elements to the questions of choice which are currently of vital concern to public education policymakers, teachers, and students. The first is an important part of the conventional wisdom: neighborhood schools. The second is the role of choice as it relates to the question of academic excellence.

It is clear, both on the basis of practice and annual surveys, that neighborhood schools are important to large numbers of parents and educators regardless of race or socioeconomic status. While this preference may be due in some measure to force of habit, it remains as a strongly held view. Both parents and educators value the convenience of neighborhood assignment. Although the limited empirical evidence from Alum Rock indicates that such views and behavior patterns can be changed, it is slow work. Parents are cautious about exercising the prerogative of choice; over time, however, the practice of selecting and attending non-neighborhood schools can become widespread.

All things being equal, then, most parents express a strong preference for the convenience and continuity of the neighborhood school. There are, however, two "naturally" occurring activities in which all things are not equal.

Choice and Integration

The continuing legal and moral pressure to end *de facto* segregation in American schools (primarily in urban centers, which are experiencing rapid decline of school-age populations) has raised the question of choice in a new and interesting way. Noting that children and parents don't object to busing if they like their destination, a number of imaginative superintendents have devised "magnet" school schemes to encourage voluntary busing and consequent integration. To date, the experience with such schemes has been modest, but the early results are encouraging: racial quotas are set and met because the "magnet" school offers special facilities and programs attractive to the community.

Easing the sting of forced busing is an objective of the highest priority for most education policymakers: the issue is a painful and confusing one for all members of the community, regardless of race, and the introduction of choice can be a real safety valve. (For a specific proposal employing choice mechanisms to encourage racial integration, see the Appendix to this book.)

The Desire for Increased Diversity

For many years the American tilt toward educational uniformity and homogeneity found no more complete expression than in the "comprehensive high school." It is designed to serve all, with a full menu of offerings from wood shop to college preparatory courses. Its objectives are as much social as educational, for the comprehensive high school is designed to be a melting pot in microcosm.

At the same time, the meritocratic aspects of modern life have led progressively more observers to the conclusion that academic high schools should be restored. In Washington, D.C., for instance, the superintendent has proposed the creation of a new academic high school, and this scheme is echoed across the nation.

Finally, large numbers of parents are concerned about questions of moral values and feel that public schools have let moral standards go by the boards. Clearly, "moral values" are a subject difficult to teach in the best of circumstances. In a pluralistic, democratic society the public schools find themselves damned if they do, damned if they don't. Private schools, formed on the basis of voluntary association, are able to squarely address questions of "moral values," however, in a way that public schools cannot. Concurrently, private schools, with discipline codes and standards of dress and conduct, are able to deal actively with questions of value.

Although the question deserves much more attention than time and space permit here, it is important to note that there is an increasing awareness that no education is "value free." Public secular education inculcates values as does private, sectarian education. In a mass society, maintaining high standards while recognizing significant but legitimate value differences is a difficult if not impossible task. Although it can be argued that the public sector's inability to deal directly with value questions has kept minority values from being overwhelmed, this is a slender reed to lean upon. A view that the public sector's clumsiness in dealing explicitly with value questions may be a mechanism for avoiding value confrontations probably has outlived its usefulness.

This suggests a small but growing interest among a broad

spectrum of educators and parents for some increased choice in American education. If this is true, the next question for those interested in vouchers is whether or not they are either necessary or appropriate at this time.

Our cultures must reflect our democratic traditions and strike some balance between the pull of pluralism and the push of a shared culture. For it is the tension expressed in the alternating attractions of maintaining diverse identities within the context of a common national community that makes the question of choice a serious one. As a society, from a moral, legal, and political perspective, the decision has been made that choice on racial grounds is unacceptable; but what of choice on the basis of curricula, religious or moral values, or intellectual ability? It is precisely along these dimensions that choice seems to be emerging as a real issue in America in the 1970s. While choice along curricular lines seems, on its face, innocuous enough, the real issue concerns the underlying reasons for selecting one curriculum as against another. Will working class parents select curricula which reinforce working class attitudes, as Henry Levin suggests? Will powerful elites perpetuate themselves by "curricular" segregation? While it is impossible to answer the question empirically, there is one important perspective on choice which deserves some attention.

CHOICE AS RESOLUTION OF LIBERTY AND EQUALITY

The narrowness of our national interest in choice, rather than reflecting the vapid fancies of intellectuals and reformers, may signal the beginning of a new awareness in our contemporary political and intellectual life. Choice may emerge as a category of resolution, binding together the divergent virtues of liberty and equality. The tension between these two ideals has been a part of the American experience since the nation's founding, even though, historically, the balance has remained tipped toward equality. It was Tocqueville's special genius to carry this idea to its fullest discussion, and America's "passion for equality" continues long after the great Frenchman's classic study.

One explanation for the strong interest in the subject of choice—as among public services, rather than among private goods—is that choice reconciles, in some measure, the tension between liberty and equality. Clearly both Friedman and Jencks saw such maximization inherent in their schemes; just as Jencks wants to insulate against freedom to fail, Friedman too proposed that vouchers equalize opportunity.

If choice is both the key to vouchers and the theme that unites thinkers as different as Jencks and Friedman, the fact that choice is still a marginal interest in American education today bodes ill for vouchers. Although choice is everywhere talked about, it is nowhere acted upon. I, for one, am convinced that Jencks vouchers are too much for the political and educational system to absorb *de novo*; what Jencks designed in 1970 is what liberals would have done to a Friedman scheme that had been in place for fifty years. It is clear that a "new deal" approach to a *laissez faire* education voucher system would be regulated and compensatory.

As Jencks vouchers are too much, Friedman vouchers are too little: their unregulated character poses too great a risk to liberal policymakers. The basic reason that policymakers will not support either Jencks or Friedman vouchers is that the dimension of vouchers that makes them interesting—choice—still threatens an egalitarian society. At the present time only one important interest group might change this, and that group is minorities in general, especially the blacks. While the traditional view has opposed choice in education on grounds that choice would increase inequality in education, there is a growing body of minority and black opinion which holds that choice itself is the key to equality—and that without choice, equal educational opportunity will remain unfulfilled. It is a theme that runs through several chapters in this book. If it should come to influence the most prominent minority and black leaders, they would have it within their power to reverse the traditional beliefs about the intrinsic antagonism between equality and choice.

CONCLUSION

Thus, it is precisely in this *a priori* sense that vouchers and what they represent—choice—are valid: avoidance of dogma, intellectual integrity, freedom of inquiry, and the spirited encounter of differing interpretations of reality. But if the idea of vouchers is sound, while their implementation is at best provisioned, how is their objective to be secured?

Two ideas which have gained some currency are worth noting. The more unlikely but perhaps most interesting of the two ideas would be a government-sponsored scholarship program for gifted or unusual youngsters. Such a scheme is already in place for handicapped children in some states, and its use is widespread at the post-secondary level. Why not a program for able students at the elementary and secondary level? In some large urban areas, for example, with public school systems in serious disarray, there is simply no public school with an adequate academic program. Only one public high school with any tradition of academic accomplishment remains in Washington, D.C., but there are a half-dozen private high schools with national reputations. St. Anselm's Abbey School has the highest proportion of Merit Scholars in its graduating class of any school in the nation and St. Alban's is second, yet poor children have severely limited opportunities to attend such schools.

In a scholarship program of this kind the administrative problems are modest, the costs small, and the potential benefits great. From a legal standpoint, so long as the number of recipients is small and distributed among secular and nonsecular schools, no claim could be advanced that the program is designed to benefit the school rather than the student.

The more realistic and perhaps more interesting approach to increasing the range of choice lies in transfer payments through negative taxation. Tax credits or deductions designed to recognize the out-of-pocket costs of tuition are easy to design, implement, and police. Further, they promise to minimize state interference with both the school and the individual.

The attractiveness of negative taxation schemes is to be found in their simplicity and directness; in them the heavy hand of government is surprisingly light. But as in so many things, their virtue is their vice. I am not convinced that they will do more than reinforce existing patterns at the margin, and ease the sting of tuition payments for those already committed to private education. What of the majority who are likely to remain in the public school monopoly—what choice are they to enjoy? Because negative taxation will have little direct effect on the public sector, a more positive and assertive approach is necessary if the benefits of choice are to be meaningfully extended to a large segment of our population.

It seems reasonably clear, then, that insofar as diversity is valued it can be secured within the context of the existing public and private systems of education. The private sector already offers a wide range if not an extensive supply of diverse offerings. And although the public sector is slow to respond, respond it must. As I have indicated, preliminary evidence suggests that a more varied array of offerings and curricula are becoming available in the public sector. This response, however, represents a sort of public sector *noblesse oblige,* and is provided the petitioner on the institution's terms. With some surprise and even consternation, we are seeing a separation between diversity and choice. Originally conceived as reciprocals, it is clear that the public sector can respond across one dimension without touching upon the other. Diversity is acceptable; choice is not.

This issue goes to the heart of the American concept of education as a technical and mechanistic enterprise, best suited to the ministrations of a rational, professional elite. Diversity fits in this context. Choice, however, directly challenges the legitimacy of the educational enterprise. As it is presently constituted, recognition of choice as valid is to assert that any parents' judgment is as sound as that of any professionals. Unlike the rationalism of the 19th century which spawned our modern system of schooling, this claim is profoundly political.

It is for this reason that choice remains as the bane and hope of vouchers: the promise of choice is what gives vouchers their profound appeal and vitality; it is the prospect of the reality of choice that makes vouchers so threatening to the system.

It may well be that the federal decision to support a program of research into the likely effects of vouchers has succeeded, but not in the way the planners had imagined. We now know, with some confidence, that American education in the 1970s is open to the idea of increasing diversity, but is still not particularly congenial to the idea of choice. But at the same time there is increasing evidence that the consumers of education—students, parents, taxpayers, policymakers—are becoming progressively more interested in choice. Thus, while the federal voucher program did not produce vouchers, it may have been an early warning signal of a more profound national interest in the idea.

CONCLUSION: SOCIAL TRUST

Almost anything that can be said about America must be said as paradox. A given assertion is seldom true, without its opposite also having considerable substance to commend it. To say, then, that we are a diverse people, proud of our diversity, requires correction. Our diversity has also made us fearful.

The central energy of this chosen nation and "almost chosen people," born in an act of revolutionary choice and living under constitutional procedures for choice, might be said to be the maximization of choice. Yet, as the essays in this book have shown, on both left and right there are serious constraints upon free choice in education. Patterns of conformity are strong.

Intellectual and social energies, however, have recently opened up new possibilities. During the past ten years, the context of discussion has been subtly and deeply altered. We are free at last to walk away from the dichotomous thinking of racial contrast—"white" and "colored," "honky" and "black." This impulse to find a new language springs from reality itself. At home, the civil rights movement found itself increasingly involved in questions of "minorities" other than blacks alone—Native Americans, Chicanos, Puerto Ricans, Asians, and (in general) Third World peoples. Even along this axis, it soon became evident that the distinctive element of coalition is not racial but, rather, cultural. And from this the full revelation about American diversity begins.

For, on the one hand, among the most successful "races" in the United States (to use the term as it was employed in the U.S. Congress prior to the immigration legislation of 1924) have been a whole series of "colored peoples" (as they were then defined): the Syrian-Lebanese, the Armenians, the Jews, the Japanese, the Chinese, the Koreans, the Italians, and the West Indian blacks. On the other hand, while conditions of slavery and reconstruction imposed upon American blacks a severity of disadvantage experienced by no other, neither blacks nor other races of "color" stand alone in facing cultural, economic, educational, and occupational disadvantage. If statistical surveys are to be done about the proportional representation of blacks on the Chicago police force, they are with equal justice to be done about the proportional representation of Polish-Americans on the Chicago police force. (The situation of Poles is even more dismal in that and in other instances.) An examination of the patterns of disadvantage in the United States reveals no stark dichotomy, based on race alone, which would supply simpler ideological needs. It reveals, instead, a large spectrum of experiences, sufferings, strengths, and weaknesses. The glory and the agony are not neatly divided.

Ideologues express concern that this more complex picture, even if more accurate, will deflate feelings of guilt, urgency, and social change. Such engines of change are far more fickle, unreliable, and suspect than ideologues have the wit to notice. In fact, the more accurate picture relieves the isolation of blacks and other racial groups, and generates among others an awareness of analogous historical experiences. It also inspires ever more exact social analyses. On such sympathies and on such concern for the exact truth—and on these alone—can one ground long-lived political coalitions.

In the international sphere, events have forced similar cultural awareness into consciousness. Most conflicts do not occur along racial lines but, rather, within them. Americans, particularly those born in the American South, may be forgiven for exag-

gerating the salience of race in human affairs. Intraracial historical enmities, however, are frequent, turbulent, and bitter, as witness the tribal wars of Africa or the bloodlettings of European
history. Arabs and Israelis are not of different races; nor are
Protestant and Catholic Irish; nor are Nigerians and Biafrans,
Katangans and Zaireans. The Germans annihilated some eigh-
teen million persons in concentration camps—Jews, Slavs, and
others—who, from the perspective of Africa, would appear to be
"white races." Whites have never wreaked so much agony upon
blacks as upon each other; and, in general, so with other races.
This is an important, but not the only, international lesson:
culture is deeper than race.

It was believed for more than one generation that the process
called modernization would homogenize the planet. The spread
of rational procedures, the development of identical tastes, and a
planetary communications network, it was assumed, would
bring the peoples of many cultures closer together. As a consequence, modernity would make them more the same. World
order, it was hoped, would become more rational. Irrational factors like blood, soil, tribal loyalties, and even nationalism would
gradually diminish. And there have, indeed, been signs that
such expectations were not entirely false. Coca Cola, Brut, Esso,
Shell, and other products are used in the most remote locations.
Where such modern products go, can managerial habits and rational arrangements be far behind? The surprising factor has
been, however, the re-emergent salience of ethnicity. Far from
being diminished by post-tribal modernization, the energies of
localism and cultural loyalty seem to have been reawakened. In
Slovakia, in Scotland, in Katanga, in Quebec, in Vietnam, in
Ukrainia, in Palestine, among Soviet Jews, and in many other
places, the desire of cultural minorities for political recognition
(for sovereignty, for the redrawing of boundaries, for linguistic
and other rights, for representation, etc., in baffling variety) has
made ethnic consciousness one of the most powerful forces in
international affairs at the end of the twentieth century.

As an hypothesis, consider three reasons why this might be
so: (1) Discontentment with the moral content of modernity

and the "new man" of the modern type; (2) the overlooked role in the human psyche of a sense of historical rootedness; (3) the capacity of modern institutions, and of the kind of consciousness appropriate for living within them, to permit differentiation and even individualization without threat to powerful bonds of social unity. Rationalistic theories, once persuasive, now seem to have been too optimistic about the moral content of the humanism actually to be produced by modern institutions. Human types like John Dean, Jeb Magruder, and others involved in "Watergate" and in similar corporate practices at every level, whether in socialist or in capitalist regimes, have not been as attractive in practice as the celebration of the secular, urban, pragmatic style had led us to anticipate.

Rationalistic theories seem also to have been too shallow in their view of human historicity. Human beings are historical animals, and the absence of a personal history is like a hunger whose filling can bring tears to the eyes: witness the emotion stirred by the TV version of *Roots,* watched by over 80 percent of all American blacks.

Finally, rationalistic theories failed to estimate the power of modern institutions—books, television, travel, the computer—to permit the individual to retain and to deepen cultural consciousness even while living among persons of a quite different culture. It is not necessary to live in a cultural enclave in order to retain one's cultural consciousness. Meanwhile, the great centripetal power of the modern state (and of other modern institutions as well) pulls so heavily in the direction of homogeneity and conformity that, as if by check and balance, individuals and local "mediating" collectivities feel freer to assert their own energies. Human liberty seems to demand it.

Historical process cyclically and slowly alternates—systole and dystole—between tendencies of unity and of diversity. (Professor Lazerson's history [Chapter I] suggests as much). At some moments, the movements are toward the center, homogenizing; at others, the center becoming too strong, resistance tends toward diversification in many directions. A system of social fear may govern such motions. When fears of division dominate, assimilation is encouraged. When fears of conformity dominate, diversity acquires partisans. We seem now to be living, both domestically and in the world at large, in an age of unparalleled "interdependence." Central governments grow stronger under liberal, as well as socialist, systems. Mass communications reflect, incite, and impose national styles. In rebellion—we may hypothesize—those institutions that mediate between the omnipotent state and the lonely individual will become the focus of increasing energy: family, ethnic group, church, neighborhood and other local associations, unions, and the like.

It is in this intellectual context that one must place the discussion of education in the United States and, in particular, the question of vouchers. Since World War II, enormous changes have taken place in American school systems. (1) Vast social migrations have occurred, especially three: that from rural to urban areas; that of blacks out of the South; and that from cities to suburbs. (2) School systems have become more centralized, professionalized, and bureaucratized. (3) The horizons for children in school have been so broadened as to change the nature of their education; it has come to be mandatory that children finish high school, and expectable that half or more will try at least some college work; education seems less and less like a privilege or a means of liberation, and more and more like an oppressive necessity. At one and the same time, schools have taken on a more complex set of tasks than occupied them prior to World War II, and parents have come to expect more and more of the schools—while providing less educational help in the home. "Consolidated" schools seem in any case more distant from the home. Education has become a specialization left to the experts.

As "modernizing" institutions *par excellence*—the institutions of passage into modernity—the schools are subject to all the aforementioned disappointments with modernity. Their moral quality is disappointing ("permissive," "progressive"); their inability to touch the moral-cultural roots of children is protested; and their capacities for developing a sound "pluralistic personality" seems to be frustrated. In part, of course, the schools are victims of their own ideology. Propelled out of the optimistic, rational hopes of the end of World War II, they have seen their task to be that of a "melting pot" in two senses: first, to mold a new undifferentiated ("unhyphenated") American characterology; and, second, to prepare millions of youngsters for the prosperity of a technical, bureaucratic, corporate civilization. (Out went the classics; in came "modern" curricula.)

The power of the upper class Anglo-Saxon elite of almost every American city and region has, I think, been exaggerated, but one area in which its hegemony has been particularly strong is that of culture, from museums and opera societies to the public schools. It could hardly be an error to see in certain forms of "Anglo-conformity" a central motif of American schooling. A few examples may be cited to establish my meaning: this nation is the third largest Spanish-speaking nation of the world; it contains more blacks than any single African nation; it contains the third-largest Eastern European Slavic community, etc. Yet the ideological slant of the curriculum looks out at the world inexorably and rather narrowly from the viewpoint of English culture in Europe and in America. Not only the language and not only the subject matter but, in addition, the emotional and spiritual style of the schools is rather more narrow than the possibilities within the population. Many millions besides blacks and Latinos have experienced discomfort in the classrooms of the "Anglo" majority. Still, recognizing that economic and political power are connected to cultural power, many parents have been grateful for the "Americanizing" efforts of the schools and have demanded such efforts. In order to notice the power of such efforts, indeed, one need not be wholly negative about them. (Although I now believe it sad, even slightly tragic, that the schools of Western Pennsylvania did not encourage me to learn the language of my grandparents, thus involving my grandparents in my education and me in Slavic culture so that in adulthood significant options would have been open to me in that direction, I am grateful for the confidence early given me that America was "mine" and that I could plunge into the stream of its language with delight.)

Three consequences, nonetheless, derive from Anglo-conformity in the schools. First, the real pluralism of American life has been lost to our view. Our eyes have been trained not to notice what they do in fact see. In fiction, the ethnic background of a character is almost always introduced, usually quite early, and is always regarded as significant. In real life (at least we tell ourselves) we do not notice; it would seem unenlightened to notice. Tolerance is a high virtue; it is higher when it is respectful without pretending to be blind.

Secondly, the nation's public language about values is impoverished. Values are learned instinctively and profoundly in the early life of the child, in families. The language for expressing values, as well as the rituals, prayers, and celebrations of the deeds of moral heroes and heroines, are passed on from generation to generation in cultural traditions. In a pluralistic society, however, in order not to give offense or to provoke division, it often happens in common endeavors that none feel free to articulate the full particularity of their own ethical commitments. "Common denominators" are sought. Refuge is taken in truisms and cant. Sentimentality triumphs over intelligence. The whole moral enterprise falls into a certain disrepute, and as soon as the ceremonies are over, the skeptical and intelligent are pleased to hurry back to their pragmatic activities.

A further result is that public language tends to be either pious, in a neutral sort of way (best exemplified by President Eisenhower's reputed observation, "Ninety-nine percent of Americans believe in God, I don't care which one you mean"); or else far more secular than are the individuals who actually speak it. Many hide their personal beliefs; the public language becomes secular by default. It seems at times to be a language that belongs to no one, with no real roots or power. Yet it has gained public dominance just the same. I am thinking here of the language that passes as "sophistication," that well-informed savviness not only of the talk shows and the celebrities, but even of college presidents, politicians, and serious journalists. Quite often in our society, public figures are not saying exactly what they themselves believe. They grope for what they take to be the consensus, for the idiom of a "sophisticated" national audience, for what "may be said." The supposed consensual audience, it turns out, can be a fiction, no single member of it being rooted in, or being fully willing to subscribe to, the consensus supposedly at work. In a pretended monoculture, false consciousness thrives.

Thirdly, the monocultural emphasis of the schools leads to profound dissatisfactions the moment the schools begin to raise serious moral issues. One citizen's enlightenment is another's subversive ideology. Let the topic be sex education, or the intellectual-moral counterculture of the urban left; or let the method of discussion exclude recourse to evangelical-biblical traditions, or to specific religious or cultural traditions, or to local mores—and one ought not to be surprised if mass meetings grow hot. In West Virginia, on such an account, school buses have been fired at. There are many different cultural traditions for the transmission of personal and social values, but under a monocultural system the schools seem oddly inept in dealing with them. Public options seem limited to whether to skip "controversial" matters entirely, or to run roughshod over minorities by ramming through a treatment of the issues, sterilized by the approval of the dominant factions. The very word "controversial," used so often in educational matters, gives away the problem. That values are nourished by contrasting traditions a thousand years (or more) old, one would think, ought to be a given of educational psychology. Naturally, people will disagree about profound issues and be uncomfortable about discussing such differences publicly; we do not have a public language for such discussions. Nonetheless, such issues are not (with its negative connotations) "controversial"; they are, rather, fundamental, instructive, and in need of exploration. Were they not so flammable, they would not be so clearly at the heart of the matter. It is a major intellectual task of our time to fashion "a public philosophy" that enables us to give tongue to our pluralism.

During a period like our own, involved in so many moral uncertainties for every tradition and yet obliged, willy-nilly, to cope with serious public problems that have a moral dimension, we should not be surprised that the cry for more "freedom" and "choice" in education should blare out over loudspeakers. When values close to the spine of a whole way of life are in question, few wish to entrust their children to just anyone. The public schools have not dealt well with problems of fundamental moral diversity. On the other hand, the public can hardly afford to permit fundamental moral issues to go by default. The educational dilemma, then, is cruel. Radicals in some places, conservatives in other places, and liberals in yet others have known what it is like to be in the minority. Evangelicals and mainline Protestants; liberal and orthodox Jews; liberal and conservative Catholics; blacks, Chicanos, and Asian Americans—nearly all Americans have had occasion to protest against the conformism of one time and place or another.

Before the advent of national magazines, the radio networks, and television, there was more reason than there is today to believe that the public schools ought to "hold us together" and to build up a "common culture." Homogenizing, rationalizing, centripetal forces are today infinitely more powerful. The inexorable formation of a "common culture" is ensured by the national merchandising of products of all sorts, by significant family mobility, and by the growing role of a national professional class (the collaborators in this book, for example). What is not so certain is how nuanced, subtle, profound, and wise that common culture will be. No doubt a law applies here: *The probabilities of creative outcomes are enhanced if the number of originating energies is very high.* Today there is less reason to fear diversity than there was. There is more reason to fear the shallowness of certain forms of homogenization. For fifteen years considerable progress has been made, at least in superficial ways, to develop "ecumenism" and elementary knowledge about each other. It is time to go deeper.

Nathan Glazer is right (above, Chapter IV) when he commends John Higham's notion of "integrative pluralism." As the generations go on, the American experience integrates all of us, through vivid memories and intense common pressures. Those who were outside the country—even for a year or so—during the assassination of John F. Kennedy or Martin Luther King,

Jr., during the riots or anti-war protests, or during Watergate—have often remarked on their return how it seemed to them that they were stepping back into a culture different from the one they had left. Strong and swift is our culture, powerful and searing, impressing upon each of us from year to year indelible experiences. These experiences may not homogenize us, but they do bind us to one another through at least analogous feelings, memories, and traumas. No one who once heard the fulsome English spoken by Martin Luther King, Jr. (or Barbara Jordan, or Yvonne Braithwaite), or heard Peter Rodino, Jr., discourse on the Magna Carta during the House impeachment proceedings, or—on a less sublime level—watched "Rhoda" and "Mary Tyler Moore" embrace, can deny that we are building here, in both a profound and subtle way, a "common culture." When I called my own book *The Rise of the Unmeltable Ethnics* (1972), I intended to suggest that Americans previously hardly heard from in the common discourse were about to "arise" and to make an important assertion, making a distinctive contribution in return for what they had been given. I had in mind, without having formulated it, something like Higham's notion of "integrative pluralism."

Such a perception of American society justifies fresh attempts to maximize choice in education. But this can be done only on a strong philosophical basis. The danger in our era is that the spiritual and moral life of our people will become banal. An homogenizing national culture, carrying no one's true voice, becomes subject to ridicule. Meanwhile, the state has grown more powerful and individuals more isolated and vulnerable. Thus, the focus and force of the liberal task has changed. In 1935 John Dewey argued that, for the first time in the history of liberalism, liberals should look to the national state not as an enemy and not only as a neutral force, but as a moral ally. Four decades later we recognize some of the costs that have accrued in the wake of the extraordinary advances made according to that choice. As Dewey once changed the goals of liberalism, so the genuinely liberal temper will once again question, reflect, and perhaps imagine a sharply different liberal future. The most promising direction, it appears, is to strengthen those "mediating institutions" that stand between the individual and the state, checking the extravagances of both. Hedonism and bureaucracy are reverse mirror images, equally restrictive of the liberal spirit.

If I am correct then, a new form of liberalism is on the horizon (and has been exhibited in many essays of this book). Superficially, its primary characteristic is its willingness to criticize the assumptions of the old liberal spirit—its own spirit of a decade or more ago—and to be just as rigorous and critical about the left as about the right. Profoundly, however, its characteristic turn is to look to social agencies outside the state for sources of renewal and strength. It is governed by a sense of modesty about what the state may accomplish; by a learned mistrust of experts or, at least, of the *hubris* of experts; by a sense of the ironies involved in every social and political policy; and by a renewed respect for what people can do for themselves, once freed from crippling circumstances, or enabled by favorable conditions. Reinhold Niebuhr in his later years often described an amalgam of classical liberalism and conservatism that, he believed, constituted a new and wiser form of the liberal spirit: a combination of the liberal's distrust of the *status quo* and its illusions, and of the conservative's sense of the tangled organic connectedness of human affairs. This combination the new liberal spirit embodies.

The matter of educational vouchers, for example, introduces a preventive *laissez faire* against the reach of the state. The state commands that children be educated, and even establishes certain standards to be met; and the state empowers parents to send their children to schools by building the schools and by offering various forms of assistance. Yet, under the voucher system, the parents would choose the actual school in which to exercise this civic right and duty. The practical design of a voucher system is not, however, simple. Conscious of the tangled history of education in America, including serious strains of racism, nativism, and exclusion, the new liberals—conspicuously in James Coleman's essay (above, Introduction)—have tried to surround the practical use of vouchers with safeguards and provisos. Their aim is to maximize liberty, uniqueness, excellence, and equality.

To recapitulate the many good points made about vouchers in the preceding essays would be to carry unnecessary coals. Their main thrust is clear. It seems within our technical capacity to design a system of education less centralized and less homogenized than the one we have, a system integrated (not only racially) and yet pluralistic, a system more representative of and nourishing to the many sorts of constituencies it serves. We can afford to have confidence in the choices of parents for their children. As Thomas Sowell has suggested (above, Chapter VIII), to seek better schooling for their children almost half of all the blacks living in the South undertook their long, difficult migration northward and westward. Indeed, to focus on the role of families in education is now timely and astute.

It is timely because there has been a tendency in Anglo-American social thought to swing back and forth between the individual and the state, to the neglect of the family, the neighborhood, the cultural society, and other small-scale institutions. Conservatives have tended to lavish passion on the individual, liberals on the government. Both have tended to regard mediating institutions as sources of prejudice, passion, bias, and constraint—as obstacles in the way of their own purposes. Neither classical conservative nor classical liberal thought has bequeathed us a strong body of theory concerning intermediate institutions.

Yet the family, in particular, has a significant and even indispensable role to play in education. The family is the original and most efficient department of health, education, and welfare. The nutritional support of the child; the development of its IQ; its nervous and emotional habits; its early lessons on how to identify letters, to read, and to compute; its motivation to read and to learn; its moral values and habits—all these are best imparted in the family and, if not there, only with difficulty elsewhere. If the family fails, society only with exceeding difficulty makes up the loss. With every new study that appears, science seems to assign the role of the family higher significance. (No wonder, under all their austere and newly recognized responsibilities, so many young people fear marriage; in the old days did parents just *do* what they did, without such exquisite scientific awareness of their possible failures?) It has been, no doubt, an error of grave consequence to have entrusted so much education to the schools, and so to have overlooked the role of the family in education.

In this respect, it is necessary to push the argument for vouchers a stage beyond the merely technical and administrative task of providing financial assistance and choice. Much attention should be given to what families can do to teach their children not only before the children begin school but in conjunction with the school. The separation of the family from the school is not a healthy step for either party. It seems preposterous that parents should expect the schools to teach their children how to read without joining in that task themselves during and after their children's preschool years. (Still at ten and twelve, kids need motivation and help in continuing to read.) It seems equally preposterous that schools should attempt all by themselves, without clear and direct communication with the homes of their students, to carry on the work of education. Home and schools are, in fact, in symbiotic relationship. The more they can do together, the better for education. In order to improve the quality of education, indeed, interventions in the home may show far more effect, more swiftly and profoundly, than interventions in the classroom. Particularly among underprivileged children, educational interventions in the home spur progress, especially if adult males are helped to work with their children. But the general point holds: throughout society, at every level, the role of parents in the education of their children is critical. Why is it so neglected in educational theory?

The notion that parents should take responsibility for helping their children to choose among competing schools does not, then, contradict the notion that the parents' role in the education of their children is indispensable. It reinforces it. To underestimate the capacities and the concerns of parents is wrong. In many families the entire strategy of where to take up residence is governed by long-range designs for the education of their children. Of course, there are many other families, themselves from traditions of peasantry, or in any case from traditions of low educational attainment, who do not so value education and whose attitudes towards the schools is one of diffidence or of indifference. Yet into such families, too, are born brilliant youngsters whose aspirations may carry them beyond their parents, and to whom the opportunity—through vouchers—of seeking out special schooling might provide a decisive breakthrough from neighborhood limits. What a scholarship once was (say) to Boston Latin for youngsters from Dorchester or Roxbury, vouchers might be today.

The California proposal by Stephen A. Sugarman and John E. Coons (Appendix A) is a further example of the new liberalism, in part because it assumes a certain basic social trust. (The "basic trust" that Erik Erikson sees as so important to personal identity has its counterpart in the "basic social trust" necessary for the health of societies; even, as St. Augustine noted, societies among thieves.) Instead of approaching integration in a punitive way, Coons and Sugarman seek an incentive, a sweetener, designed to attract citizens (and schools) to do what they would probably be inclined to do, and what in their ideal selves they would approve of themselves doing. This incentive gives them a practical spur to overcome both past injustices and the expectable inertia of social systems. By contrast, many of those involved in problems of integration have come out of evangelical religious backgrounds. Guilt is their rhetorical staple, and their proposals for remediation are tinged with a punitive character. But guilt feelings in political and social matters often have ironic effects, deepening the very condition they propose to heal. Neither coercion nor punishment is the ideal liberal instrument. Each generates effects counter to its intention.

The new liberals, then, while remarkably more modest than they were fifteen years ago about the capacity of governmental social policies, are more sanguine about the good instincts of many citizens. What they have lost in trust in massive government interventions, they have gained in basic social trust. They tend to seek ways of *enabling* and *empowering* individual citizens and small-scale mediating institutions to act for themselves. "Ask not what your government can do for you. Ask what you can do better than the government." The role of government, in this view, is less arrogant and obtrusive.

The new liberals thus tend to place government in a less salient role than did the old liberals. They prefer it to play the role of a *removens prohibens,* a secondary, supportive role. In a sense, they have borrowed a leaf from the movement toward "participatory democracy"; they define social problems as very largely enabling problems. Buried here, as well, is the ancient Catholic notion of "subsidiarity" which holds that each social problem should be addressed upon its own social level; a higher agency should be called in only when the lower has exhausted its possibilities. Higher agencies, simultaneously, must take care not to weaken local agencies by taking too much responsibility and too many resources from them.

In a word, a new direction for liberalism is in the air. Assaulted by radicals on the one side and by an assertive conservatism on the other, liberals during the past decade have by now had a chance to get a fresh grip upon "the liberal mind." Much wisdom has been wrested from the struggles of the last few years. In 1963 John F. Kennedy in an address at Yale suggested that, given modern social knowledge, we knew what needed to be done; all we lacked was will. Such *hubris*—and the buoyant programmatic manifestos that went with it—are absent now. The newly skeptical eye searches for the possible unintended consequences of proposed courses of action. Governmental initiatives are still promoted, but both in their design and in the tone in which they are presented distinctive notes are heard: Consider the qualities of mind and spirit exerted in the preceding essays. Running through each of them is an activism tutored by respect for the intricacies of social reality.

Perhaps at no point has the liberal mind undergone a more profound change than in its perception of cosmopolitan atmosphere and felt most at home in it. Such an atmosphere is usually urban and somewhat continental, as in New York, Cambridge, and San Francisco. Yet cosmopolitanism in some respects falls short of pluralistic consciousness. To be cosmopolitan is to be surrounded by and experienced in cultural variety. But to exhibit a pluralistic consciousness is to become more sharply aware of one's own finitude, of one's own particularity and unique roots, while (a) respecting the uniqueness of others and (b) recognizing the many diverse sources from which one draws one's own spiritual nourishment.

The cosmopolitan experiences the many, and yet remains rather vague about his relation to the many. The cosmopolitan may glory in a kind of tolerance and practice benign neglect of differences. A sense of world-weariness may well afflict him. He takes differences for granted and does not perceive the threat that arises among the managers and mass-producers. The new managerial class, equally at home in any of the world's major cities, is not really cosmopolitan. It carries homogenization like a virus. By contrast, the pluralistic personality is *changed* by contact with the many. It internalizes diverse insights and virtues learned from others, while remaining sharply faithful to the traditions of the self. The pluralist is aware of the many social influences upon the self; his own personality draws—and knows that it draws—nourishment from several streams. The pluralist knows, as well, that diversity today is threatened.

Another significant contrast emerges from the theme of relativism. Since the cosmopolitan has seen much and experienced much, he has a tendency, confronted with variety, to shrug his shoulders as if to say, "Everything is relative." The cosmopolitan is eager to differentiate himself from the merely provincial, the narrow, the inexperienced. But the pluralistic personality is concerned not simply with the contrast on that side, but also with the contrast on the other. The pluralistic personality fears the mush of mere tolerance, the flaccid sentimentality of homogenization, and the sheer potential evil of "anything goes." Hence, the pluralistic personality respects the finite human need to be who one is, to take a stand, to make commitments, to define the self—while grasping clearly the risks and losses inherent in free choices, in the necessary self-limitation, and in unchosen alternatives. A swift stream runs in narrow channels. This personality, deep in its own traditions and yet· open to those of others, evokes a new form of morals and religion.

The pluralistic personality could only have come into existence in a nation like our own. It is the distinctive American type. It is the distinctive American gift to civilization. In a book far too criticized along merely partisan political lines, a book of vast conception, *The Cultural Contradictions of Capitalism,* Daniel Bell has written of the need for our civilization to make contact once again with the clear streams of its basic religious impulses. He is not thinking of an instrumentalist use of religion. He means that every vital civilization has an implicit historical scheme, some way of understanding its relation to other civilizations and to the future. It has, as well, some implicit sense of what is sacred, what is truly "being," and what is a waste of time or a diversion. It gives to individuals deep instinctive ("gut") feelings about what is good, right, fitting, appropriate. A pluralistic society like ours, of course, requires a most sophisticated and complex scheme of values, feelings, and visions. But Professor Bell's point is that we cannot pretend not to have such a scheme, or not to need one. We shall have one, willynilly. Either it will be profound, creative, and inspiring of life, or it will be shallow, destructive, enervating and confusing. Have one we shall.

No society as free as ours has ever existed before. The economic system is more open, the social system is more open, and the cultural system is more open than any the earth has ever seen. Consequently, the task of articulating a religious system as open to freedom and choice as our institutional life demands is no modest task. It must be attempted.

This attempt, moreover, cannot take the form of some all-embracing "religion-in-general." There is no such religion. Historical religions, which take history seriously, are particular, embodied, limited. The genius of our culture has been to elicit enormous dynamism out of our religious particularities. Atheist, Protestant, Catholic, Jew (each in several varieties) contribute special impetus to the culture of which we are a part. We learn from each other, without ceasing to be different from each other. Each is check-and-balance to the others. Slackness in one injures all. Massive indifference corrupts all together, and each individual person singly.

It may be wise here to distinguish between two forms of atheism. There is a false form of atheism, which is really a hidden form of belief disguised by dislike for religious institutions and traditions. Such atheists show confidence in progress, history, socialism, science, art, or moral enlightenment. Such atheism is a form of deism. An editorialist's religion, the religion of commencement speakers, its universe is benign and moral. (What do they lack, such humanists, seeking justice and loving the poor and all the rest, but Sunday collections to distinguish them from being Christians?) The religious impulse in American life runs close to the skin among millions who call themselves nonbelievers. Such atheists, in the words of G.K. Chesterton, "do not believe in nothing; they believe in anything"—from Tarot cards, to the environment, to socialism, to the divinization of Me. Tremendous religious energies roam America unmoored. By contrast, the genuine atheist has a sense of what he has rejected and its costs. Such atheism, like true belief, is a long-term project, requiring painful discipline, commanding a long scorching journey through the desert. In such an atheism the human spirit can also be renewed; it carries to the depths. (Between true belief and true unbelief there are many dark parallels; as there are many between happy piety and happy atheism.)

Liberalism can no longer allow itself to be confused with a shallow cosmopolitanism, an easy tolerance, an inexpensive disbelief. The vital human spirit sharpens edges. If one fears organized religion because it is narrow and "divisive," one should also fear the power of the state to become a religion of its own. In all nations, a kind of "civil religion" (Rousseau) develops through the grandeur and ritual of state display. In democratic states, in which church is separated from state—and in the United States, where the sense of developing a "new man" and a "new woman" in a "new world" is acute—this tendency of the state (and its accompanying culture) to develop its own religious symbolism is particularly strong. On the popular level, "the American way" carries religious connotations. On a sophisticated level, moral outrage and the urge for moral reformation prove that the itches of the Puritans live on in consumer advocates, environmentalists, champions of sundry rights, and critics of the nation's failings. Those who evince disdain for organized religion appear to park their unarticulated religious passions wherever they find space.

The problem of values and moral vision in American life is directly related to the problem of choice in education. One's sense of values and moral vision is "grounded" in a world view (atheistic or theistic), not in the sense that a conclusion is "grounded" in a premise, but in the sense that a stage play is "grounded" in a particular cast, a set, a stage, a theater, and spoken lines. World views, like dramatic traditions, have a history. They are concrete. There is no "religion in general," or "ethics in general," or "drama in general." Human cultures in their variety display the record of human liberty, the particularizations that human imagination and ingenuity shape from the materials of human life. Every human being in every culture is born, suffers, loves, dies. There are constants in the human condition everywhere. Yet even the constants—pain, irony, tragedy—are differently experienced through each form of the cultural imagination, are given a somewhat different meaning and a different reverberation in the sensibility. A funeral is not the same in Sicily and in Des Moines.

The attempt of American schools to proceed as if diversity did not exist has deprived the nation of many sources of nourishment for the spirit. If students cannot explore in depth the particularities of the culture of their own homes and linked families, what will be substituted is the thin gruel of "lowest-common-denominator" piety. Students will be graduated morally illiterate. Worse than that, they will have learned no language appropriate to the history and tradition of their own roots. Their own instinctive aspirations and inhibitions will be shortcircuited, stunted, and struck dumb. The contradictions between what they have learned at home, often unconsciously, and what they learn from teachers and peers, television and cinema, will go unnoticed and unexamined. Many will collapse in moral confusion. The allure of whatever morality happens to sway their crowd or their surroundings is likely to seem to them compelling. Thus did Jeb Magruder and John Dean describe the moral imperatives they too easily obeyed, and thus, perhaps, are we to understand the phenomena of sudden conversions and counterconversions sweeping through a confused population.

An education in values and in moral vision can only be conducted if pluralism is respected. Such respect demands that its workings be clearly understood. The pluralistic personality has two strengths: (a) clarity and depth about its own roots and particularity; (b) openness to and interest in sources of strength beyond its own traditions. A system of education designed to nourish the pluralistic personality must itself comprehend the diversity of the moral roots of the American people. It should not attempt to develop a "common culture" that would represent a watering down of each participant culture, but rather a "common culture" that arises out of a shared, common knowledge of the analogies and the differences between moral traditions. To take a thoroughly complex example like abortion, for example: it is not necessary for everyone within the school system to hold the same views; nor for the view of the majority, nor the views of minorities, to be accorded higher status than any other view. But it would be appropiate for all students to understand clearly the history and the forms of life from which present positions on this important public issue derive. Both those in favor and those opposed to abortion would benefit by a clear understanding of the way the world looks from where the other stands. It is an old American tradition to "walk in the other's moccasins a moon" before casting judgment.

The question of choice in education, then, is not only a question of where one chooses to send one's own children to school. It is also a question of what sort of schooling in choice goes on in the schools. One ideal form, particularly appropriate for schools that belong to and serve the whole public, would strengthen two skills: (a) the ability of children to understand, to articulate, and to think critically about the traditions in which they have been reared (and thus to supply some continuity between the home and the school); and (b) the ability of children to detect, to penetrate, to learn from, and to respect the internal power of traditions not their own.

There is, we have seen, an unfortunate tendency in the American public schools to assume that the values and vision of the secular-Protestant upper class of the Northeast represent morality simply, and to imagine that the moral task consists of enlightening the others accordingly. (To speak of a "blue-ribbon" commission is to describe a commission composed predominantly of members of that class, whose presence *ipso facto* bestows moral legitimacy and public trustworthiness.) This tendency runs against the best intentions and traditions of that class, and could not succeed except for the fact that we are each so close to our own moral vision that it always appears to us as the countenance of reality itself; we do what we think is right without noticing how different that appears to others. The cure is *not* to become relativistic, *not* to surrender our values. The cure is to become self-conscious, articulate, and self-critical about our own moral vision; to see both its strengths and its limits; to assess its trade-offs and its losses, as well as its gains. We can be who we are without insisting that others be like us, and without dismissing our own highest standards. For our own most highly developed upper class, too, the pluralistic personality represents a moral gain. The choices of that class, too, need to be deepened and strengthened. The nation would not be served by its loss of nerve, weakening of faith, or lowering of standards. A renewed emphasis on choice in education will help the members of every social class.

This nation is slowly acquiring, then, a public philosophy proper to the composition of its own people. This public philosophy is not a common set of values imposed upon all. It is, rather, a world view patiently acquired through which each participant comes to recognize the diversity of the whole. Even the simplest and most basic of values are understood differently in the light of different traditions. But there are sufficient "family resemblances" among these diverse points of view for skillful citizens to learn a public language for understanding both the self and others. The writers in this book, for example, have not had to be unfaithful to their own visions and traditions in order to speak intelligibly to each other. As the decades go on, the many American peoples discover each other, learn more about each other, and build up, slowly, social devices for attaining a maximum of cultural unity consistent with maximal respect for differences. Unity in diversity is the highest possible attainment of a civilization, a testimony to the most noble possibilities of the human race. This attainment is made possible through passionate concern for choice, in an atmosphere of generous social trust.

APPENDIX A

CHOICE AND INTEGRATION: A MODEL STATUTE

JOHN E. COONS   STEPHEN D. SUGARMAN

In Chapter VI we described the political, legal, and demographic realities limiting the prospects for racial integration in education. The cities appear to be losing their white pupil population. The federal courts are reluctant to order metropolitan desegregation by compulsory interdistrict busing. Unless political forces enter and change the rules by legislation, segregated urban districts will be required by federal law to do what they can on their own, an undertaking which may only accelerate the process of resegregation. Well-drafted state or federal legislation could involve the suburbs; but while the polls support integrated education, the support for "forced busing" among the districts is very thin.

In this context, systems of voluntary transfer could represent a new political option based upon a symbiosis of choice and integration. Public support for integration may well justify an effort to encourage families to choose integrating transfers. At the same time resistance to educational freedom might be blunted; many mistrust the judgment of the poor, but few will publicly prefer segregation to family choice. Thus an important obstacle to choice may at least be neutralized wherever it can be made to harmonize with and to advance integration. There is, in short, political hope for a well-tempered combination of integration and choice.

This hope might be enlarged by the provision of carrots offered to existing institutions. These could include rewards to school districts for integrating their own schools, as well as for contracting with other public districts to provide for voluntary transfers with an integrating effect. In some areas an even more promising opportunity for such transfers would come from the participation of private schools located in or out of a segregated district.

In this appendix we offer a legislative proposal designed to further integration, in part by choice. It would provide dollar bonuses to school districts which achieve integration in a variety of ways ranging from traditional bureaucratic assignment to various voluntary transfer plans. While the prospect of traditional bureaucratic assignment may seem problematic to those who object to compulsion of any sort, it seems to us a pragmatic concession to political reality. But, as indicated, a district need not integrate its own schools through force; it may employ a voluntary transfer plan. Or it might integrate some of its students through compulsory out-of-neighborhood assignment—say, when schools elect to be paired—while at the same time supporting extradistrict integrating transfers by its other students. This illustrates how compulsion and choice can coexist, complementing one another in their effects. Furthermore, conceding that some districts might not take full advantage of the integration bonus program, we have included provisions (in Section 4) by which the family itself holds the key to an integrating transfer.

In California some device of this sort is ripe for legislative consideration because of two decisions of the California Supreme Court, both based on the state constitution and thus in-

sulated from federal review. First, *Serrano v. Priest* has initiated
an unprecedented legislative reexamination of the system of
school finance. The principle adopted by the court has left the
legislature a very wide discretion in its choice of reforms. Hence
change is both necessary and unpredictable in form. Literally
any well-argued and plausible proposal should receive attention
in the next two years. In fact, the model here proposed, in a
slightly revised form, has just been introduced as a bill in the
California legislature.

Second, in *Crawford v. Los Angeles Unified School District,* the
court jettisoned the distinction between *de facto* and *de jure*
school segregation and held the Los Angeles district to be—
simply—segregated. Other urban districts are in the same boat.
The court has not yet decided whether, as a remedy for segregation, state judges should decree compulsory metropolitan (interdistrict) assignments; the trial court judge who must fashion the
remedy in the *Crawford* case is now considering that issue.
Whatever decision is reached about the use of compulsion, it
seems likely that the court could, if it chose, order the Los
Angeles district to seek the cooperation of other districts in
receiving transfers of minority children when these would help
to desegregate both sending and receiving schools.

Minority groups in California are urging the court to make
such use of its equity power to promote voluntary transfers. Indeed, in an *amicus curiae* brief they have gone further, asking the
court to require the defendant district to pay the tuition of
minority children who wish to make integrating transfers to private schools (see Appendix B). This minority perception of the
hope that lies in a system of educational liberty is enormously
significant. Voluntarism is no longer perceived exclusively as a
racist ploy, but as a plausible strategy to desegregate, and to do
so in a way that promises stability and orderly change. The chief
sponsors of the Model Integration Incentive Act now before the
California legislature are black and Chicano legislators.

A MODEL INTEGRATION INCENTIVE ACT

[Introductory comment: This Act commits the state to the payment of bonuses designed to further school integration. The first three sections together present local school districts with financial incentives to provide integrated educational experiences for their students—either in public schools within the district or in other public or private schools. The fourth section (included here in two versions) is intended to give individual families leverage against districts otherwise unwilling voluntarily to provide the experience desired for their children. Detailed commentary follows each section. The data, illustrations, and references to local law are taken from California to give a sense of realism; however, the system is easily adapted to the law and demography of most states.]

Section 1.

Pursuant to regulations to be issued by the Superintendent of Public Instruction, elementary and secondary school pupils shall be classified into five groups: Asian American, Black, Native American, Spanish-surnamed, and Other.

[COMMENT. The five classified groups established by the Act are those commonly employed in California school matters that concern ethnic minority groups. "Other" means white, plus those few additional pupils who might not fit one of the other classifications. It is integration among these five groups that the Act seeks to stimulate. Of course, policymakers might wish to add to or delete from the list; certainly this is likely in states other than California.]

Section 2. Intradistrict Integration Bonuses

(a) Definitions. For purposes of this section,

(1) a pupil is a minority group member if, in his district, pupils of his classified group (see Section 1) do not comprise the largest classified group of pupils attending the public schools in his district;

(2) a school district has a concentration of minority group pupils if two or more of the five classified groups of pupils each constitutes at least five percent (5%) of the pupils attending the public schools in the district; and

(3) a pupil is attending an integrated district school if pupils in his classified group attending his public school comprise no more of the enrollment of that school than the greater of (i) twenty-five percent (25%) or (ii) ten (10) percentage points more than the percentage his classified group represents in the district.

(b) Bonuses.

The Superintendent shall apportion to each school district with a concentration of minority group pupils $500 annually for each pupil who is minority group member in that district and who is attending an integrated district school.

(c) Spending of Bonus.

School districts shall spend all bonus dollars in the individual schools where they are generated; such spending shall be in addition to all other funds to which such schools would otherwise be entitled in the ordinary course of administration.

(d) Regulations.

The Superintendent of Public Instruction shall issue regulations implementing this Section.

[COMMENT. This Section is designed to provide an incentive to local school districts to desegregate their schools without a court order. From the perspective of state-local relations, it is a program that emphasizes decentralized choice. Districts already integrated to any degree will automatically qualify for bonus money; others, it is hoped, will be enticed by the program.

As drafted, a district qualifies for the bonus by sheer body mix, however achieved. It may, for example, simply assign its pupils to schools, giving children and their families no choice in the matter; in some communities the incentive bonus could move the existing political balance to such an imposed solutions. In other districts it is assumed that private choice would be preferred; public schools in such communities would be opened to children from outside the neighborhood whose families decide to make integration-advancing transfers. The transfering minority student will be attractive to white segregated schools because of the new state money he brings; indeed, some such schools could be expected to recruit minority families.

The Section could be limited to programs of family choice, thus excluding from the bonus plan those districts that simply assign children compulsorily on the basis of race. This could be accomplished by adding a proviso to Section 2(b) so that it would read: "The Superintendent shall apportion to each school district with a concentration of minority group pupils $500 annually for each pupil who is a minority group member in that district and who is attending an integrated district school; provided that if a pupil is attending a school that is not his neighborhood school, he is attending with the informed consent of his parent or guardian." (Presumably the Superintendent would issue regulations defining "neighborhood school.") An even further emphasis upon free choice would restrict the bonus to cases of voluntary *transfers* of minority pupils out of their neighborhood school to an integrated school.

The program is "color blind"; the bonus is not paid for the integration of ethnic minorities defined statewide, but for the integration of whatever students are minorities within their local district. That is, bonuses can also be triggered by whites when they are the district minority, as in Oakland.

The program does not apply to districts whose pupils are essentially all members of one ethnic group; there must be first at least 5 percent representation of each of two groups. Once a district qualifies for the program based upon two groups, however, all of its minorities may generate bonuses no matter how few their numbers.

The Section does not actually define an integrated school directly, describing rather the several conditions under which bonuses may be triggered. Thus, under certain circumstances, schools may receive bonuses for some minority group pupils but not for others. Here follow increasingly complicated examples of how the plan would work.

If a district enrolled 65 percent white and 35 percent black students, it would receive $500 each year for every black student attending a school that is 45 percent or less black (that is, the 10 percent overrepresentation rule would apply). If a district enrolled 90 percent Spanish-surnamed and 10 percent white students, then it would receive a bonus for each white student attending a school that is 25 percent or less white (the 25 percent rule would apply). Many districts have three or more groups prominently included so that no group is a majority. In that case, the bonuses apply with respect to students in all those groups except the largest. Thus if the district had 40 percent white, 30 percent Spanish-surnamed, 28 percent black, and 2 percent Asian American students, funds would be distributed with respect to Spanish-surnamed students attending schools with fewer than 40 percent Spanish-surnamed, with respect to black students attending schools with fewer than 38 percent black, and with respect to Asian American students attending schools with fewer than 25 percent Asian Americans. Suppose, then, a school in such a district were 5 percent Asian and 95 percent white; it would receive bonuses for its Asians. Now suppose another school in that district had 5 percent Asian, 50 percent black, 40 percent Spanish-surnamed, and 5 percent white students. It would receive bonuses for its Asian and Spanish-surnamed students, but for *none* of its black, since their percentage exceeds the allowable 38 percent (district-wide percent plus ten).

From these examples it should be clear that the more racially diverse the district, the greater its potential in bonuses. This concentrates funds in districts more likely to find it difficult to integrate. As was illustrated, however, the program applies to any school in an eligible district that qualifies any of its minority students. If desired, a stronger rule could be substituted; for example, one that released funds only if, say, 80 percent of the minority group members in the district qualified for bonuses by attending what for them are integrated schools.

The 25 percent and 10 percent overrepresentation figures are somewhat arbitrary (as is the 5 percent minimum concentration rule) for defining when a student's experience is integrated. Other rules are certainly possible. For example, bonuses could be paid for any minority group member in whose school he is not in the majority. The definition provided in Section 2 seeks instead a rough ethnic balance, considering the character of the district's population, while at the same time permitting modest densities of minority pupils (e.g., 25 percent when a group's district-wide proportion is 10 percent). The latter is likely to be desired by many minority group members in preference to being thinly spread throughout the district. Indeed, this is why the program pays only when minority group members are integrated; an alternate rule might require majority group integration as well. But the policy emphasis here is less upon "total" integration and more upon the objective that minority groups not be isolated in segregated schools; the isolation of some members of the majority seems less worrisome.

The Superintendent would issue rules for determining, among other things, how and at what date (or dates) attendance is to be measured and the counts to be taken of the five classifications. He would, for example, develop rules respecting transiency and transfers within the year. He would also adopt accounting regulations designed to assure that the state funds represent extra dollars for the individual integrated school. Federal Title I rules and other maintenance-of-effort models can be copied here.

Table 1 displays a rough indication of the potential eligibility of a number of California's largest districts. The figures are based on 1973-74 data, the latest currently available. There have been some significant shifts since then, but the general picture is still the same. It is noteworthy that, in a few districts such as San Francisco, blacks have replaced whites as the largest classified group; thus in 1977-78 funds in that district would be generated by the integration of whites but not of blacks.

Total California public school ADA in 1973-74 was 4.5 million. Of that number Native Americans, Asians, black, and Spanish-surnamed totaled 1.35 million. If whites were always the largest group in the individual district and if all districts with minorities had a 5 percent or larger share of minorities, this 1.35 million figure would represent the outside limit on eligible pupils under the Section as it is now drafted. However, since

Table 1

Potential Eligibility for Intradistrict Bonuses

Selected Large Districts	Number of Students[a] (in 1,000s)	Number and Percentage of Students by Classfied Group[b] (number [in 1,000s]/percent)				Number of Potentially Eligible Students (in 1,000s)
		Black	Spanish-surnamed	Asian	White[c]	
Los Angeles	620.0	155.0/25%	155.0/25%			310.0
San Francisco	80.0	24.0/30	11.0/14	20.0/25%		55.0
San Diego	123.0	16.0/13	14.0/12			30.0
Oakland	60.0	(38.0/62)	4.5/8	3.5/6	14.0/24%	22.0
Sacramento	50.0	8.5/17	6.0/13	4.0/8		18.5
Fresno	50.0	5.0/10	12.0/22			17.0
Richmond	38.0	12.0/32	2.5/6			14.5
Santa Ana	27.0	2.5/9	11.0/40			13.5
Pasadena	25.0	10.0/40	3.0/12			13.0
Long Beach	62.0	7.5/12	5.0/8			12.5
San Bernardino	32.0	5.0/16	7.0/20			12.0
Stockton	30.0	4.5/15	7.0/24			11.5
Pomona	20.0	5.5/27	4.5/21			11.0
Hacienda	30.0		10.0/33			10.0
Montebello	24.0		(14.5/60)	1.5/6	8.0/34	9.5
San Jose	36.0		9.0/25			9.0
Alum Rock	16.0	2.0/11	(8.0/50)		6.0/39	8.0
Norwalk	27.0		8.0/28			8.0
Bakersfield City E.	19.0	3.0/16	5.0/27			8.0
Berkeley	14.0	6.0/44	1.0/5	1.0/6		8.0
E. Side Union	17.0	1.5/8	5.5/32			7.0
Riverside	25.0	2.5/10	4.0/15			6.5
Vallejo	15.0	4.0/28	1.0/5	1.5/8.5		6.5
Hayward	24.0	1.5/7	4.5/19			6.0
Garden Grove	50.0		6.0/13			6.0
Sweetwater U.	23.0		6.0/27			6.0
Baldwin Park	12.0		5.0/42			5.0
Total number (in 1,000s)	1,549.0	276.0	307.5	31.5	28.0	644.0

[a]1973-74 data used throughout.
[b]No entries in the black and Asian columns mean less than 5 percent of that group. This omission is a result of data availability; the few in those groups would qualify for bonuses if integrated.
[c]Entries are in the white column only when whites are not the largest group.

neither of these assumptions is true, the potential maximum of eligible pupils is smaller. For example, about 55,000 Spanish-surnamed pupils attended districts in which they were 60 percent or more. (Therefore, these districts might contribute, say, 20,000 non-Spanish-surnamed pupils to the list of potential eligibles.) So, too, about 80,000 black pupils attended districts in which they were 60 percent or more. (Similarly, these districts probably could contribute about 33,000 non-black pupils to the list of eligibles.) In addition, about 144,000 black, Spanish-surnamed, Asian, and Native American pupils attended districts in which they were less than 5 percent. Many of these, of course, would turn out to be in districts that include more than 5 percent of one of some other group and thus are districts eligible to participate. But some would reside in 95-plus percent, hence noneligible, white districts. Roughly, we estimate the total potential pupils in eligible districts to be about 1.2 million in 1973-74. The twenty-seven listed districts in the table account for a little more than half of this number. They also account for (nearly) all the districts in which any minority group has at least 5,000 members; note that one possible means of reducing cost would be to limit the plan to such districts.

Taking potential eligibility at 1.2 million students, the likely cost to the state must be based upon predictions of district integration patterns. It is safe to assume that the $600 million upper limit would not be reached or even approached. One salient fact is that although Los Angeles by itself could qualify in theory for about 25 percent of those dollars, given its 1976-77 attendance patterns and its early response to court desegregation orders it would qualify for very little. What would remain to be seen is how Los Angeles would respond to the bonus plan. By contrast, in San Francisco, given its already well-integrated schools, the district would probably immediately qualify for much of its potential ($27.5 million in 1973-74, although the maximum available dollars would be reduced in view of recent enrollment declines).]

Section 3. Extradistrict Integration Bonuses

(a) Definitions. For purposes of this section,

(1) a qualifying school may be either (i) any public school outside the district of a pupil's residence or (ii) any private school;

(2) a qualifying integrated school is a qualifying school whose tuition-paid pupils do not belong to the classified group that is the largest group in the school;

(3) a tuition-paid pupil is one whose school district, pursuant to this Section, pays his full tuition at a qualifying integrated school.

(b) Permission to contract for tuition.

In order to participate in the program established by this Section, school districts and qualifying integrated schools are hereby authorized to contract for the purpose of providing pupils with an education in an integrated environment, and pursuant to such contracts, sending school districts are authorized to pay an amount equal to the full tuition of the qualifying integrated school; provided, however, that (1) in the case of a public qualifying integrated school, the contract shall be made on its behalf by its school district and full tuition shall be no more than the average expenditure per pupil in the district in which the qualifying integrated school is located; (2) in the case of a private qualifying integrated school, full tuition shall be no more than the full tuition amount charged its other students; and (3) for all qualifying integrated schools, the tuition amount shall be supplemented so that transport of the child to the school shall be guaranteed at no cost to him or to his family.

(c) Bonuses.

The Superintendent shall apportion to each school district $500 annually for each pupil who resides in the district and who is attending a qualifying integrated school as a tuition-paid pupil.

(d) State aid allocation.

A tuition-paid pupil shall be counted as part of the average daily attendance of the school district that contracts for his education at a qualifying integrated school and pursuant to that contract pays the agreed tuition.

(e) Interaction of Sections 2 and 3.

A pupil who is a tuition-paid pupil in a public school under this Section shall not generate an integration bonus paid under Section 2 for any school district. Such pupils, however, shall be

counted in the district where they attend for purposes of determining whether the school of attendance is integrated so as to
generate Section 2 bonuses for its own students.

(f) Voluntary requirement.
   The bonuses provided by this Section shall be paid only with
respect to tuition-paid pupils whose claiming districts have obtained the informed consent from a parent or legal guardian of
the tuition-paid pupil to the contract placement.

(g) Regulations.
   The Superintendent of Public Instruction shall issue regulations implementing this Section.

[COMMENT. This section is designed to provide an incentive
to districts to send students to nondistrict schools in order that
they may enjoy an integrated educational experience. These
"transfers" to both public and private schools may be initiated
by either the family or the local district, but the placement must
be agreed upon by both. In contrast to Section 2, this Section is
not limited to pupils who are minority group members in their
district. Any student may participate in the program and earn
his contracting district a bonus—so long as he is a minority
group member in the school he actually attends.
   The bonus money does not move to the district in which the
integrating child attends; rather, it stays in the district in which
he resides; nor is it given to a specific school, but is for general
use of the district. Moreover, for purposes of other state aid
allocations, his sending district keeps him as its pupil and
receives the aid. Of course, the district must pay his tuition
elsewhere. An alternate financial arrangement is discussed at
the end of this Comment.
   The fiscal *raison d'etre* behind the bonus arrangement in this
Section is to remove the financial pinch a district would otherwise feel at the margin if it shipped out students in this way.
Surely, tuition costs are likely to exceed costs saved by its not
having to educate the child itself; this is especially so where stag-
nant or declining enrollments face the district with the problem
of too many tenured teachers. Therefore, the bonus should not

only relieve the financial bind of the sending district, but hopefully, at least in many places, serve as a clear sweetener. Moreover, the sending district can also protect itself financially by contract, by bargaining about tuition with the receiving districts and private schools, and by favoring those that have low tuition. (Some private schools fall into that category.) Such bargaining and selectivity are permitted by the Section. It is only required that the sending district pay the full tuition in the sense that the family must not be asked by the receiving school to pay any itself—even if it were willing. This protects poor and average families.

A receiving school—public or private—is under no obligation to admit would-be tuition-paid pupils. For such schools, the attraction of a full tuition-paid pupil who would improve the racial balance of the place would have to be incentive enough. Very likely many private schools would welcome such contract students. Public schools seeing nearby private schools choosing to further integration in this manner would probably follow suit, if for no other reason than out of a sense of public duty and embarrassment. Even without that spur, many public schools, especially those with excess capacities, would welcome minority students in their classrooms. Apart from the advantage of integration, the marginal cost to educate the contract student is very likely to be less than the amount of tuition he brings. There obviously is room for some price haggling here between sending and receiving districts. The Superintendent's regulations would, among other things, establish rules for determining the permitted range of tuition payments. In any event, since the receiving school could take just as many minorities as it wished (until they ceased to be the minority), one would expect to see some communities recruit minority families, urging them to induce their own district to permit them to in-transfer their children.

One additional issue is whether to restrict the right of receiving schools to pick and choose among their tuition-paid applicants; for example, it could be provided that once a school accepts any contract pupils under this Section it must do so on a first-come basis so long as there is space.

Sending districts might not be very enthusiastic about farming out students already attending integrated schools in the district. Those students would already attract intradistrict integration bonuses under Section 2, and those bonuses would be lost if they attended elsewhere; thus, the bonus provided by this Section would just keep the district even. The district would be in the position of having to pay full tuition in another place when, as noted, the marginal costs saved by the student's exit would probably be less. Still, there is reason to believe that some such transfers would be made when the district realized that if a family dearly preferred another school, it was probably a better place for the child. Such possibilities would be enhanced if a trade could be engineered; that is, where the sending school discovered there was someone who wished to shift from the receiving school. Furthermore, once a tuition-paid pupil left, this would open up a classroom seat that the sending district might fill with one of its own pupils from another school and thereby earn itself an intradistrict bonus under Section 2.

More commonly, however, one would predict that the contracted students would be those otherwise assigned to schools in which they did not already produce bonuses under Section 2. Although whites would, of course, qualify for transfers to places where they were not the largest group, in practice most of the transferring would probably be done by blacks, Asian, and Spanish-surnamed children. An example of the kind of place where this could easily occur is Los Angeles. Black and Spanish-surnamed children, for example, might find it preferable to integrate nearby suburbs than to attend white-dominated schools that, while in the Los Angeles district itself, are much further away. And in some cases these minorities might find a warmer reception in neighborhoods outside their district; in that event, by cooperating with the transfer rather than employing intradistrict integration, the district is making for smoother and probably more successful integration.

As already noted, Section 3 may be employed to further integration by districts with predominately black and Spanish-surnamed pupils. Oakland is such an example; rather than (or in addition to) trying to spread its less than 25 percent whites around to earn Section 2 bonuses, it might choose to encourage those of its more than 60 percent blacks who desire integration to attend elsewhere.

It might be desirable to impose some requirements on participating private schools. It probably would suffice, however, simply to demand both that they meet the minimum requirements already imposed upon them by state law, and that they agree not to discriminate on the basis of race with respect to the rest of their admissions—their in-transfers being limited by Section 3 to minority group members.

Under Section 3 school districts could, of course, arrange contract placements with religious schools. Some might wonder at the constitutionality of this. It would, however, seem a bizarre interpretation of federal or state Establishment Clauses to conclude that a plan plainly designed to serve the high policy of desegregation has the "primary effect" of aiding religion. Surely the principal impact would be to provide a child with an integrated educational opportunity at a school chosen by his family and his district. That the receiving schools may also benefit from the placement is but an incidental effect. By definition, only its minority students could be tuition-paid pupils. Moreover, were religious schools precluded from serving as hosts for contract placements, not only would this itself raise First Amendment issues—here, Free Exercise rights—but, perhaps more important, it could have the effect of barring minority children from an integrated education. How could the Constitution mean that? Nonetheless, some observers of the U.S. Supreme Court's hostility towards previous modest state efforts in support of family choice in education might feel more comfortable were Section 3 recast in "child benefit" terms; certainly the contracting out concept could easily be modified to embrace that form. In a model statute such cosmetics seem unnecessarily distracting.

The treatment of minority children already enrolled in private schools is a thorny issue. As drafted, the Section would allow a district to contract with respect to all such children—thereby generating for itself both the bonus dollars and regular state aid funds—even though this does not achieve any net increase in integration. This behavior would be most likely to occur in instances in which the cash intake from the state equaled or exceeded the district's tuition costs, since the district would not be educating such children anyway. This is by no means an undesirable outcome—even though it is costly to the state. After all, these are families whose children are doing just what the state's extradistrict integration is designed to reward. Besides, if some, but not all, minority children who reside in the same district and attend a given private school are tuition-paid pupils, this might produce perceptions of unfairness.

Nevertheless, this lack of uniform treatment is plainly permitted by the Section as now drafted. Under the Section a district could, for example, individually size up an applicant family and make a judgment as to whether it would send its child to the private school anyway; on that basis it might or might not decline to contract for his education. If the arbitrariness inherent in such an arrangement seems to raise serious due process concerns, the district might set a specified number of contract students to be placed in a given private school and then award the contract positions by lottery among applicants.

Another tough issue is the propriety and constitutionality of a district deciding that it will only contract for students belonging, say, to one classified group; for example, suppose Oakland agreed to send only its blacks out to schools where they are minorities. Such a racially based rule of exclusion seems insupportable, despite one's initial sympathy for the city's desire to hold onto its relatively few whites. As to those whites who are in basically white schools in Oakland, what is gained by not allowing them to shift to white minority schools elsewhere? Those few whites who are already integrated could be held in place by a more nearly neutral rule that contract arrangements will not be made for anyone presently generating a Section 2 bonus.

Where receiving schools enrolled a large number of contract pupils, the question of just who would qualify as tuition-payable minority groups could be put in doubt. Minorities at some point become majorities. The easiest rule to administer would simply eliminate the bonus if the contract pupils' group became the largest group; with such a clear rule, the sending and receiving schools could contract in their self-interest to police mutual attendance patterns to assure continued entitlement. Of course, the transfer out from the receiving school by the majority group students would threaten an imbalance and a consequent loss of eligibility that is beyond the school's control. Where this occurred, a less draconian rule could be applied to terminate only a portion of the bonus.

It should be understood that under this Section it would not matter whether a student—say, a black student—had been attending a 10 percent black or 90 percent black school; his district would qualify for a Section 3 bonus so long as he had transferred to a school in which blacks were not the largest group. Of course, his district's willingness to agree to such a transfer may depend whether in his current situation he generates a Section 2 bonus. It would, however, be possible to restrict the district's leeway by providing, for example, that bonuses under Section 3 will be paid only for contracts entered into on behalf of students otherwise overrepresented in their neighborhood school—with over-representation measured by their group's proportion in the sending district.

Section 3 could be designed so that (as in Section 2) the receiving school gets the integration bonus and, in the case of a public school, the general state aid money as well; in that event, no tuition would be paid. This version would not be as attractive to receiving private schools, except to those for whom the bonus is as much as their tuition. Its relative attractiveness to receiving public schools would depend in large part upon what portion of their costs are funded by state per-pupil funds and what portion by local funds. If state per-pupil payments plus the bonus exceed what they would charge in tuition, this version would probably be favored; if not, the drafted Section probably would be. It is the position of the sending district that causes the most alarm under this alternate approach, which treats the district as if the student moved away. While in theory one might think that the district's voters generally ought to be happy just to have one less child to educate, in practice the district bureaucracy is not likely to act this way. If the child is treated as having moved, the district loses state per-pupil funds and, given its perceptions of teacher tenure, in effect the district may lose more than it saves. Also, if the pupil is "no longer there," probably no local funds could properly be raised for him; while this may help the voters, for the bureaucracy the financial bind then is even tighter. Put differently, if the bonus is needed to entice the sending district to agree to placement, the alternative version is probably too weak. In short, too many sending districts may not participate.

Yet too much should not be made of this. For if receiving and sending schools can rather cheaply bargain over the amount of tuition actually paid under Section 3 as drafted, and the receiving school can also pay a "placement fee" to the sending school under the alternate version, then the parties could negotiate the same solution regardless of the rule, since the state is paying one per-pupil allotment and one bonus in either case. To be sure, if in each case the per-pupil allotments vary in amount, the districts will want the solution which assigns the pupil to the district with the larger allotment, as this increases the state share; but to the extent that districts are stuck with one rule or another, there are probably as many barriers to effective agreements under one version as under the other. To repeat, however, private school placements—generally cheaper for the state—are more difficult under the alternate version since schools would have no way of reaching a price settlement that exceeded the bonus amount. For that reason alone one might prefer the Section as drafted.

It is impossible to estimate the costs to the state of Section 3 without reliable empirical estimates of the behavior of families and districts. One possibility would be for the state to limit the number of bonuses to a fixed maximum—to be awarded to applying districts on a first come-first served basis—until experience with the program was obtained. Perhaps the maximum for Section 3 should be tied to the use of Section 2. Or perhaps a sum of money could be assigned to Section 3 with the $500 pro-

portionally reduced if applications are made for too many
pupils.]

Section 4. (Version A) The Right to Freedom from Segregation

[COMMENT. Sections 1-3 provide districts with incentives;
they give families no rights (except the right to refuse a contract
placement). This may not be enough leverage to give an integrated educational experience to all pupils desiring it. Section 4,
therefore, is designed to strengthen individual family autonomy.
It is set out in both a weaker form (Version A) and a stronger
form (Version B).]

(a) Definition.
A pupil is assigned to a segregated district school if his
classified group is not the largest in his district and if, in addition, his attendance at such school would not generate an intradistrict integration bonus for his district under Section 2.

(b) Transfer right.
Any pupil assigned to a segregated school may, through his
parent or guardian, request to be transferred to a nonsegregated
public school in his district; if such request is not granted, his
district, at the demand of his parent or guardian, shall be obliged
to contract for his education, pursuant to Section 3 and the rules
thereof, as a tuition-paid pupil in any qualifying integrated
school public or private to which he has been accepted and within which school he will not be a member of the largest classified
group, provided that his classified group is proportionately
smaller in the receiving school than in the sending school; and
provided further that while the contract shall be for his full tuition, it shall be in an amount that does not exceed his district's
average expenditure per pupil.

(c) Information.
The Superintendent of Public Instruction shall assure through
appropriate regulation that, by action of the districts and otherwise, all families shall be informed of the opportunities available
for integrated education under this Section.

(d) Regulations.
The Superintendent of Public Instruction shall issue regulations implementing this Section.

[COMMENT. Version A of Section 4 is designed to force a district to make an integrated educational experience available to any minority group child whose family desires it. This is not guaranteed by Sections 2 and 3. The intradistrict and extradistrict provisions of those sections are not mandatory, and the politics of some district will leave individual minority families in their present assignments. In many cases, families of students who are *minority* group members in the district will genuinely prefer the neighborhood school, even if segregated, to a more distant one. Others, however, may resent the district's inaction, and Section 4 gives them the right to do something about it. In this Version A, the minority group family may first seek an integrated experience in the district's schools—one that will qualify the district for an intradistrict integration bonus under Section 2. If the district has no place available or prefers not to make the assignment, then, provided the family can find a qualifying extradistrict placement open to it, the district is obligated to contract for such placement under Section 3. The full tuition for the child at such placement may not exceed the district's average spending on its pupils. By making the contract, the district will earn the extradistrict bonus provided by Section 3.

Two things about the limited nature of the right established by Version A should be well noted. First it is cast only in favor of those who are minorities in their district. Hence those in the largest group in the district, even if black, Spanish-surnamed, etc., would have no enforcible transfer privilege (although the district still may elect to contract them out under Section 3); their rights are left to the local political process where they should, after all, have some power. Second, if the family winds up exercising the extradistrict option under Section 4, it must select a school in which not only is the child not in the largest group, but in which the proportion of his own group in the new school must be less than in the originally assigned school. Thus, for example, if blacks are 20 percent in the local public school district and the child is assigned to a 40 percent black school, a transfer could be made to a school in which blacks are both not the largest group and less than 40 percent. In that way all transfers under Section 4 would improve racial balance.

Some might wish to make stronger the right under this Section with respect to intradistrict placements. For example, if the district initially assigns the child to other than an integrated district school, perhaps the family should be able to demand placement in *the* integrated district school of its choice, or else be entitled to employ the contracted-out alternative. The need for such a rule, as opposed to the one drafted that allows the district to place the child in *any* integrated school, would depend in large part on how districts reacted to demands under this Section. If they regularly responded with the option to attend very out of the way, thoroughly unfriendly, or plainly lower quality schools—in effect, hoping the family will withdraw its demand—then the stronger rule would be appropriate for this Version A of Section 4. But perhaps much of this bad faith behavior could be precluded, even under current wording, by regulations of the Superintendent.

Minority group students already attending private schools can also make demands under Section 4, in order to try to have their tuition paid for; but in Version A the district can, of course, respond by offering an integrated place in its system.]

Section 4. (Version B) The Right to Chosen Integration

(a) Any pupil may, through his parent or guardian, demand that the school district in which he resides contract for his education, pursuant to Section 3 and the rules thereof, as a tuition-paid pupil in any school, other than the district's public schools, into which he has been accepted and in which he will not be a member of the largest classified group; districts are required to honor that demand so long as his full tuition may be paid in an amount that does not exceed the district's average expenditure per pupil.

(b) Information.

The Superintendent of Public Instruction shall assure through appropriate regulation that, by action of the districts and otherwise, all families shall be informed of the opportunities available for integrated education under this Section.

(c) Regulations.

The Superintendent of Public Instruction shall issue regulations implementing this Section.

[COMMENT. Version B of Section 4 gives a very strong right to all families both to patronize the extradistrict integrated school of their choice and to use that power as leverage to induce the district to provide a more attractive local option. Note that, in contrast to Version A, *all* pupils in any district—not just district minority group pupils—may become tuition-paid pupils, so long as they are admitted to and attend an eligible school. Furthermore, in Version B (again in contrast to Version A) the receiving school need not be one in which the tuition-paid pupil's group is less represented than in his assigned school; the only limit is that his group not be the largest at that school. Version B (provided the tuition is low enough) would make all the minority group members now attending private schools eligible for tuition-paid status. It could also start a serious recruiting drive by numerous schools seeking to attract minority students—and unlike Section 3 alone or Version A of Section 4, the campaign could be directed solely at the family since the cooperation of the sending district need not be obtained.

The ability to force contracting out upon a district under the terms of Version B might be thought to create financial difficulties for some communities. But since the full tuition it must pay is limited to its average expenditure per pupil, the sending district is put more or less in the Section 3 posture which should not be financially difficult for any district; it would gain $500 plus the costs saved by not educating the child, but it would be short the tuition amount.]

APPENDIX B

AMICUS BRIEF SUPPORTING COURT-ORDERED VOLUNTARY INTEGRATION PLAN IN
CRAWFORD V. LOS ANGELES UNIFIED SCHOOL DISTRICT (1977)

H. ELIZABETH HARRIS
Attorney at Law
Education Finance Reform Project
4401 Crenshaw Boulevard, Suite 212
Los Angeles, California 90043
(213) 294-0051

Attorney for:
Robert Farrell
Education Finance Reform Project

SUPERIOR COURT OF THE STATE OF CALIFORNIA

FOR THE COUNTY OF LOS ANGELES

Mary Ellen Crawford, et al.,)) Plaintiffs,)) vs.)) Board of Education of the) City of Los Angeles,)) Defendant.))	No. 822 854 *AMICI CURIAE* BRIEF

TO THE HONORABLE JUDGE PAUL W. EGLY:

On April 1, 1977, this Court granted to Robert Farrell and the Education Finance Reform Project the right to file a brief as *Amici Curiae* in the above captioned matter.

Through the filing of this brief, *Amici* now moves this Court for permission to argue the herein brief and the right to place before this Court evidence which would support *Amici* purposed remedy in the above captioned matter.

This motion is made upon the grounds that the Court's decision in this matter will establish important legal precedent having community-wide impact and affecting the interests of persons other than the parties hereto.

Amici Curiae respectfully submitted May 18, 1977.

By   H. ELIZABETH HARRIS
Attorney for Robert Farrell and
Education Finance Reform Project

Interest of *Amici*

The Education Finance Reform Project (EFRP) was created after the decision in *Serrano v. Priest* (Cal. 3d; P. 2d [1971]). Its purpose was and is, through research and education, to assure that the promise of the *Serrano* decision for educational reform is fully realized on behalf of minority children. The EFRP has participated as *Amicus* in several test cases with significance for the improvement of primary and secondary education.

Robert Farrell is a member of the City Council of the City of Los Angeles. As an individual and official he is deeply concerned both with the quality of city life in general and the quality of education in particular. The task of serving the people of the city is immensely complicated and burdened by the continuation of racial segregation in education.

Introduction

This Court must supervise the desegregation of one of the largest school districts in the country, the Los Angeles Unified

School District (hereinafter LAUSD). The task is rendered discouraging by severe residential segregation and by the unwillingness of LAUSD to offer creative desegregation alternatives. *Amici* here propose to this Court a remedy emphasizing individual choice and cooperation. Insofar as desegregation and free choice are compatible they represent a stable educational order and wise policy.

I. UNDER APPROPRIATE ARRANGEMENTS LOS ANGELES SHOULD BE ORDERED TO PROVIDE TUITION AND TRANSPORT FOR ITS MINORITY STUDENTS WHO CHOOSE TO MAKE INTEGRATING TRANSFERS TO OUT-OF-DISTRICT PUBLIC SCHOOLS OR TO PRIVATE SCHOOLS.

Amici propose that, as part of any remedy in this case, minority families residing in defendant district who seek integrated education in schools other than those of the LAUSD be permitted to exercise that choice with defendant providing the cost of tuition and transport. This right should at least be extended to all those minority children currently attending defendant's segregated schools. Throughout Section I of this brief *Amici* will assume that participation in such a plan by receiving schools would be voluntary. In Section II, *Amici* will alter this assumption and argue that neighboring public school districts are obligated to receive voluntary integrating transfers and to respect and facilitate the choice of their own minority children to make integrating transfers out.

In Section I, frequent reference will be made to three classes of schools: 1. Schools of Defendant Los Angeles Unified School District. 2. Schools of other public school districts in the Los Angeles area. 3. Private schools in and near Los Angeles. For convenience these three classes of schools often will be referred to as "Defendant schools," "Other-public schools," and "Private schools," respectively.

A. IT IS PROBABLE THAT SPACE IS AVAILABLE IN
   BOTH OTHER-PUBLIC AND PRIVATE SCHOOLS,
   THE CHOICE OF WHICH BY MINORITY PUPILS
   WOULD ENHANCE INTEGRATION.

Amici have conducted a preliminary survey of Other-public and
Private schools located within a reasonable distance of predominately minority neighborhoods in Los Angeles hoping to
determine in a rough way the amount of space potentially
available for voluntary transfers by minority students that
would have an integrating effect.

One thing is clear. Whites dominate the student population in
many of the public school districts surrounding LAUSD. Examples of some sizeable districts for which this is true are illustrated in the . . . table [Table 2].

Second, to anyone even slightly familiar with the geography of
Los Angeles, it is obvious that for the bulk of both LAUSD's
black children (those who live in central and south central Los
Angeles) and LAUSD's Chicano children (those who live in
East Los Angeles) many of the districts listed in the table are
physically closer than are the great mass of LAUSD's white
children who live in the San Fernando Valley. Thus, these and
other districts represent a potential for integrated education that
might be far more appealing to minority families than would be
a bus ride to the Valley.

Third, inasmuch as school districts around the state in general
are experiencing declining enrollments, especially in the elementary grades, there is good reason to believe that the type of
district illustrated by those in the table either has or can easily
make available space for additional students.

Fourth, although *Amici* have thus far been able to obtain only
sketchy data, it is nonetheless highly probable that many opportunities for integration-enhancing placements exist in the private schools located both within and outside of the LAUSD
boundaries. There are, for example, more than 250 Catholic
schools under the auspices of the Archdiocese of Los Angeles,
and those schools have more than 100,000 students enrolled in

Table 2

Large Districts with Sizeable "White" Student Population

District Name	Approximate Average Daily Attendance 1975-76	Approximate Percentage "White" 1973-74*
Long Beach Unified	60,000	76%
Torrance Unified	33,000	86
Glendale Unified	24,000	85
Downey Unified	17,000	87
Palos Verdes Peninsula Unified	18,000	95
Burbank Unified	15,000	85
Santa Monica Unified	14,000	74
Centinela Valley Union High	9,000	76
South Bay Union High	9,000	90
Beverly Hills Unified	7,000	93
Redondo Beach Elementary	7,000	85
South Pasadena Unified	4,000	83

*"White" means non-Spanish-surnamed whites. 1973-1974 data is the latest year's racial/ethnic count available to *Amici*.

them. Many of such schools are integrated already; others, it appears, would be happy to be. Since Catholic schools have been hit by declining enrollments, nationally at least, among these two hundred and fifty plus schools there is very likely space for racial balancing transfers. We assume that this reflects the situation in other private schools in the Los Angeles community as well. Whatever space is currently available, that space is likely to increase given present birth rates and demographic patterns; spaces might also increase if new opportunities for integrated private education stimulate the opening of new institutions.

Amici believe that this Court should obtain more precise information by ordering the defendant to determine: (1) About how many places are presently available and are likely to become available in the next five years in Other-public and Private schools? (2) What is the approximate racial composition of such schools with space? and (c) which of these Other-public and Private schools with substantial white majorities would be prepared to receive voluntary minority transfers assuming reasonable tuition terms could be arranged?

This portion of the brief is grounded on the assumption of available classroom space having potential for racially integrating transfers.

B. A PROGRAM OF VOLUNTARY TRANSFERS IS CRUCIAL TO SUCCESSFUL DESEGREGATION

The ultimate constitutional objective is an educational system that remains desegregated after judicial compulsion terminates. The goal is stability, and voluntary integration is the definition of stability. It should be a high judicial priority to secure the opportunity freely to choose among a wide variety of integrated schools. *Amici* believe that if given the opportunity many minority families, properly informed and provided with transport, would make transfers to Other-public and Private schools which would increase integration. Reputation, location, the reception offered and other factors ought to make many of these schools particularly attractive—more so than many

LAUSD schools. The extent of such transfers that would occur could be made a matter of judicial inquiry in the present hearings through the techniques of social science; or the Court could experiment directly with a preliminary order directing the adoption of a system of voluntary transfers for a portion of defendant district. (We postpone the question of the relation between such transfer programs and co-existing involuntary programs).

With stability as the goal, it is important to perceive the special role to be played by Private schools. When integration occurs in a private institution, it has been achieved not only by the choices of minority families, but as well by the free choice of majority families; these remain in the school despite their financial ability to leave. Thus, the decision of a Private school to participate in a voluntary transfer plan would reflect a vote of confidence in integration by the school and its white clientele; the school would be betting its very life upon its capacity to attract families from all races, believing with them that integrated education is superior education. No stronger guarantee of stability can be imagined; private school space is a crucial resource in the building of a permanent solution.

C. THIS COURT IS EMPOWERED TO REQUIRE DEFENDANT TO FACILITATE THE VOLUNTARY ENROLLMENT OF ITS MINORITY PUPILS IN COOPERATING OTHER-PUBLIC OR PRIVATE SCHOOLS UNDER APPROPRIATE CONDITIONS.

The opinions by the Court above both in the instant case and the *San Bernardino* case have clarified the appropriateness of free choice as a remedy for segregation. See *N.A.A.C.P.* v. *San Bernardino City Unified School District,* 17 C. 3d 311, 327-28 (F.N. 19) (1976). In the *San Bernardino* case, the Supreme Court stressed the strong and positive impact of the voluntary "controlled open enrollment" plan. *Id.* at 316. In the instant case the Court above noted the employment of "magnet" schools as an accepted means of desegregation. 17 C. 3d at 305 (text and F.N. 17). It also excoriated Defendant for its failure to make its transfer policy truly voluntary and effective so as to ". . . provide a realistic opportunity for minority children in segregated schools voluntarily to integrate other schools in the district." *Id.* at 307-8.

It is equally clear that this Court may take both Other-public and Private schools into account in fashioning its order. Since the Court above rejected the *de facto/de jure* distinction, the constitutional wrong is simply racial separation; that is, the obligation of the Defendant is not to undo the effects of racist motivation, but " . . . to undertake reasonably feasible steps to alleviate school segregation, regardless of its cause." *Id.* at 292. Plainly the constitutional right of the minority child declared by *Crawford* includes the opportunity for an integrated education if he wishes it. It is not enough, however, solely to make available transfer options within LAUSD. If other schools promise to achieve additional integration by choice, the Defendant surely can be ordered to make that integration possible—even if its realization requires schools other than those it administers. And since *Amici* have assumed that the receiving schools are not being ordered to do anything—they participate voluntarily—the Court can, for this section of the brief, ignore the problems raised by coercive "metropolitan" proposals of the sort considered in *Milliken* v. *Bradley,* 418 U.S. 717 (1974).

Requiring the LAUSD to employ Other-public and Private schools in its remedy, therefore, is plainly consistent with footnote 14 of the opinion above. *Id.* at 303. True, the California justices "have not considered" the matter of an interdistrict *remedy.* But note that their restraint in addressing this question is expressly limited to the *assignment* of pupils—compulsory interdistrict transfers. Programs of outward *voluntary* transfers were ignored in footnote 14 presumably because no one could question their propriety. Such programs would be judged solely by the capacity of free emigration to contribute to desegregation. And, of course in some districts such programs would be the only hope. Where minority children are isolated from majority children by district lines, the alternative to crossing those lines and/or using private schools could be to abandon the enterprise of desegregation *despite its feasibility.* It could not be supposed that this was the Court's intention. Thus, one need take no position on the Court's power to *compel* cross-district transfers in order to recognize the more limited power to provide opportunities outside the district's own schools which the family itself may freely choose.

The propriety of including Other-public and Private schools in a voluntary remedy is further supported by the rejection above of the racial balance rule. *Id.* at 303. The Supreme Court is not interested in quotas; it is interested in equality of opportunity and in genuine desegregation precisely of the sort that voluntary action would entail. Presumably the exercise of freedom of choice would produce schools with minority cadres of various sizes (up to a maximum to be set by the Court). Such an outcome is not only tolerable but wholly desirable.

The *Crawford* opinion supports *Amici's* argument in yet another respect. In rejecting the *de jure* principle, the Supreme Court noted that ". . . retention of a rigid neighborhood school policy would impermissibly grant to private individuals the power to exclude . . . " by their capacity to control residence patterns. *Id.* at 300. Plainly this private power over residential patterns does not stop at district boundaries. Thus, in order to help counteract that power, it is important to reject both LAUSD's "rigid neighborhood policy" and its rigid *district* policy and to allow its minorities to seek admission at both Other-public and Private schools.

Therefore, by the Court's decision, the district has adequate power to contract with other public and private institutions to effect desegregating transfers. Not only would an assertion of *ultra vires* be an inadequate excuse for unconstitutional behavior, but in the present case, there is statutory authority. We note that as a result of the Independent Study Program, school districts are empowered by California law to contract with private persons and institutions to secure all or part of the education of any individual student. See Ed. Code 11251 (a).

D. THE INCLUSION OF PRIVATE ELEMENTS WITHIN

PUBLIC EDUCATIONAL STRUCTURES IS TRADI-
TIONAL AND LEGITIMATE IN CALIFORNIA AND
COULD IN THIS CASE BE THE KEY TO SUC-
CESSFUL DESEGREGATION.

Private schools and other private institutions play various and
important roles in promoting the public policies of California.
For example, the parents of some handicapped children are
given grants by the state in order to enroll their children in private schools and thus alleviate the burden of the public system.
Ch. 8.2 Ed. Code §6871. The training of these children is a function that, in the judgment of the Legislature, cannot be well dis-
charged in all cases by the public schools; the same could be said
in the instant case.

The state also provides scholarships for higher education
which are usable in private colleges and universities. Ed. Code
§41000 et seq. (§40400 et seq. starting in fiscal 1977-78). Thousands of young Californians have thereby been enabled to enroll
at Claremont, USC, Loyola and other private institutions. Other
state scholarships have supported the enrollment of individuals
in private vocational schools. Ed. Code §41400 et seq. (§40410
starting in 1977-78). In 1973, the Legislature also added provisions to the Education Code which permit school districts to experiment with educational vouchers spendable in private
schools under certain conditions. Ed. Code §31180 et seq.

There are constitutional considerations, of course. The
California constitution imposes limitations on the relation between private institutions and the state; and, if religious schools
participate, both state and federal constitutions will be concerned with the nature of the connection. But, as *Amici* will explain, an order employing both private and religious schools as
the state's instruments of desegregation will not violate these
constitutional provisions.

As far as the *private* character of such schools is concerned,
the relevant constitutional language is in Article IX, section 8, of
the California constitution:

No public money shall ever be appropriated for the support of . . .

any school not under the exclusive control of the officers of the public schools; . . . .

This language has never been directly construed by the California Supreme Court. Surely its objective is to preclude appropriations whose *purpose* is to aid private schools. After all, public appropriations to pave streets in front of private schools benefit those schools but are not unconstitutional. Thus, this provision is inapplicable to the proposal here because the public purpose of the remedy does not fall with the prohibition. That is, the purpose of tuition payment is to provide desegregated schooling to plaintiff children, and not to benefit any institution whatsoever.

This provision of Article IX, section 8, has been implicitly construed to this effect by the Court of Appeals for the Fourth District in *Bowker v. Baker*, 73 C.A. 2d 653, 167 P. 2d 256 (1946). There the court approved the expenditure of public funds for busing children to parochial schools. Plainly that program could be said to have the incidental effect of benefitting private schools. Even so, that plan was upheld, for the purpose was not to support the private institution but only the children who wished to use it.

Where the private school being used for desegregation is a *religious* school, four additional constitutional provisions must be consulted. There are the "Establishment" clauses of the state constitution (Article I, section 4) and the federal constitution (Amendment I) plus two parallel provisions of the California constitution relating to schools. These are Article XIV, section 5, and a provision of Article IX, section 8, different from that just discussed. These latter provisions have been analyzed by the Supreme Court and the Attorney General in the same terms as the Establishment clauses. See *Cal. Educ. Facilities Auth. v. Priest* 12 C. 3d. 593 (1974); *Bowker v. Baker, supra;* Ops. Cal. Att'y Gen. 25:214; 29:91; 39:149; and 45:89. Hence all four may be treated for present purposes as equivalent.

Once again the decisive element of the remedy proposed is the character of the purpose to be served. By adopting the proposed order this Court would be pursuing a public purpose of the highest order; it would be employing for a public end an efficient institution that happens to be private and religious. Just as religious schools presently provide services under federal programs for children disadvantaged by family poverty, so may those schools be employed by the state to aid children disadvantaged by race. See 20 U.S.C. §241a et seq; *Wheeler v. Berrera,* U.S. 402 (1974). It would be a bizarre interpretation of either constitution which would close them to a black or Chicano child seeking an integrated education.

This use of private schools may not be rejected because a cost accountant might discover some very indirect aid to religion. No one would deny that, in some remote sense, there would be a "benefit" to the religious institution; else why would it accept the child? But that is not the test. Not every governmental act that benefits a religious school is forbidden; government builds sidewalks, puts out fires, and purifies the air, all to the benefit of these schools. As our Supreme Court recently noted, ". . . . a law which confers indirect, remote, or incidental benefits upon religious institutions is not, for that reason alone, constitutionally defective under either Establishment clause." *Cal. Educ. Facilities Auth. v. Priest,* 12 C. 3d at 600.

The *Priest* case involved a legislative program which permitted private educational institutions to use the authority of a state agency to issue tax exempt bonds. The Court emphasized in *Priest* that no judgment of the establishment issue is possible without considering and weighing the public purpose at stake. With great import for the present case, it emphasized that educational opportunity is fundamental in the scale of constitutional values and noted that ". . . The significant contribution of private schools to providing such educational opportunities is well recognized." 12 C. 3d at 600, citing *Board of Education v. Allen,* 392 U.S. 236 (1968). No doubt lines must be drawn. Yet where the state's purpose is desegration and where the payment to the private school does not exceed the cost to be borne by the school, it would be hard to imagine the proposed order to be an establishment of religion.

Amici concede that there is language in federal decisions which, if taken literally, would embarrass existing California programs as well as what is here proposed. It is enough, however, to note that in every instance in which a program has been struck down, the prominent policy objective and primary effect has been "parochaid"—the provision of economic assistance to struggling religious schools and their clientele. See *Committee for Public and Religious Liberty v. Nyquist,* 413 U.S. 756 (1973). In *Sloan v. Lemon,* 413 U.S. 825 (1973), Justice Powell emphasized that the "State has singled out a class" of users of religious schools "for a special economic benefit. . . .its intended consequence is to preserve and support religion-oriented institutions." *Id.* at 832. And recently in *Meek v. Pittinger,* 421 U.S. 349, 364 (1975), the Court saw the primary intended beneficiaries of certain programs to be "nonpublic schools with a predominate sectarian character." Where, by contrast, the purpose and primary effect is to discharge *the state's own duty to provide desegregated education* the matter stands differently. This is a far cry from programs conceived by sectarian educators, lobbied by sectarian politics, seeding sectarian objectives, and primarily benefiting sectarian schools. Here the protagonists are black and Chicano children seeking their acknowledged constitutional rights.

Indeed, because a state responsibility is involved, the proposed order is not only proper, but could even be constitutionally required. Under the opinion above, the plaintiff children may well have a right to this Court's employment of all relevant educational opportunites. Calkins and Gordon, "The Right to Choose an Integrated Education: Voluntary Regional Integrated Schools—A Partial Remedy for De Facto Segregation," 9 Harv. Civ. Rights-Civ. Liberties L. Rev. 171 (1974).

Providing plaintiffs with a private school remedy is reminiscent of governmental provision of a chaplain or a chapel to soldiers, prisoners or state hospital patients. All these religion-supporting activities withstand attack under the Establishment clause because of (a) the importance of the individual right the government is pursuing—there the right to the free exercise of religion—together with (b) the necessity for the government to act in view of the "captive" status of the individual as a result of governmental action itself. See *Abington School District v. Schempp,* 374 U.S. 203, 226 n. 10 (1963), Ops. Cal. Att'y Gen. 45:89; Ops. Cal. Att'y Gen. 15:214. Here too the right to desegregated education is a fundamental right that defendant has denied, and will continue to deny so long as plaintiffs are assigned to neighborhood schools. See also the opinions of the attorney general upholding loans of public textbooks to religious colleges, Ops. Cal. Att'y Gen. 29:91, and upholding propriety of full-time students in sectarian schools receiving part-time instruction in public school, Ops. Cal. Att'y Gen. 39:149.

There are two further considerations relevant to the Establishment question. The first is merely mechanical or structural in character. An order from the Court presumably would limit the number of minority transfers to any school so as to maintain desegregation. The Court could, for example, forbid transfers into any school beyond the proportion of minority children in the metropolitan area—say, 30%. In that event, no sectarian school could qualify for more than a relatively minor portion of its total budget in public scholarships. And because of numerous state curriculum requirements the cost of the school's expenditure for religious instruction could never approach 70%. Hence, the state would get its money's worth in the purely secular coin of integration and state curriculum.

Nor is the "excessive entanglement" proscription to be feared. Were it necessary, a considerable degree of administration would be excused by the state's own duty to employ these schools to desegregate; but it is plain that very little intrusive administration would in fact be required. Even admissions of minority transfers to private schools could be handled quite separately by the school district. The student would disclose his choice of private school; the district would inform the school and provide the appropriate scholarship. No doubt some additional monitoring would be appropriate but certainly no more than is currently involved in the program for college scholarships and less than in the textbook loan program approved in *Meek v. Pittinger,* 421 U.S. 349 (1975).

E. VOLUNTARY TRANSFER RIGHTS CAN CO-EXIST WITH A COMPULSORY PROGRAM AND EXTEND ITS CAPACITY TO DESEGREGATE.

Compulsory and voluntary programs can articulate in a variety of ways depending upon both the demography of the schools and the manner in which the programs are designed. Suppose, for example, that, by using only Defendant's own schools, it would be feasible, by mandatory busing and assignments, to achieve a minority/white ratio in all schools that reflected the district-wide Los Angeles proportion—about 40% white, 60% non-white. For various reasons—white flight included—this might be thought an unstable outcome. And it would seem particularly imprudent as an *exclusive* remedy if "whiter" Other-public and Private schools stood at hand and availble to accept voluntary minority transfers. If such neighboring schools, for example, were 10% minority and 90% white, a minority transfer program could provide the key to stability in the Los Angeles remedy. To generalize the point, so long as minority children transferred exclusively to schools with a lower percentage of the same minority it would *always* be desirable to add such a transfer opportunity whatever system of initial assignment may be adopted. This is *a fortiori* in the instant case, for racial balance in all the LAUSD schools cannot be achieved.

F. OUTLINE FOR AN ORDER

Whatever else it may order, this Court should require the Defendant to facilitate access on a voluntary basis for its minority students to all desegregating educational opportunities in the Los Angeles area. *Amici* will now outline such an order in a form that runs only against the present Defendant. The order must attend to a number of separable issues such as definition of the class of student eligible for transfer, the responsibility for information and transportation, and other administrative matters.

1. Eligibility Rules: Pupils.

The class of persons eligible for transfer could be defined in a relatively simply two-part rule:

Blacks, Chicanos, and members of other identifiable minority groups shall be eligible for transfer

    a. *From* any school in which their group constitutes a proportion larger than its total proportion in Defendant's schools;
To any eligible Other-public or Private school in which pupils of the applicant's minority group constitute a proportion smaller than that group's total proportion in Defendant's schools.

    b. *From* any school in which white pupils constitute a proportion of the student body smaller than the total white proportion in Defendant's schools;
To any eligible Other-public or Private school in which (1) pupils of the applicant's minority group constitute a proportion smaller than that group's total proportion in Defendant's schools, *and* (2) white pupils constitute a proportion equal to or larger than the total white proportion in Defendant's schools.

[Comment: The basic rule is that minorities that are overrepresented in a school may transfer to schools in which they are underrepresented. However, the refinement in Rule *b* is required where, for example, a school is 80% Chicano and 20% black; the Chicanos could transfer under Rule *a,* but the blacks could not. Hence, Rule *b* permits the blacks to transfer since whites are *under*represented.]

2. Eligibility Rules: Schools.

All schools, Other-public and Private, which meet minimum state standards shall be eligible to receive transferring students under the following conditions:

    a. *Tuition*—The tuition charge shall not exceed the lesser of (1) the per pupil expenditure of Los Angeles public schools of similar grade level, and (2) (i) in the case of Other-public schools, the average per pupil expenditure of similar grade level; or (ii) in the case of Private schools, the tuition charged other students. No additional charges shall be permitted. All receiving schools shall agree to refund the tuition pro-rata if the student subsequently retransfers.

[Comment: In the case of private schools that subsidize all their students, the Court should consider whether it would be fairer to allow actual cost to be charged.

Note that the Court will be unable to control the payment of state aid based upon ADA unless the state is made a party. This is discussed in Part II of *Amici's* brief. Here, we assume the Defendant will continue to receive ADA funds for students who transfer; it can probably protect this outcome by an agreement with the receiving schools that treats the relationship as a subcontract.]

  b. *Admissions*—Admissions should be either on a first-come, first-served basis or—where applications exceed space in the school—on the basis of a random selection among those applying.

[Comment: Other-public and Private schools should not have the opportunity to turn away applicants they find unattractive. If they enter the program, schools should be required to accept those who apply to the extent of the space available.]

3. Affirmative Action by Defendant.

The Court should order the Defendant to facilitate the transfer opportunity in general and in several particulars. *First,* Defendant should be ordered to use its best efforts to stimulate the provision of as many openings as possible by Other-public and Private schools. *Second,* it should be ordered to advertise those openings in an effective manner to the eligible population; its action should include the use of all media and the development of systems of direct personal communication to parents. *Third,* it should be ordered to plan and promptly develop a system of transport to secure efficient travel to the chosen receiving schools. *Fourth,* Defendant should adopt and publicize whatever regulations will support the objective of voluntary integration.

[Comment: Regarding the costs of transportation, if LAUSD is not ordered to provide free transport, at least students should be required to pay no more than they do now.]

II. AS DEFENDANTS ARE ADDED AND/OR REMEDIAL LEGISLATION ADOPTED, TRANSFER OPTIONS MAY BE ALTERED AND EXTENDED BY THE COURT.

Amici have thus far assumed that the Los Angeles Unified School District would remain the sole defendant subject to the Court's remedial power. Plainly, this could change; under the theory of the opinion above, both the state and neighboring districts are potential defendants. With the requirement of racial motivation absent, the extent of racial separation becomes the only constitutional inquiry. The proof or disproof of this illegal condition requires only racial headcounts in the schools of neighboring districts; in this section it will be assumed that such headcourts would show additional districts to be so segregated. It is not too early, then, to consider what desegregating role might be played by voluntary transfers under an order of this Court binding all those districts found with Los Angeles to be cotenants of a zone of segregation.

Setting fiscal consequences to one side, it appears that, with certain adjustments, the remedy suggested in Part I of this brief would respond effectively to the multidistrict wrong. Two main alterations would be required. First, the other districts would cease to be voluntary participants in the transfer plan; they would be required to accept minority students wishing to transfer to their white majority schools, at least where space is available. Indeed, it would be appropriate for each receiving district to be ordered to make room for minority transfers to at least a certain percent—say 10%—of its total enrollment. Second, the order suggested in Part I could be made reciprocal, each district being required to afford its overrepresented minorities, if any, the option to transfer out.

In shifting to a voluntary interdistrict remedy, there is another element the Court would need to consider. At least until the Legislature adopts a new school finance system, interdistrict spending differences and differences in state subventions based upon ADA would require a decision locating responsibility for the transferring child's tuition and transportation. This issue is not so complex as it first appears. The rule suggested in Part I could apply to all transfers in which the receiving institution is a public school. Tuition would be paid by the sender but limited to the lesser of the average per pupil expenditures of the two districts. The sending district would continue to receive the state aid. For transfers from lower spending to higher spending districts—transfers which could no longer be refused—such a solution could sometimes impose a modest burden on the receivers, though the marginal cost of the extra students actually incurred by such districts would depend greatly upon numbers and other factors. Indeed, in the typical case, it would be the sending districts who would face net losses when students transferred out; costs saved might well not equal the tuition charge incurred. Perhaps the best solution, short of new legislation, would be for the State Department of Education, either on its own motion or as an impleaded defendant to assume regulation of the fiscal aspects of transfers. It is precisely the kind of technical administrative responsibility that should be assigned to a party accountable to the Court but standing in a disinterested relationship to the districts whose interests are in conflict.

The Department also could be useful in proposing to the Court common and intelligible standards to be applied to all defendants. It could, for example, suggest criteria by which the capacity of schools is to be measured; it could also assist the Court, the districts and the private schools in designing and implementing a system of transport consistent with the aims of the Court's order. Equally important the Department could act as the central agency for assembling and disseminating information about space available and about other information regard-

ing schools and transportation; the information system would
be crucial to parents and children in a voluntary program. The
Department could also be ordered to propose to the Court (and,
given approval, to seek from federal authorities) whatever adjustments would be necessary and permitted under federal law
in order to distribute fairly the moneys available under federal
programs.

Finally, whoever the defendants may be, this Court should
design its order with concern for the possibility that relevant
proposals of the sort now before the Legislature may become
law. S.B. 1064 (Greene), if adopted, would provide to all the districts of California a structure of dollar incentives to carry out
programs of integration, voluntary and involuntary, within and
outside the district in both public and private schools. Under SB
1064, the employment of this range of legislated devices might
be discretionary to the district at least in part. It would, however,
be the prerogative of this Court to require the effective employment of such devices by those districts that are subject to its
order to desegregate.

Amici take no position here on the propriety of desegregation
by crossdistrict compulsory assignments. Plainly, arguments
make in this brief support the Court's power to order such a
remedy and suggest that, under some circumstances, the Court
has the duty to do so. Nevertheless, *Amici* respectfully recommend that the Court hold such an interdistrict order in abeyance
to observe first the results of the voluntary interdistrict program
here proposed.

NOTES

I. Marvin Lazerson: "Consensus and Conflict in American Education: Historical Perspectives"

1. On the reorganization of work at the turn of this century, Oscar and Mary Handlin (1975, p. 149) have written,

> Only military officers and the masters of plantations had previously dealt with numbers in the hundreds; and their management experience, grounded on the threat of coercion, did not fit the circumstances of a labor force which was not servile.

II. John P. O'Dwyer: "Classroom Collage: One Perspective"

1. Shapiro includes a discussion of her research into space and behavior in the classroom.

2. Class size in Lodi, California, is determined on the basis of "weighted factors" which consider the special needs of some children.

3. The concept of cross-fertilization has been a major factor in eliminating ability/achievement tracking from California schools.

4. As part of the grant application procedure for state and federal monies, districts are required to prepare a community/school "needs assessment." Much of the community-related data throughout this chapter is drawn from a 1975 needs assessment done in my district.

5. A higher incidence of physical problems is to be expected among kindergarten students (1976-1977). Speech, vision, gross motor, and dominance problems are often developmental in nature and disappear with maturity.

6. Estimate was derived by multiplying the district per pupil expenditure by the average enrollment and adding the class share of special project monies.

7. Control, of course, varies from district to district. Teachers frequently serve on hiring, text selection, grant application, and student placement committees, either in an advisory capacity or as voting members. Membership, however, may be mandatory, district-wide, and without regard for qualifications or compensation.

8. The administration may argue that the existence of Parent Advisory Committees, parent education, and classroom volunteer programs serve this purpose. None of these, though, serves the function of helping parents establish specific goals for their child.

IV. Nathan Glazer: "Public Education and American Pluralism"

1. The main themes of cultural pluralism, as presented by Kallen and Bourne, were first published as magazine articles early in World War I. The best account of the developments of American attitudes toward diversity in the period since, roughly, the turn of the century is that by Higham (1975).

2. See Christian (1971) for a full bibliography of Adamic's many publications.

3. I do not know of a general history of the intercultural education movement, but Goodenow (1975) gives a good account of that part of the movement that was linked to the progressive education movement, along with important references in his footnotes. Some of the works preparing curricula or evaluating work in the schools included that of Vickery and Cole (1943), with a foreword by William Heard Kilpatrick, which listed in its introductory pages eight other books that were being prepared for the Service Bureau for Intercultural Education as part of "Problems in Race and Culture in American Education: A Series of Teachers' Manuals and Resource Units." I am not sure all were published. In the American Council of Education was to be found a unit dealing with Intergroup Education in Cooperating Schools; those listed under IECS 1949, 1951, 1952, all had Hilda Taba as first author.

4. The quotation from Herman (1974) is taken from the full statement published in the *Bulletin* of the American Association of Colleges of Teacher Education, November 1972.

5. These documents are quoted from a convenient compilation made by the Center for Law and Education (CLE), Cambrige, Mass., published in December 1975.

V. Richard E. Wagner: "American Education and the Economics of Caring"

1. The replacement of tuitions by taxes is documented in West 1967, 1975.

2. For an examination of some these implications as they pertain to the inheritance of material wealth, see Wagner 1977.

3. For particularly valuable surveys of education in ancient Greece, see Castle 1965, and Marrou 1960.

4. On some of these matters of choice and knowledge, see Staaf 1976.

5. This general theme about competition and monopoly in government is explored in Wagner [forthcoming].

6. For some general treatments of the problem of monopoly in government, see Breton 1974; Niskanen 1971, 1975; Wagner and Weber 1975.

7. See the general conceptual discussion in Alchian 1965.

VI. John E. Coons and Stephen D. Sugarman: "A Case for Choice"

1. This chapter is drawn in part from our forthcoming volume, *Choice*. The authors gratefully acknowledge the generous support of the Ford Foundation and the Carnegie Corporation of New York made available through the Childhood and Government Project, University of California, Berkeley.

2. See *Pierce v. Society of Sisters,* 268 U.S. 510 (1925).

3. For a sense of how that system has operated and its impact upon racial clustering, see the symposium, "The Courts, Social Science, and School Desegregation," *Journal of Law and Contemporary Problems* 39 (1975): 1-431.

4. The classic study of the limitations and biases of counseling is Cicourel and Kitsuse (1963).

5. *Hobsen v. Hansen*, 327 F. Supp. 844 (D.D.C. 1971); and see Kirp (1973).

6. Our own research has identified substantial positive effects from additional voluntary programs in Richmond and San Bernardino, Cal., Portland, Ore., Milwaukee, Wis., and elsewhere.

7. See also U. S. Commission on Civil Rights, *Statement on Metropolitan Desegregation* (1977). and Coleman, "School Desegregation and Loss of Whites from Large Central-City School Districts" (unpublished).

8. *Village of Arlington Heights v. Metropolitan Housing Development Corp.*, 97 Sup.Ct. 555 (1976); *Milliken v. Bradley*, 418 U.S. 717 (1974); *Spangler v. Pasadena Unified School District*, 427 U.S. 424 (1976).

9. Coons and Sugarman (1071) give a detailed statutory model of intervention.

10. This is a primary fault of the widely publicized suggestion of Friedman (1962).

11. See old Section 214 and new Section 44A of the Internal Revenue Code.

12. See Appendix to this volume.

13. *Goss v. Lopez*, 419 U.S. 565 (1975); *Wood v. Strickland*, 420 U.S. 308 (1975).

14. See e.g. the system specified in Coons and Sugarman 1971, pp. 30-32.

15. 18 Cal. 3d 728, 557 P. 2nd 929 (1976).

IX. Andrew M. Greeley: "Freedom of Choice: 'Our Commitment to Integration.' "

1. Another question, beyond the scope of this article and completely free from the issue of racial integration, is how do we educate the children of the very poor and deprived? Suffice it to say that the educational technology currently available to the public school monopoly has shown itself quite incapable of dealing with the problem.

2. My own personal conviction, incidentally, is that this should also be true of private schools, including religious schools. They should all be under some constraint (not necessarily court-ordered) to actively recruit students from minority groups.

3. In this paper the assumption is that integration will be between black and white; but there is no reason in principle why the voucher system described above could not be expanded to include other minorities.

X. R. Kent Greenawalt: "Voucher Plans and Sectarian Schools: The Constitutional Problem"

1. For those interested in referring to cases cited in this article, I am listing the cases alphabetically with full citations:

> *Abington School District v. Schempp*, 374 U.S. 203 (1963)
> *Board of Education v. Allen*, 392 U.S. 236 (1968)
> *Committee for Public Education and Religious Liberty v. Nyquist*, 413 U.S. 756 (1973)
> *Everson v. Board of Education*, 330 U.S. 1 (1947)
> *Hunt v. McNair*, 413 U.S. 734 (1973)
> *Lemon v. Kurtzman*, 403 U.S. 602 (1971)
> *Levitt v. Committee for Public Education*, 413 U.S. 472 (1973)
> *Meek v. Pittinger*, 421 U.S. 349 (1975)
> *Soan v. Lemon*, 413 U.S. 825 (1973)
> *Tilton v. Richardson*, 403 U.S. 672 (1971)
> *Walz v. Tax Commissioner*, 397 U.S. 664 (1970)

XI.   Denis P. Doyle: "The Politics of Choice: A View from the Bridge"

1. An earlier article by Jencks in the *Saturday Evening Post* made some of the same points, but it seems that no one at OEO read the *Post* (or admitted to it.)

2. Though education is the constitutional responsibility of the state, with few notable exceptions (such as Title I, the federal compensatory program for disadvantaged children) most educational activities in this country are in the hands of locally selected boards of education. In addition to this sharp political decentralization, there is little federal financial support for lower education. Of the total elementary and secondary school cost, the federal government pays for less than 8 percent—which, for the most part, is targeted to specific populations. Moreover, the biggest federal program, Title I, may be more accurately conceptualized as a civil rights than an education program.

REFERENCES

AASA (American Association of School Administrators). 1947. *From Sea to Shining Sea: Administrators Handbook in Intercultural Education.* Washington, D.C.: AASA.

Adamic, Louis. 1940. *From Many Lands.* New York: Harper.

————. 1938. *My America, 1928-1938.* New York: Harper.

————. 1945. *A Nation of Nations.* New York: Harper.

————. 1942. *What's Your Name?* New York: Harper.

Ahlbrandt, Roger. 1973. Efficiency in the Provision of Fire Services. *Public Choice* 16.

Alchian, Armen A. 1965. Some Economics of Property Rights. *Il Politico* 30.

Anderson, James D. 1973. Education for Servitude: The Social Purposes of Schooling in the Black South, 1870-1930. Doctoral dissertation, University of Illinois.

Armor, David J. 1972. The Evidence on Busing. *The Public Interest* 90.

Axtell, James. 1974. *The School upon a Hill: Education and Society in Colonial New England.* New Haven: Yale University Press.

Banfield, Edward. 1958. *The Moral Basis of a Backward Society.* New York: Free Press.

Barker, Ernest, ed. and trans. 1946. *The Politics of Aristotle.* Oxford: Oxford University Press.

Barton, Josef. 1975. *Peasants and Strangers: Italians, Rumanians and Slovaks in an American City, 1890-1950.* Cambridge: Harvard University Press.

Beecher, Lyman. 1835. *Plea for the West.* Cincinnati: Truman and Smith.

Bell, Robert R. 1975. Waiting on the Promise of Brown. *Journal of Law and Contemporary Problems* 39.

Bodnar, John. 1976. Materialism and Morality: Slavic-American Immigrants and Education, 1890-1940. *Journal of Ethnic Studies* 3.

Bond, Horace Mann. 1969. *Negro Education in Alabama: A Study in Cotton and Steel.* New York: Octagon.

Borcherding, Thomas E., ed. Forthcoming. *Budgets and Bureaucrats.* Durham, N.C.: Duke University Press.

Bourne, Randolph. 1956. Trans-National America. In *The History of a Literary Radical and Other Papers.* Reprint. New York: Russell and Russell.

Bowles, Samuel, and Gintis, Herbert. 1976. *Schooling in Capitalist America: Educational Reform and the Contradictions of Economic Life.* New York: Basic Books.

Breton, Albert. 1974. *The Economic Theory of Representative Government.* Chicago: Aldine.

Bromsen, A. 1935. The Public School's Contribution to the Maladaptation of the Italian Boy. In *Greenwich Village, 1920-1930,* ed. Caroline F. Ware. Boston: Houghton Mifflin.

Buchanan, J., and Tullock, G. 1962. *The Calculus of Consent.* Flint, Mich.: University of Michigan Press.

Carlson, Robert A. 1975. *The Quest for Conformity: Americanization through Education.* New York: John Wiley.

Castle, Edgar B. 1965. *Ancient Education and Today.* Baltimore: Penguin Books.

Christian, Henry Arthur. 1971. *Louis Adamic: A Checklist.* Kent, Ohio: Kent State University Press.

Cicourel, Aaron, and Kitsuse, John I. 1963. *The Educational Decision Makers.* New York: Bobbs.

Civil Rights, U.S. Commission on. 1977. *Statement on Metropolitan School Desegregation.* Washington, D.C.: Government Printing Office.

CLE (Center for Law and Education). 1975. *Bilingual-Bicultural Education: A Handbook for Attorneys and Community Workers.* Cambridge, Mass.: CLE.

Cohen, David K. 1970. Immigrants and the Schools. *Review of Educational Research* 40.

Coleman, James S. 1975. School Desegregation and Loss of Whites from Large Central-City School Districts. Consultation to the U.S. Commission on Civil Rights, 8 December, Washington, D.C.

——et al. 1966. *Equality of Educational Opportunity.* 2 vols. Washington, D.C.: Department of Health, Education and Welfare.

Coons, John E. 1976a. Law and the Sovereigns of Childhood. *Phi Delta Kappan* (September).

———. 1976b. The Rise of the Parental Class. *Phi Delta Kappan* (October).

———, and Sugarman, Stephen D. Forthcoming. *Choice.* N.p.

———. 1971. *Family Choice in Education.* Berkeley, Ca.: Institute of Government Studies.

Covello, Leonard. 1967. *The Social Background of the Italo-American School Child.* Leiden, Netherlands.

Cross, Robert D. 1965. Origins of the Catholic Parochial Schools in America. *American Benedictine Review* 16.

Davies, David G. 1971. The Efficiency of Public Versus Private Firms: The Case of Australia's Two Airlines. *Journal of Law and Economics* 14.

Dawley, Alan. 1976. *Class and Community: The Industrial Revolution in Lynn.* Cambridge, Mass.: Harvard University Press.

———, and Faler, Paul. 1976. Working Class Culture and Politics in the Industrial Revolution: Sources of Loyalism and Rebellion. *Journal of Social History* 9.

DeLoria, Vine. 1970. *Custer Died for Your Sins.* New York: Avon.

Demos, John. 1970. *A Little Commonwealth: Family Life in Plymouth Colony.* New York: Oxford University Press.

Elson, Ruth Miller. 1964. *Guardians of Tradition: American Schoolbooks of the Nineteeth Century.* Lincoln, Neb.: University of Nebraska Press.

Farley, Frank H. 1975. Residental Segregation and Its Implication for School Integration. *Journal of Law and Contemporary Problems* 39.

Fiss, Owen. 1975. The Jurisprudence of Busing. *Journal of Law and Contemporary Problems* 39.

Friedman, Milton. 1962. *Capitalism and Freedom.* Chicago: University of Chicago Press.

Genovese, Eugene D. 1974. *Roll, Jordan, Roll: The World the Slaves Made.* New York: Pantheon.

————. 1969. *The World the Slaveholders Made.* New York: Pantheon.

Goodenow, Ronald K. 1975. The Progressive Educator, Race and Ethnicity in the Depression Years: An Overview. *History of Education Quarterly* 15.

Graglia, Lino A. 1976. *Disaster by Decree: The Supreme Court Decisions on Race and the Schools.* Ithaca, N.Y.: Cornell University Press.

Graham, Patricia Albjerg. 1975. *The Community and Class in American Education, 1865-1918.* New York: John Wiley.

Greeley, Andrew M., McCready, William C., and McCort, Kathleen. 1976. *Catholic Schools in a Declining Church.* Kansas City, Mo.: Sheed and Ward.

Greeley, Andrew M, and Rossi, Peter H. 1966. *The Education of Catholic Americans.* Chicago: Aldine.

Gutman, Herbert G. 1973. Work, Culture, and Society in Industrializing America, 1915-1919. *American Historical Review* 78.

Hall, G., et al. 1972. *A Guide to Education Performance Contracting.* R-955/1-HEW. Santa Monica, Ca.: The Rand Corporation.

Handlin, Mary, and Handlin, Oscar. 1975. *The Wealth of the American People.* New York: McGraw-Hill.

Harlan, Louis R. 1972. *Booker T. Washington: The Making of a Black Leader, 1856-1901.* New York: Oxford University Press.

————. 1969. *Separate and Unequal.* New York: Atheneum.

Hendrick, Irving G. 1976. Federal Policy Affecting the Education of Indians in California 1849-1934. *History of Education Quarterly* 16.

Herman, Judith, ed. 1974. *The Schools and Group Identity: Educating for a New Pluralism.* New York: Institute on Pluralism and Group Identity.

Higham, John. 1958. Another Look at Nativism. *Catholic Historical Review* 44.

————. 1975. Ethnic Pluralism in Modern American Thought. In *Send These to Me: Jews and Other Immigrants in Urban America.* New York: Atheneum.

IECS (Intergroup Education in Cooperating Schools). 1951. *Diagnosing Human Relations Needs.* Washington, D.C.: American Council of Education.

————. 1952. *Intergroup Education in Public Schools.* Washington, D.C.: American Council of Education.

Jones, Douglas L. 1975. The Strolling Poor: Transiency in Eighteenth Century Massachusetts. *Journal of Social History* 8.

Jowett, Benjamin, ed. and trans. 1892. The Republic. In *The Dialogues of Plato.* Vol.1. London: Macmillan.

Kaestle, Carl. 1974. *The Evolution of an Urban System: New York City, 1750-1850.* Cambridge, Mass.: Harvard University Press.

Kallen, Horace M. 1924. *Culture and Democracy in the United States.* New York: Boni and Liveright.

Katz, Michael B. 1971. *Class, Bureaucracy and Schools: The Illusion of Educational Change in America.* New York: Praeger.

———. 1976. The Origins of Public Education: A Reassessment. *History of Education Quarterly* 16.

———. 1975. *The People of Hamilton, Canada West.* Cambridge, Mass.: Harvard University Press.

Kerber, Linda K. 1975. The Abolitionist Perception of the Indian. *Journal of American History* 62.

Kirp, David L. 1973. Schools as Sorters: The Constitutional and Policy Implications of Student Classification. *University of Pennsylvania Law Review* 121.

Klitgaard, Robert, and Hall, George. 1973. *Are There Unusually Effective Schools?* Santa Monica, Ca.: The Rand Corporation.

Lazerson, Marvin. 1971. *Origins of the Urban School: Public Education in Massachusetts, 1870-1915.* Cambridge, Mass.: Harvard University Press.

———, and Grubb, W. Norton. 1974. *American Education and Vocationalism: Documents in the History of Vocational Education, 1870-1970.* New York: Teachers College Press.

Litwack, Leon. 1961. *North of Slavery: The Negro in the Free States, 1790-1860.* Chicago: University of Chicago Press.

McAdams, Tony. 1974. Can Open Enrollment Work? *The Public Interest* 69.

McCready, W., and McCready, N. 1973. Socialization and the Persistence of Religion. *Concilium* (January).

Marrou, Henri I. 1960. *Histoire de l'education dans l'antiquite.* 5th ed. Paris: Editions du Seuil.

Meier, August, and Rudwick, Elliot M. 1967a. Early Boycotts of Segregated Schools: The East Orange, New Jersey, Experience, 1899-1906. *History of Education Quarterly* 7.

———. 1967b. Early Boycotts of Segregated Schools: The Alton, Illinois, Case, 1897-1908. *Journal of Negro Education* 36.

Mnookin, R. 1975. Child Custody Adjudication: Judicial Functions in the Face of Indeterminacy. *Journal of Law and Contemporary Problems* 39.

Monroe, Paul. 1970. *A Textbook in the History of Education* [1905]. New York: AMS Press.

Morrissey, Timothy H. 1975. Archbishop John Ireland and the Faribault-Stillwater School Plan of the 1890's: A Reappraisal. Doctoral dissertation, University of Notre Dame.

NAC (National Advisory Council on Bilingual Education). 1976. *Second Advisory Report.* Washington, D.C.: NAC.

———. 1942. *Americans All: Studies in Intercultural Education.* Washington, D.C.: Department of Supervisors and Directors of Instruction.

NEA (National Education Association). 1968. *Class Size: A Research Summary.* Washington, D.C.: NEA, Research Division.

Nicols, Alfred. 1967. Stock Versus Mutual Savings and Loan Associations: Some Evidence of Differences in Behavior. *American Economic Review, Proceedings* 57.

Niskanen, William A. 1971. *Bureaucracy and Representative Government.* Chicago: Aldine.

——. 1975. Bureaucrats and Politicians. *Journal of Law and Economics* 18.

Ohlson, Audrey. 1977. Lodi Teachers Win Class Size Battle. *OTA/NEA Action* (18 March).

Olneck, Michael R., and Lazerson, Marvin. 1974. The School Achievement of Immigrant Children: 1900-1930. *History of Education Quarterly* 14.

Olson, M. 1965. *The Logic of Collective Action.* Cambridge, Mass.: Harvard University Press.

Pettigrew, Thomas, Useem, Elizabeth, et al. 1973. Busing: A Review of the "Evidence." *The Public Interest.*

Public Policy, Center for Study of. 1970. *Educational Vouchers.* Washington, D.C.

Ravitch, Diane. 1974. *The Great School Wars: New York City, 1805-1973.* New York: Basic Books.

Rothman, David J. 1971. *The Discovery of the Asylum: Social Order and Disorder in the New Republic.* Boston: Little, Brown.

Rudolph, Frederick, ed. 1965. *Essays on Education in the Early Republic.* Cambridge, Mass.: Harvard University Press.

Sanders, James W. 1976. *The Education of an Urban Minority: Catholics in Chicago, 1833-1965.* New York: Oxford University Press.

Schlossman, Steven L. 1974. The "Culture of Poverty" in Ante-Bellum Social Thought. *Science and Society* 38.

Schultz, Stanley K. 1973. *The Culture Factory: Boston Public Schools, 1789-1860.* New York: Oxford University Press.

Scott, Joan W., and Tilly, Louise A. 1975. Women's Work and the Family in Nineteenth-Century Europe. *Comparative Studies in Society and History* 17.

Shanabruck, Charles H. 1975. The Catholic Church's Role in the Americanization of Chicago's Immigrants: 1833-1928. Doctoral dissertation, University of Chicago.

Shapiro, Silvia. 1975. Some Classroom ABC's: Research Takes a Closer Look. *Elementary School Journal* (April).

Shapson, Stanley M. 1972. *Optimum Class Size: A Review of the Literature.* Toronto: Board of Education.

Sizer, Theodore, and Whitten, Phillip. 1968. A Proposal for a Poor Children's Bill of Rights. *Psychology Today* 2.

Smith, Timothy L. 1967. Protestant Schooling and American Nationality, 1800-1850. *Journal of American History* 53.

Spann, Robert M. Forthcoming. Public Versus Private Provision of Governmental Services. In *Budgets and Bureaucrats,* ed. Thomas E. Borcherding. Durham, N.C.: Duke University Press.

Staaf, Robert J. 1976. Political Economy and the Right to Choose: Public Education. In *Financing Public Schools in Virginia,* ed. Stephen B. Thomas. Vol. 5. Madison, Va.: Virginia Institute for Educational Finance.

Stewart, Richard B. 1975. The Reformation of American Administrative Law. *Harvard Law Review* 88.

Stolarik, Marian Mark. 1974. Immigration and Urbanization: The Slovak Experiences, 1870-1918. Doctoral dissertation, University of Minnesota.

Sugarman, Stephen D. 1974. Family Choice: The Next Step in the Quest for

Equal Educational Opportunity? *Journal of Law and Contemporary Problems* 38.

————, and Kirp, David L. 1975. Rethinking Collective Responsiblity for Education. *Journal of Law and Contemporary Problems* 39.

Taba, Hilda, and Van Til, William. 1945. *Democratic Human Relations: Promising Practices in Intergroup and Intercultural Education in the Social Studies.* Washington, D.C.: National Council for the Social Studies.

Thomas, Stephen B., ed. 1976. *Financing Public Schools in Virginia.* Madison, Va.: Virginia Institute for Educational Finance.

Troen, Selwyn. 1975. *The Public and the Schools: Shaping the St. Louis System, 1838-1920.* Columbia, Mo.: University of Missouri Press.

Tuerck, David G., ed. Forthcoming. *The Political Economy of Advertising.* Washington, D.C.: American Enterprise Institute.

Tyack, David B. 1966. The Kingdom of God and the Common School: Protestant Ministers and the Educational Awakening in the West. *Harvard Educational Review* 38.

————. 1974. *The One Best System: A History of American Urban Education.* Cambridge, Mass.: Harvard University Press.

————. 1967. *Turning Points in American Educational History.* Waltham, Mass.: Blaisdell Publishing Company.

Unger, R. 1975. *Knowledge and Politics.* New York: Free Press.

Vecolli, Rudolph J. 1964. *Contadini* in Chicago: A Critique of *The Uprooted. Journal of American History* 51.

————. 1969. Prelates and Peasants: Italian Immigrants and the Catholic Church. *Journal of Social History* 2.

Vickery, William E., and Cole, Stewart G. 1943. *Intercultural Education in American Schools: Proposed Objectives and Methods.* Foreword by William Heard Kilpatrick. New York: Harper.

Wagner, Richard E. Forthcoming. Advertising and the Public Economy: Some Preliminary Ruminations. In *The Political Economy of Advertising,* ed. David G. Tuerck. Washington, D.C.: American Enterprise Institute.

————. 1977. *Inheritance and the State: Tax Principles for a Free and Prosperous Commonwealth.* Washington, D.C.: American Enterprise Institute.

————, and Weber, Warren E. 1975. Competition, Monopoly, and the Organization of Government in Metropolitan Areas. *Journal of Law and Economics* 18.

Ware, Caroline F. 1935. *Greenwich Village, 1920-1930.* Boston: Houghton Mifflin.

Washington, Booker T. 1963. *Up from Slavery.* Reprint. New York: Bantam.

West, E.G. 1975. *Education and the Industrial Revolution.* London: B.T. Batsford.

————. 1967. The Political Economy of American Public School Legislation. *Journal of Law and Economics* 10.

Wolf, Eleanor. 1976. Classrooms and Courtrooms. In *Education, Social Science and the Judicial Process.* Washington, D.C.: National Institute of Education.

Wolff, R. 1968. *The Poverty of Liberalism.* Boston: Beacon Press.

ABOUT THE AUTHORS

JAMES S. COLEMAN, Professor of Sociology at the University of Chicago, holds the John Dewey Society Award for Distinguished Service to Education and the Nicholas Murray Butler Medal from Columbia University. He has published widely in both public and professional journals on sociology and on education; his recent books include *Power and the Structure of Society* (1974), and *Youth: Transition to Adulthood* (1974) which he authored with others as Chairman of the Panel on Youth for the President's Science Advisory Committee.

JOHN E. COONS is Professor of Law at the University of California, Berkeley, and is Director of the Childhood and Government Project. He has written and coauthored numerous articles on school integration, finance, and the *Serrano* case. One of his most recent articles is "The Rise of the Parental Class" (1976).

WILLIAM H. CORNOG, former Superintendent of the New Trier Township High School in Winnetka, Illinois, served as vice chairman of the Committee on Examinations, College Entrance Examination Board, from 1969 to 1973, and is a former trustee of the American Field Service. He is the author of books and articles on medieval Latin, modern literature, and educational philosophy.

DENIS P. DOYLE is Chief, School Finance Division, National Institute of Education. He is a former director of the Voucher Project for the OEO, and is educational consultant to several national and state organizations including the Ford Foundation, the California Joint Committee on Teacher Licensing, and the Academy for Educational Development. He is the author of numerous articles on educational financing and teacher evaluation.

E. BABETTE EDWARDS, consultant to several universities, colleges, community agencies and parent organizations, and to the New York City Board of Education, is Administrator of the Harlem Parents Tutorial Project. She is the founder of the Harlem Parents Union, and a member of the National Urban Coalition Task Force.

NATHAN GLAZER is Professor of Education and Sociology, Harvard University, and coeditor of *The Public Interest*. A former editor at Doubleday and Random House, his recent publications include *Affirmative Discrimination:*

Ethnic Inequality and Public Policy (1976) and, with Daniel P. Moynihan, he coedited *Ethnicity: Theory and Experience* (1975). His current research is in urban social policy and ethnic and race relations.

ANDREW M. GREELEY, Director, Center for the Study of American Plural-ism at the National Opinion Research Center, University of Chicago, received his Ph.D. in sociology at that university. He has written widely on education, ethnicity, religion, and sociology, his most recent book being *The American Catholic: A Social Portrait* (1977).

R. KENT GREENAWALT is Professor of Law, Columbia University, and former Special Assistant at the Agency for International Development. He has contributed to a number of legal publications, and with Walter Gelhorn coauthored *The Sectarian College and the Public Purse* (1970).

MARVIN LAZERSON, Associate Professor of Education at the University of British Columbia, was Research Fellow at the Immigration History Research Center, University of Minnesota. His recent publications include "Continuity and Conflict in Urban Education" in *Reviews in American History* (1976), and "Rally 'Round the Workplace: Continuities and Fallacies in Career Education" with W. Norton Grubb in *Harvard Educa-tional Review* (1975).

WILLIAM C. McCREADY, Associate Program Director, Center for the Study of American Pluralism at the University of Chicago, holds a Ph.D. in Sociology and is Managing Editor of *Ethnicity.* The most recent of his many publications include *The Ultimate Values of the American Population* with Andrew M. Greeley (1976), and *Changing Attitudes of American Cath-olics toward the Liturgy* (1976).

MICHAEL NOVAK holds the Watson-Ledden Chair of Religious Studies at Syracuse University. He is the author of many articles in *The Commonweal,* the *New Republic,* and other journals. Among his books is *The Rise of the Unmeltable Ethnics* (1972), and "The People and the News" in *The Fifth Alfred I. duPont-Columbia University Survey of Broadcast Jouralism,* ed. Mar-vin Barrett (1975).

JOHN P. O'DWYER holds teaching credentials in reading, administrative ser-vices, and in both elementary and secondary standard teaching. He began his career in 1967 as a teaching assistant at the University of Nebraska, taught junior high school and nursery school, and at present teaches kin-dergarten in a suburban California school district.

ROBERT SINGLETON has been director of the Education Finance Reform Project, Los Angeles, since 1972. He is founder and chairman of the board for the *Journal of Black Studies,* is a member of the Urban Education Task Force and the National Urban League Education Task Force, and has writ-ten extensively on economics, school finance, and court decisions affecting education.

THOMAS SOWELL, a Fellow at the Center for Advanced Study in the Behavioral Sciences at Stanford University, is Professor of Economics at the University of California, Los Angeles. Among his many publications are *Race and Economics* (1975) and *Black Education: Myths and Trag-edies*(1972). He has written for U.S., Canadian, and British journals.

STEPHEN D. SUGARMAN is Professor of Law, University of California,

Berkeley. He was acting director of the New York State Commission on the Cost, Quality and Finances of Elementary and Secondary Education, and has spent considerable time in international research. His published writings are concerned with legislative reform of education and with educational consumerism and the rights of parents and their children.

RICHARD E. WAGNER, Professor of Economics at Virginia Polytechnic Institute and State University, has taught at both the graduate and undergraduate level on micro- and macroeconomic theory, public finance, and urban economics. In addition to articles published in journals of economics and public policy, he is the author of several monographs and books including *Democracy in Deficit: The Political Legacy of Lord Keynes,* written with James M. Buchanan (1977).

SELECTED PUBLICATIONS FROM
THE INSTITUTE FOR CONTEMPORARY STUDIES
260 California Street, San Francisco, California 94111

NO TIME TO CONFUSE—A Critique of the Ford Foundation's Energy Policy
Project: *A Time to Choose America's Energy Future.*
$4.95. 156 pages. Publication Date: 2/25/75. ISBN 0-917616-01-4
Library of Congress #75-10230
Contributors: Morris A. Adelman, Armen A. Alchian, George Hilton, M. Bruce
Johnson, Walter J. Mead, Arnold Moore, Thomas Gale Moore, William
Riker, Herman Kahn, James DeHaven.

NO LAND IS AN ISLAND: INDIVIDUAL RIGHTS AND GOVERNMENT
CONTROL OF LAND USE
$5.95. 190 pages. Publication Date: 11/19/75. ISBN 0-917616-03-0
Library of Congress #75-38415
Contributors: Benjamin F. Bobo, B. Bruce-Briggs, Connie Cheney, A. Lawrence
Chickering, Robert B. Ekelund, Jr., W. Philip Gramm, Donald G. Hag-
man, Robert B. Hawkins, Jr., M. Bruce Johnson, Jan Krasnowiecki, John
McClaughry, Donald M. Pach, Bernard H. Siegan, Ann Louise Strong,
Morris K. Udall.

GOVERNMENT CREDIT ALLOCATION: WHERE DO WE GO FROM
HERE?
$4.95. 208 pages. Publication Date: 11/20/75. ISBN 0-917616-02-2
Library of Congress #75-32951
Contributors: Karl Brunner, George Benston, Dwight Jaffee, Omotunde
Johnson, Edward Kane, Thomas Mayer, Allan H. Meltzer.

THE POLITICS OF PLANNING: A REVIEW AND CRITIQUE OF
CENTRALIZED ECONOMIC PLANNING
$5.95. 352 pages. Publication Date: 3/3/76. ISBN 0-917616-05-7
Library of Congress #76-7714
Contributors: B. Bruce-Briggs, James Buchanan, A. Lawrence Chickering,
Ralph Harris, Robert B. Hawkins, Jr., George Hilton, Richard Mancke,
Richard Muth, Vincent Ostrom, Svetozar Pejovich, Myron Sharpe, John
Sheahan, Herbert Stein, Gordon Tullock, Ernest van den Haag, Paul H.
Weaver, Murray L. Weidenbaum, Hans Willgerodt, Peter P. Witonski.

THE CALIFORNIA COASTAL PLAN: A CRITIQUE
$5.95. 192 pages. Publication Date: 3/31/76. ISBN 0-917616-04-9
Library of Congress #76-7715
Contributors: Eugene Bardach, Daniel Benjamin, Thomas Borcherding, Ross
Eckert, H. Edward Frech, M. Bruce Johnson, Ronald N. Lafferty, Walter
Mead, Daniel Orr, Donald M. Pach, Michael Peevey.

NEW DIRECTIONS IN PUBLIC HEALTH CARE: AN EVALUATION OF
PROPOSALS FOR NATIONAL HEALTH INSURANCE
$5.95. 265 pages. Publication Date: 5/17/76. ISBN 0-917616-06-5
Library of Congress #76-9522
Contributors: Martin S. Feldstein, Thomas D. Hall, Leon R. Kass, Keith
Leffler, Cotton M. Lindsay, Mark V. Pauly, Charles E. Phelps, Thomas C.
Schelling, Arthur Seldon.

PUBLIC EMPLOYEE UNIONS: A STUDY OF THE CRISIS IN PUBLIC
SECTOR LABOR RELATIONS
$5.95. 295 pages. Publication Date: 6/23/76. ISBN 0-917616-08-1
Library of Congress #76-18409
Contributors: Jack D. Douglas, Raymond Horton, Theodore W. Kheel, David
Lewin, Seymour Martin Lipset, Harvey C. Mansfield, Jr., George Meany,
Robert Nisbet, Daniel Orr, A. H. Raskin, Wes Uhlman, Harry Wellington,
Charles Wheeler, Ralph Winter, Jerry Wurf.

THE CRISIS IN SOCIAL SECURITY: PROBLEMS AND PROSPECTS
$5.95. 214 pages. Publication Date: April 1977. ISBN 0-917616-16-2
Library of Congress #77-72542
Contributors: Michael J. Boskin, George F. Break, Rita Ricardo Campbell, Ed-
ward Cowan, Martin Feldstein, Milton Friedman, Douglas R. Munro,
Donald O. Parsons, Carl V. Patton, Joseph A. Pechman, Sherwin Rosen,
W. Kip Viscusi, Richard J. Zeckhauser

DEFENDING AMERICA: A NEW INTERNATIONAL ROLE
AFTER DETENTE
$13.95 (hardbound only). Publication Date: April 1977 by Basic Books
(New York). ISBN 0-465-01585-9
Library of Congress #76-43479
Contributors: Robert Conquest, Theodore Draper, Gregory Grossman, Walter
Laqueur, Edward M. Luttwak, Charles Burton Marshall, Paul H. Nitze,
Norman Polmar, Eugene V. Rostow, Leonard Schapiro, James R.
Schlesinger, Paul Seabury, W. Scott Thompson, Albert Wohlstetter.

PARENTS, TEACHERS, AND CHILDREN: PROSPECTS FOR CHOICE IN
AMERICAN EDUCATION
$5.95. 250 pages. Publication Date: June 1977. ISBN 0-917616-18-9
Library of Congress #77-79164
Contributors: James S. Coleman, John E. Coons, William H. Cornog, Denis P.
Doyle, E. Babette Edwards, Nathan Glazer, Andrew M. Greeley, R. Kent
Greenawalt, Marvin Lazerson, William C. McCready, Michael Novak,
John P. O'Dwyer, Robert Singleton, Thomas Sowell, Stephen D. Sugar-
man, Richard E. Wagner.